JUNG'S
INDISPENSABLE
COMPASS

Also by James Graham Johnston

THE CALL WITHIN
Navigating Life with Inner Guidance

JOSHUA
The Light of the World

THRIVING ON COLLABORATIVE GENIUS
The Art of Bringing Organziations to Life

JUNG'S INDISPENSABLE COMPASS

A Guide to Navigating the Dynamics of Psychological Types

James Graham Johnston

Excerpts from the Collected Works used with permission of
Princeton University Press

Cover and text design by Jennifer Shoffey Forsythe

ISBN-10: 0-9979700-0-6
ISBN-13: 978-0-9979700-0-5

MSE Press

Contents

And so one must be what one is; one must discover one's individuality, that center of personality which is equidistant between the conscious and the unconscious.
—C. G. Jung

Preface

I HAD COME TO ZURICH, much like Dorothy seeking the Great Oz, to find one last answer in my quest to understand Jung's theory of psychological types. I had designed an online self-assessment for getting oriented to one's preferred types; now I wanted to know how that instrument could be used for individuation—the centerpiece of Jung's Analytical Psychology. Surely in Zurich, the city of countless conversations about the human psyche, the human experience, and the nature of consciousness I would find the answer I sought.

My question seemed simple. Jung's book on psychological types was Volume 6 in a long series of books that dealt primarily with the unconscious and individuation. He had subtitled the first edition of Volume 6 *The Psychology of Individuation.* It did not, on the surface, appear that my question could strike at the root of a troubling quandary. Individuation is the centerpiece of Jung's depth psychology—the psychology of the unconscious. I just wanted to know how his psychological types—the psychology of consciousness—could be fruitfully linked to his psychology of the unconscious.

On a hazy summer evening, on an outdoor terrace overlooking the rambling, winding streets and rooftops of historic Zurich, from conversations with people from the International School of Analytical Psychology (ISAPZurich), I discovered that my simple question did not have a clear and present answer. To the three people who met with me that evening, Stacy Wirth, Stefan Boëthius, and Nathalie Boëthius-de Béthune, I owe many thanks. After our lengthy conversation, where my unanswered question hung like a stubborn piñata, I returned to the United States and redoubled my search through *The Collected Works of C. G. Jung* to discern an answer. This book consolidates my findings.

Along the course of that journey further into Jung's work, Jungian analyst Stacy Wirth was an especially steady and patient supporter. I am deeply indebted to her for our many illuminating conversations and for her perpetual encouragement.

My associate Margie Spino brought a steady, insightful, and systematic approach to Jung's theory of psychological types that generated the comparative categories used to analyze the types and relationships among them.

My friend Angelo Spoto, author of *Jung's Typology in Perspective*, cultivated my interest in Jung long before my journey to Zurich. Our conversations and his informative seminars provided a helpful framework for delving into Jung's types

Several people read "preview editions" and offered comments that have helped to improve the book's content and structure. In alphabetical order, they include Janice Bachman, Diplomate Jungian Analyst (US); Lindsay Chant, DPhil (UK); Margareta Ehnberg MSc, Training Candidate, ISAP-Zurich (FI); Andrew Fellows, PhD, Dunelm, Diplomate Jungian Analyst (UK); Michael Glock, PhD (NZ/US); Thayer Greene, Diplomate Jungian Analyst (US); Vicki Hart, MSW, LCSW, Diploma Candidate Jungian Analyst (US); Sharon Heath, Diplomate Jungian Analyst (US); Karen Hermann, Diplomate Jungian Analyst (US); Anne Hoagland, Diplomate Jungian Analyst (US); Monika Lanz, body therapist, Cert. in Jungian Psychology (CH); Dean Ludwig, PhD (US); Christopher Mead, PhD, Diplomate Jungian Analyst (US/NL); Elena Mikhaylova, PhD (RU/CA); Barbara Helen Miller, Diplomate Jungian Analyst (US/NL); Kathleen Moreau, Diplomate Jungian Analyst (US); Peter Mudd, Diplomate Jungian Analyst (US); Marianne Peier-Baer, lic. phil. I, Diplomate Jungian Psychologist, FSP (CH); Anita Putignano (US); Dennis Pottenger (US); Bernie Pursley (US); Vanessa Prins-Goodman, Diplomate Jungian Analyst (NL); Susanna Ruebsaat, PhD(c) (CA); David Marcus Schmid, JD, Diploma Candidate, ISAPZurich (CA); Thaddeus A. Schnitker, PhD (DE); Jeanne Schul, PhD (US); Maggie Stanway, IGAP Advanced Candidate, (UK); Nancy van den Berg-Cook, PhD, PsyD, Diplomate Jungian Analyst (NL/US); Don Wukasch, MD, Diploma Candidate (US); Norman S. Wolfe (US); Cristina L. M. Xavier, MD (BR); Jan Zalla, Diplomate Jungian Analyst (US); and Sheila Zarrow, Diplomate Jungian Analyst (US).

A faculty of Jungian analysts formed to deliver the training were also quite helpful in refining and critiquing the book. They included Murray Stein, Andrew Fellows, Mary Tomlinson, Stacy Wirth, Barbara Helen

Miller, Vanessa Prins, Misser Berg, Kathryn Cook-Deegan, and David Schmid.

Psychologists Pedro Mendes and Anne Rodrigues, hosts to our online training groups, helped to deepen and clarify my understanding of Jung's model through our many conversations. Sónia DaVeiga perceptively and assertively identified key additions, clarifications, and deletions that made the book more useful to practitioners.

I am especially indebted to Jungian analyst Andrew Fellows who meticulously and comprehensively edited the final version of the book. His editorial guidance, challenging critiques, and foundational understanding of Analytical Psychology have strengthened and simplified the book. Margaret Diehl, professional copy editor, meticulously combed the manuscript for editorial corrections. The talented graphic artist Jennifer Forsythe created the cover design and attended to the fine-tuning of the interior layout and typesetting. Naturally, any remaining errors or weaknesses in the book are to my credit and not theirs.

Many of Jung's terms, sometimes used ambiguously by that bold and brilliant pioneer, are still the subject of much debate. The inclusion of a person's name in this acknowledgment does not necessarily indicate agreement with the contents of this book.

– JGJ

Introduction

THIS BOOK WAS WRITTEN to affirm and help clarify Jung's original model of psychological types. I have done my utmost to return to the "classical" Jung and his original, astonishing insights into orientations of human consciousness.

This book evolved through dialogue. The aim of that dialogue was to understand the dynamics of the types and their important linkage to a centerpiece of Jung's Analytical Psychology—individuation. Individuation embraces the process of integrating diverse and often opposing psychological types for the realization of *unique personality.*

If you are a more casual reader, simply reading this book to gain a better overall sense of Jung's model of psychological types and their dynamics, you may not want to read the whole book. Chapters 2 and 5 are meticulously technical. You should be able to skip those chapters and still gain a general working understanding of Jung's types and their relationship to individuation.

The section "Terms," at the back of the book, could be a helpful reference for you, should you have questions about particular terms as you read. A few terms are quite important for understanding Jung's model. They include the terms *orientation, attitude,* and *collective unconscious.*

An *attitude* is a readiness to act. Each of the types will have an attitude, a readiness to act. An *orientation* is what the attitude is acting upon.

It is not possible to fully understand the attitudes of the four introverted types without understanding their mutual orientation to the *collective unconscious.*

We are oriented, in the human experience, to two synchronized worlds. We all acknowledge the world outside of us as one world. Yet, with the introduction of the *collective unconscious*, Jung acknowledged a second, inner world to which we are also oriented.

The dynamics of Jung's model of psychological types are born from the tension of living between these two worlds: the world without, and the world within.

✻

THIS BOOK, IN ITS ENTIRETY, is also the training guide for professional practitioners in the use of the Gifts Compass Inventory (GCI), an online instrument that profiles dispositions for each of Jung's eight types. To learn more, please see the section "The Gifts Compass Inventory" at the back of the book.

1

The Theater of Individuation

SHE WAS BORN LONELY. From the earliest age she could remember, her mother ridiculed her and found her wanting. The early unfulfilled yearning for a mother's tender care haunted her with a longing that would detach her from her own children later in life. Seeds of early melancholy found fertile soil.

Her mother was a comely woman of high society—charming, socially accomplished, and intelligent—who responded quickly to the smallest change in the social environment, adjusting with an uncanny empathy to the values and viewpoints of others and navigating effortlessly among people wherever she went.

She, her mother's counterpoint, could hardly respond at all—tongue-tied, painfully shy, too sensitive—she could not begin to measure up to her outgoing mother's social ease. Her mother was strikingly attractive; she was uncommonly plain. Artists sought to capture the classical grace and beauty of her mother. Her mother mockingly called her "granny" and thought her "old-fashioned."

She never measured up to her mother's lofty expectations of a socially precocious child. Her mother tried to teach her good manners to compensate for her homely appearance, but all those makeover efforts left her even more keenly aware of her shortcomings. She languished in the shade of her gregarious and popular mother.

Conscious of her shortcomings, she worked diligently to excel at school, seeking her mother's unattainable approval. She wanted to compensate for all her felt inadequacies.

She found solace in the warm comfort of her innermost feelings and imagination, so naturally available to her. She was trapped by her own obsessive introspection and withdrew into injured melancholy.

Her father was her salvation. She worshipped him, and he adored her. Her father called her his "little Nell." During his frequent and extended absences from their home, he wrote her often. He was the tangible, living embodiment of an idealized masculine figure who hovered, like a phantom, in her soul. He brought to life a transcendent dream of being fully and unequivocally loved. Through him, she gained a clearer image of her own destiny.

She saved his letters and read them over and over, even as an adult. She carried them with her for the rest of her life. Each time she read them, they invoked the magic of his fatherly presence. Her brief and intense enthrallment with her father ignited an attachment to vital masculine qualities that would permeate all of her later relationships with men. She would be readily drawn to those inaccessible younger men who revived a thrilling relationship with her memories and images.

Her father kindled the ideals to which she would aspire; he ignited magical associations that resonated deep within her psyche. The image she carried—part vision, part memory—would influence her all her life. It would personify her motivating ideals, her dream of happiness and unconditional love, and her unquenchable fire for living a significant life. She had been chosen—by her adoring father and by a fatherly image within—and she would not let them down.

As an adult she would write, "I have lived a dream life with him; so his memory is still a vivid, living thing to me." Her connection to her father brought her strength and courage. She strove to be noble, studious, brave, and loyal because he wanted her to be. By her life she would both affirm his love and refute her mother's rejection.

Her father was better in her dreams than in her waking life. He was also the one who sent her messages that he was coming but then let her down, who abandoned her in the dark cloakroom of his club, who obsessively sought entertainment and indulgence, who caroused and drank to the depths of despair.

The family moved to France for his convalescence, and she was cast into a strange new environment—new school, new language, new religion, new people—and again she felt miserably isolated and rejected. Her adult passion for aiding the poor, the dislocated, and the rejected in society was fueled by her own experience of a dislocated childhood.

Her parents' marriage had been teetering on the verge of collapse for years, and they separated after her second sibling was born. Not long after their separation, when she was eight years old, her mother died of diphtheria. Her father was hospitalized. She was moved again, this time to live with her maternal grandmother in New York.

No one can fully understand the shock, grief, and confusion that she felt at the age of ten when her father died after he jumped from the window of his sanitarium. Eleanor remained under the watchful care of her grandmother in a luxurious brownstone row house in Manhattan. She would be brought up in elite New York society, but the memories of a conflicted and disconsolate childhood; the painful, deeply ingrained memories of rejection and grief; and the enduring bond of her father's love would remain with her all her life.

Thus began the life of one of the most remarkable women of the twentieth century. Her disposition toward an introverted psychological type, oriented to feeling life deeply, was intensely charged in the first ten years of her life with the stuff of human grief, rejection, isolation, and despair. Yet she did not give up. She moved on and through life, finding women of like mind, meeting guiding mentors, discovering new capabilities within herself, enduring more grief, suffering more disappointments from the men she loved, selflessly supporting and encouraging a crippled husband, becoming a voice for the poor and the downtrodden, and orchestrating diplomacy at the inception of the United Nations. Spouse to the most popular president in American history, beloved by millions around the world, supporter of troops at war, writer, social advocate, and political mentor, Eleanor Roosevelt grew to become one of the most dearly loved women of her age. People from Chicago to New Delhi adored her, and President Harry Truman declared her "First Lady of the World."

Eleanor Roosevelt, 1884–1962

She began shy, awkward, aloof, clumsy, slow, and tortured by grief and rejection; yet through personal transformation she acquired greater resolve and determination, more capabilities, and even gregarious and administrative aptitudes that were opposite her own natural disposition. She lived by her own advice: "You must do the thing you think you cannot do."

In the language of Carl Gustav Jung's psychology, we could say she *individuated.*

INDIVIDUATION AND PSYCHOLOGICAL TYPES

The path of greatest personal fulfillment, the experience of life-giving energy and connection with the cosmos, *individuation* is available to us all. In the social and life sciences, this term could refer to the process of uniting disparate elements into an integrated whole or to differentiating one's individual attributes from the attributes of others. For Jung, individuation is both. A person develops unifying balance *simultaneously* with uniquely differentiated individuality.

Individuation is a central theme, both in Jung's depth psychology and in his "psychology of consciousness"—psychological types. Jung studied psychiatry, medicine, philosophy, alchemy, physics, life sciences, Eastern and Western religions, occult phenomena, astrology, literature, and anthropology, all in pursuit of a fuller understanding of the human experience. Individuation emerged as a central unifying theme of his psychology.

> The meaning and purpose of the process is the realization, in all aspects, of the personality originally hidden away in the embryonic germ-plasm; the production and unfolding of the original, potential wholeness. (Collected Works [CW], Volume 7, §186)

A close associate of Sigmund Freud for six years, Jung pursued with him their common interest in the nature of the unconscious. The elder Freud had high expectations of his protégé. He saw Jung as an ambassador for his newly born psychology, but they separated acrimoniously when their views and purposes diverged irreconcilably.

The dissolution of their relationship occurred congruently with, and may even have been precipitated by, Jung's midlife crisis. He fell into a period of deep personal reflection that he called his "confrontation with the unconscious." From that intense crucible of inner inquiry, his profound new model of psychology emerged; its development and elucidation would consume the remainder of his life.

> All my works, all my creative activity, has come from those initial fantasies and dreams which began in 1912. . . . Everything that I accomplished in later life was already contained in them, although at first only in the form of emotions and images. (*Memories, Dreams, Reflections,* p. 192)

Much of Jung's writing, subsequent to this crucial phase in his life, revolves around the task of individuation—personal transformation toward one's unique potential. This vital journey is largely shaped by unconscious patterns and powers. Jung's insights and observations open an uncanny window to the domains of the unconscious psyche. Building both on the insights of philosophers and visionaries and on his experiences of himself and with his patients, he developed a psychological model that recognizes the existence and influence of frameworks beneath the surface of consciousness. He delved more deeply, and drew from resources more broadly, than any other inquirer into the human condition, before or since.

Jung's approach to depth psychology, now known as Analytical Psychology, has inspired practitioners around the globe. Analysts and therapists trained in his vast body of work assist people in navigating the passages of individuation. Theirs is not the traditional medical model of curing illness but Jung's more holistic approach to the progressive self-actualization of the unique individual.

To guide the journey of individuation, Jung's psychology of the unconscious is complemented and illuminated by his model of psychological types. Psychological types cannot be understood apart from their integral relationship with the larger model of depth psychology. To separate them would be like disjoining *diastole* from *systole* or *yin* from *yang*. Conscious and unconscious processes are complementary and dynamically intertwined elements of the whole psyche.

While Jung's *The Red Book,* begun in 1913 and finally published in 2009, reveals the initial fantasies and dreams of his own liminal experiences with the unconscious, his book *Psychological Types,* published in 1921, was the first consolidated expression of his conceptual architecture of the psyche.[1]

---

[1] The content of Jung's Collected Works (CW), Volume 7 (*Two Essays on Analytical Psychology*), which was actually written before that of Volume 6 (*Psychological Types*), also presents his emerging model of Analytical Psychology. The essays in Volume 7 were written prior to and during Jung's "confrontation with the unconscious" from which key elements of Analytical Psychology emerged. Volume 6 is a more complete presentation of the full model by virtue of

Now Volume 6 of his Collected Works, it not only articulates the functions of consciousness but also provides a thoroughly developed reference to the ideas that would distinguish his model of depth psychology. The definitions in Chapter XI still serve as a glossary of terms for his entire Collected Works and beyond.

Chapters I through IX set the context for understanding the types as dynamic oppositions, while Chapter X describes the types themselves. If taken alone, Chapter X, "A General Description of the Types," presents only an isolated and partial view of the model and has unfortunately been widely misinterpreted as a means of classifying people by "personality type." This was clearly not Jung's intent.

> People often ask me, "now is So-and-So not a thinking type? I say, "I never thought about it," and I did not. It is no use at all putting people into drawers with different labels. (CW 18, §34)

Jung was dismayed by the attention given preeminently to that chapter. In the 1934 foreword to the Argentine edition of CW 6, he wrote:

> Far too many readers have succumbed to the error of thinking that Chapter X ("General Description of the Types") represents the essential content and purpose of the book, in the sense that it provides a system of classification and practical guide to a good judgment of human character. . . . This regrettable misunderstanding completely ignores the fact that this kind of classification is nothing but a childish parlour game.

He went on to note that Chapters II and V were of greater importance. Each deals with the dynamics of psychic oppositions and their integration—essential elements of individuation.

> I would recommend the reader who really wants to understand my book to immerse himself first of all in Chapters II and V. He will gain more from them than from any typological terminology superficially picked up, since this serves no other purpose than a totally useless desire to stick labels on people. (CW 6, Foreword to the Argentine edition, p. xv)

Significantly, Jung clarified the comprehensive intent of *Psychology Types* with its original subtitle: *The Psychology of Individuation.*

Chapter XI therein with its lengthy definitions of terms, Chapter X for its full presentation of the types that were only partially developed in Volume 7, and Chapters II and V with their in-depth review of the union of opposites. If Volume 7 is like a useful pencil sketch, then Volume 6 is like a finished painting.

THE TYPES AND LIFE EXPERIENCE

South American Jungian analyst Raphael Lopez-Pedraza suggested that Jung should have received the Nobel Peace Prize for this theory of psychological types, for it so clearly illustrates and acknowledges the diversity of human experience.

We interact with others on the unspoken or unconscious assumption that they see things the same way we do. When they don't, we may become bewildered, frustrated, or judgmental—reactions that can easily lead to misunderstanding and conflict. With an understanding of Jung's type orientations, we can more readily learn to appreciate how others may see the world differently. The type model can help us heal conflict, correct misunderstanding, and smooth some of the rough edges of relationships.

Each of the type dispositions carries inherent aptitudes—gifts—that can guide an individual's life choices. Understanding one's type dispositions can be quite helpful in navigating career development.

The type dispositions less engaged by life or career tend to remain undeveloped. They are the types that will contribute to the contents of what Jung called *shadow,* and they will provide the impelling oppositions for individuation. In meeting the challenges and oppositions posed by the shadow, Eleanor Roosevelt strove valiantly toward a highly individuated life.

Sometimes people "falsify" their type dispositions in response to social, commercial, or family pressure. They pursue a life inconsistent with their true nature, and their natural type disposition will often disrupt their chosen life. Jung's model helps us understand the nature of those disruptions.

People with introverted dispositions process information in ways radically unlike those with extraverted dispositions. Understanding how students are primarily oriented helps teachers both to adjust their teaching style to their students' needs and also to become more conscious of their own predisposition to teach in a certain way.

Jung's type model helps us understand unconscious factors in the dazzling experience of "falling in love." It also helps us understand how friendships tend to form more readily between some people than others.

Psychologists have found that affirming personal connections in early childhood beneficially influence a child's development. The type model could help parents appreciate and relate to their children, especially if the children have type dispositions quite different from the parents'.

Early responses to trauma, rejection, and loss are influenced by type disposition. A child with an introverted disposition, for example, may withdraw in response to a traumatic event, while one with an extraverted disposition may try to actively engage to oppose or stop the trauma. The complexes formed through childhood experiences will be colored and shaped by the child's early orientations to type.

Organizations can use Jung's model to build more dynamic and collaborative teams, to identify work compatible with people's gifts, and to promote cooperative understanding. As organizations mature and leaders discover that organizational vitality is directly linked to their own personal growth and the personal growth of others, the type model, as a compass for individuation, can help engender robust organizational vitality.

Like individuals, organizations, too, may become overly one-sided, oppressing the "shadow side" that is inconsistent with their cultural norms. The type model helps to understand both the one-sidedness and the ensuing disruptions that may ensue. Nations, too, like any group or individual, can become detrimentally one-sided. We will consider the implications of one-sidedness in Chapter 6.

All of these are useful applications of Jung's type theory, but first and foremost his type model is important for charting the life experience of individuation. To understand how the type model could usefully augment Jung's depth psychology, we now turn to his conceptual architecture of the psyche to see how his psychology of consciousness and of the unconscious are conjoined. We could think of that architecture as a "psychic theater."

THE PSYCHIC THEATER

The psyche, in Jung's model, is the totality of all psychic processes and contents, conscious and unconscious. We could imagine the psyche to be an interactive theater in which many psychic actors play their roles. This imagined theater has two stages: a conscious one and an unconscious one (Figure 1-1).[2]

On the conscious stage, two "actors" play their roles. At the apron of the conscious stage we meet the first actor: the *persona*—the personal façade turned to the audience of social interaction in the world. The persona is like an actor's mask held up to the audience, and it is thus useful for creating a desired impression.

> The persona is a complicated system of relations between the individual consciousness and society, fittingly enough a kind of mask, designed on the

---

[2] Figure 1-1 is the first in a series of diagrams of the "Psychic Theater" that are adapted from Jung's 1925 Seminars. See C. J. Jung, *Introduction to Jungian Psychology: Notes on the Seminar on Analytical Psychology Given in 1925*; Lecture 16, Diagram 9, ed. Sonu Shamdasani and William McGuire (Princeton: Princeton University Press, 2012).

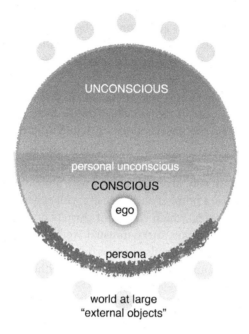

Figure 1.1 The Conscious Stage and the Personal Unconscious

one hand to make a definite impression upon others, and, on the other, to conceal the true nature of the individual. (CW 7, §305)

Behind the persona, we find the lead actor on this stage—the *ego*. The ego exerts its influence as the lead identity of consciousness. The orientations of psychological types, for the ego, are orientations to life experience that will determine the sort of role the lead is destined to play.

The ego orientations will influence behavior but do not in themselves constitute the unique person. They might be considered expressions of the developing individual, but those ego-based expressions will change as she or he matures. Although each individual begins life with certain predisposed ego orientations, the goal of individuation is to gain greater access to all of the orientations, even the opposing ones.

The conscious audience—the world at large or "outer objects"—is not passive in the drama of individuation; it will directly influence plot development. Unlike the audience in a conventional theater, the audience here—the noisy, tumultuous, and sometimes unpredictable audience of the world—will interact with the actors on stage, sometimes applauding, sometimes booing, conversing, taunting, rallying, opposing, ignoring, or supporting them.

Behind the lead actor on this stage is a vague psychic scrim that conceals the *personal unconscious*. A scrim in a theater is a lightweight transparent curtain that conceals actors or objects behind it when they are *not* illuminated but reveals them if light is cast upon them. Likewise, memories of past personal experiences are concealed from the conscious stage *unless* they are illuminated.

Memories will often unexpectedly light up and, like the audience of the world, interrupt the play of individuation on the conscious stage. The ego would like to control the interruptions caused by spontaneous memories, but it is often powerless to suppress them. The memories are thrust upon it, and it must adjust its script in response to what appears.

These memories may arrive uninvited and incognito as *autonomous complexes* that grow in number and intensity with experience in the world. Autonomous complexes, which consist of clusters of often long-forgotten memories and associations, carry unusual weight or intense emotional content and may trigger compulsive urges or reactions. As their name suggests, they seem to come and go as they please, either hindering or reinforcing the ego's role.

The ego, which Jung termed a *functional complex,* may be frequently upstaged by these interventions in the play. Sometimes autonomous complexes thrust themselves onto the conscious stage, commandeering the action. They may appear as irrational fears, disproportionate reactions, intense attractions or aversions to certain people, motivating memories, and obsessive personal attachments. They can be as unpredictable as the rowdy audience of the world in shaping the story of individuation.

As we stumble through the backstage of the personal unconscious, cluttered over the course of many productions with its memories and complexes, we are surprised to step onto yet another stage, this one a seeming mirror image of the first, but having a quieter and more ethereal quality. This is the unconscious stage (Figure 1-2). Just as the conscious stage includes perceptions of, and interactions with, the world at large (outer objects), this audience includes perceptions of, and interactions with, images from the *archetypes* of the *collective unconscious* (inner objects).

This stage also has its principal actors. The unconscious stage seems relatively quiet because it is hidden, but it is far from uneventful. The actors on this stage perform their own play that complements the action on the conscious stage. At the center of the unconscious stage, a shadowy figure is antagonist to the chief actor on the other stage.

Illuminated by the many stage lights and spotlights of conscious experience, the ego casts a *shadow* on the rear stage. Whatever attributes the ego has adopted, this shadowy twin adopts the opposite attributes behind the scrim. If the ego is emboldened with pride, the shadow is timid and incompetent. If the ego is productive, the shadow is reflective. If the ego is oriented to the world, the shadow will be oriented to the inner life.

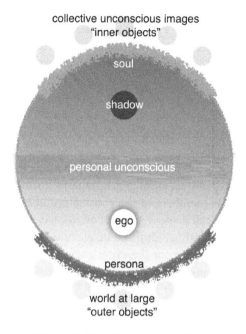

collective unconscious images
"inner objects"

soul

shadow

personal unconscious

ego

persona

world at large
"outer objects"

Figure 1.2 The Unconscious Stage

If the shadow is ignored and repressed in the backstage of consciousness, it can become an unruly phantom, interrupting the conscious stage as an adversary. The ego may discover the attributes of its unwanted counterpart among the audience of the world. If the ego's rejected sibling is thrust onto others, rather than embraced as a fellow actor, the play will be no comedy. In the larger social arena of history, unbridled shadow projections have been the root of ugly discrimination, violent personal hatred, mass persecutions, and even horrendous genocide.

However, if the shadow is regularly acknowledged as a legitimate actor in this theater, the play of individuation continues apace; progressive personal growth ensues toward the emergence of the whole person.

> There is no light without shadow and no psychic wholeness without imperfection. To round itself out, life calls not for perfection but for completeness; and for this the "thorn in the flesh" is needed, the suffering of defects without which there is no progress and no ascent. (CW 12, §208)

The persona, too, has its complement in the unconscious—the *soul*.[3] It is

---

[3] Because *persona* is a singular term, denoting either a masculine or a feminine personality, we will use the singular term *soul* to denote the compensatory masculine or feminine personality. Many use the more precise terms *anima* or *animus*. Jung later used the term *syzygy* for the

a psychological, not a religious, term that refers to an inner "personality." The soul plays a compensatory role to the persona on the conscious stage. Just as the persona presents a sort of personality at the threshold of the outer world, the soul presents a personality at the threshold of the inner archetypal world. If the persona is masculine, then the personification of soul is feminine (*anima*). If the persona is feminine, then the personification of soul is masculine (*animus*). The soul, as anima or animus, is a powerful but silent player, mysterious and alluring, which charms the ego forth to an individuated destiny.

Like the shadow, the soul can also be projected onto the conscious audience, and inevitably so, as long as it remains unconscious. Unlike the shadow that brands members of the conscious audience as undesirable, adversarial, or even evil players, the soul often casts a favorable aura onto others, projecting a dazzling, idealized image onto some lucky beneficiary.

This is often the trigger for the experience of "falling in love." Dante's beloved Beatrice was just such a beneficiary. Though he met her only twice, just a distant glimpse of her was sufficient for him to project upon her his own unconscious anima: "Behold," he wrote, "a deity stronger than I; who coming, shall rule over me." Such is the power of this actor at the very recesses of the unconscious, who stands upon an apron to yet another audience in our theater.

Just as the persona is positioned at the apron of the conscious stage as a means of relating to the audience of the world at large, the soul (anima or animus) assumes a position at the edge of the unconscious stage where it serves as the interface to the audience of the *collective unconscious*—an array of archetypal patterns and powers that will have their influential say in the production.

This archetypal audience also shapes the drama of individuation, for it is the psychic complement to our waking experience of the world. Whereas the outer world comprises people, events, and circumstances that influence the development of the individual, the collective unconscious

---

anima/animus. With an emphasis on Volume 6 of the Collected Works in this book, we will use the term *soul*, which he defines extensively in Chapter XI of Volume 6. There Jung speaks of the soul as a functional complex. While the persona is a functional complex that engages the outer object—the world—the anima and animus are also functional complexes that relate to the inner object—the collective unconscious. Either complex could be considered a personality or a subset of the true personality. A person might behave inconsistently: at work he might present one personality, yet while at home, relaxed and in the company of a spouse, quite another. In the former case he would be presenting the persona's personality, and in the latter, possibly the personality of the anima. In this book I will use the term *soul* for that functional complex, or *sub-personality*, that engages the inner object—the collective unconscious. To be technically accurate, in Jung's definition, it appears that he might also apply the term *soul* to persona, using the term to denote a functional complex that acts as a personality. The problem is further compounded by the fact that *soul* is not an exact translation of the German term *Seele* in Jung's original writing, as noted by the translators in a lengthy footnote in Volume 12 (§9 n) of the Collected Works.

provides a deep structure of patterns and powers that shape human development. Like Kant's meticulously defined a priori categories that frame conscious perception and judgment, Jung's a priori archetypal categories loosely frame all of human experience.

> The form of the world into which he is born is already inborn in him as a virtual image. Likewise parents, wife, children, birth, and death are inborn in him as virtual images, as psychic aptitudes. (CW 7, §717)

Nations, clans, families, and individual progenitors—the long trail of evolutionary experience—have representative archetypes in the audience. In a series of seminars delivered in 1925,[4] Jung likened these levels of archetypes to archaeological strata.

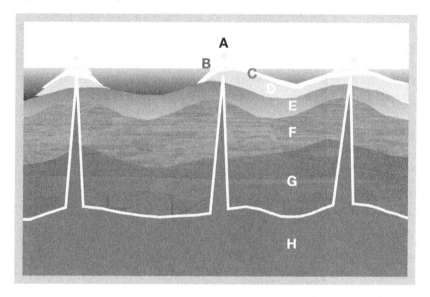

Figure 1.3 The Conscious Stage and the Personal Unconscious

Unconscious archetypes underpin a person's life from built-up layers of ancestral experience. In Figure 1-3, starting with the "central fire" (H) at the bottom, the layers progressively move up from animal ancestors (G), to primate ancestors (F), to large groups (e.g., European) (E), to nations (D), to clans C, to families (B), and finally to individuals (A), depicted as round objects on the small mounds of family lineage.

Archetypes precondition the individual's response to their environment. Jung followed Kant and Plato in recognizing preestablished frameworks for interpreting and differentiating the mass of conscious experi-

---

[4] See Jung, *Introduction to Jungian Psychology,* Lecture 16, Diagram 10.

ence. The mind is not a blank slate—a tabula rasa—at birth.

> What Kant demonstrated in respect to logical thinking is true of the whole range of the psyche.... [The archetypes are] a kind of pre-existent ground-plan that gives the stuff of experience a specific configuration, so that we may think of them, as Plato did, as *images*, as schemata, or as inherited functional possibilities. (CW 6, §512)

The archetypes are activated and engaged in response to the drama being enacted on the stage of consciousness. For example, the quality of a mother's touch, care, support, and compassion provide the experiential substance for a child's predisposition for the archetypal experience of a mother. The tangible elements of that relationship form complexes that will shape and influence development, even into later adulthood. For Eleanor Roosevelt, early natural bonding was stunted, affecting her whole life course and likely diminishing her capacity to bond with her own children.

A penchant for any particular conscious disposition is not a conscious choice but an expression of an unconscious *predisposition*. The archetypes structure and shape the ego complex like "the axial system of a crystal, which, as it were, preforms the crystalline structure in the mother liquid, although it has no material existence of its own" (CW 9i, §155).

The archetypes perform an unseen directive role offstage, and the play could not go on without them.

> We can see [man] in a new setting which throws an objective light upon his existence, namely as being operated and maneuvered by archetypal forces instead of his "free will," that is, his arbitrary egoism and his limited consciousness. (C. G. Jung as quoted in Miguel Serrano, *C. G. Jung and Herman Hesse: A Record of Two Friendships*, 1968; p. 86)

With the addition of the archetypal audience, or "inner objects," we have constructed the full theater. It could be thought of as two semicircular stages, together forming a theater-in-the-round. On one side of this theater we have the conscious story being enacted; on the other, unconscious side, we have the hidden but mighty complementary story. We could call the theater the *theater of individuation* (Figure 1-4).

Psychological type dispositions in this theater are not limited to ego consciousness. All the elements of the psychic theater, from the persona to the soul, have typological orientations that will substantially influence the life of the individual. As the persona and ego share type dispositions in

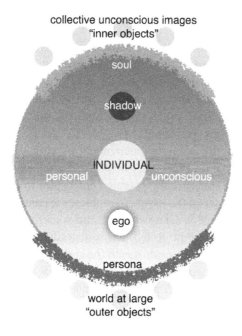

collective unconscious images
"inner objects"

soul

shadow

INDIVIDUAL
personal   unconscious

ego

persona

world at large
"outer objects"

Figure 1.4 The Theater of Individuation

common, so too do the soul and shadow. The nature of these oppositions will substantially influence the life of the individual.

The continuous life-giving threads of initiation, reorientation, and rebirth are imbued with type dispositions that weave the fabric of individuation. The types in the shadow are just as important as those most accessible to consciousness, for they constitute the threshold to the riches of the unconscious and, with their integration in the life of the individual, the pathway to wholeness.

The *individual* is the very subject of individuation. At the schematic center of the psyche—midway between the conscious and unconscious audiences, with access to both, the individual personality has the central place in this theater.[5] The person is neither the ego, nor the persona, nor

---

[5] Jung's diagram (Figure 1-4) uses the term *individual* at the center, yet his discussion of that element of the diagram suggests that he could have been referring to the archetypal Self. The line of demarcation between the archetypal Self and the individual self is not well articulated; they could be considered congruent. Jung uses the term *personality* widely and imprecisely to refer to the person individuating, the shadow as the "objective personality," the ego as the "subjective personality," the soul as a personality, and so forth. He does not include the term *personality* among his many definitions in Chapter X of *Psychological Types*. For clarity in this book, the term *personality* is used to refer only to the individuating person, the individual deemed to be

the shadow, nor the soul. The individual is found at that balanced mid-point with access to them all.

The goal of individuation is to "become whole"—to achieve coherence and equilibrium with an authentic personal position at the center. The ego is the main actor of consciousness, and the shadow occupies center stage in the unconscious; but the individual is the one for whom the whole theater has been built. The developing person unites the many psychic actors as one integrated, unique individual.

The roles of all the formerly independent psychic identities are transformed as individuation proceeds. The persona gradually presents a more authentic face. The superficially sovereign ego begins to defer to the legitimate heir at the center of the psyche. Troublesome complexes become less disruptive. The shadow is acknowledged, and sometimes even embraced, rather than suppressed or projected. The soul gradually becomes more of a mediator of a two-way relationship with the archetypes.

We could be tempted to say, "All's well that ends well," but the performance of individuation does not end. People continually move through pathways of personal transformation—sometimes painful and arduous—as individuation presses on.

Individuation can be a tumultuous struggle, sometimes full of gut-wrenching anguish. If not for the *Self*, the journey might careen wildly off course. The *Self* is the ordering archetype of individuality in the theater of individuation. The Self offers a teleological framework for personal growth; it holds the potential for wholeness for the evolving unique individual. We might think of the Self as the play's "producer"—the one who considers all aspects of the play and theater as a whole. When we consider the question of "becoming whole" in Chapter 7, we will turn more fully to the Self and its functional accomplice, the *transcendent function*.

"THE COMING TO BIRTH OF PERSONALITY"

Individuation is the self-actualization of the unique person. By the mid-nineteenth century, the idea seemed to be "in the air." Ralph Waldo Emerson and the American Transcendentalists had promoted the value of the individual. In the twentieth century, humanistic psychologist Abraham Maslow would also pick up the standard of individuation with the new

---

at the center of Jung's diagram of the psyche, guided in development by its pattern potential, the "center and circumference" of the whole person—the Self. Post-Jungian terminology often refers to an *ego-Self axis*; it seems more fitting to refer to a *personality-Self axis*.

language of the human potential movement.

Some of the fundamental precepts advocated by Emerson, Jung, and Maslow are so similar that one can scarcely tell them apart.

> There is a time in every man's education when he arrives at the conviction that envy is ignorance; that imitation is suicide; that he must take himself for better or for worse, as his portion; that though the wide universe is full of good, no kernel of nourishing corn can come to him but through his toil bestowed on that plot of ground which is given to him to till. . . . Not for nothing one face, one character, one fact, makes much impression on him, and another none. This sculpture in the memory is not without pre-established harmony. . . . Trust thyself: every heart vibrates to that iron string.[6]

> Man should live according to his own nature; he should concentrate on self-knowledge and then live in accordance with the truth about himself. . . . And so one must be what one is; one must discover one's individuality, that center of personality which is equidistant between the conscious and the unconscious; we must aim for that ideal point towards which nature appears to be directing us. Only from that point can one satisfy one's needs.[7]

> What man can be, he must be. This need we may call self-actualization. It refers to the desire for self-fulfillment, namely, to the tendency for him to become actualized in what he is potentially. This tendency might be phrased as the desire to become more and more what one is, to become everything that one is capable of becoming.[8]

Though all three of these men advocated the development of the distinct individual, it was Jung, more than anyone else, who delineated the psychological depth and breadth of self-actualization. In Jung's model, the dynamic interplay of growth-engendering oppositions serves as protagonist and antagonist for the story of individuation. These oppositions—dominant and repressed types, ego and shadow, persona and soul, numinous and objective experience, individual and collective, nature and culture—generate psychic tensions perpetually seeking resolution. With each resolution, each integration of oppositions, the locus of personal

---

[6] Ralph Waldo Emerson, "Essay on Self-Reliance" ([1841]; The Domino Project, 2012).

[7] C. J. Jung, quoted from Miguel Serrano, *C. G. Jung and Herman Hesse: A Record of Two Friendships* (1968), p. 91.

[8] Abraham Maslow, "Toward a Psychology of Being," *Psychological Review* 50: 370–96 (Hoboken, NJ: Wiley, 1998).

identity shifts from a one-sided ego toward a fuller realization of personality at the center.

> This something is the desired "mid-point" of the personality, that ineffable something betwixt the opposites, or else that which unites them, or the result of conflict, or the product of energetic tension: the coming to birth of personality, a profoundly individual step forward, the next stage. (CW 7, §382)

A predisposed orientation to certain types will tend to shape the course of individuation by determining what will be of early interest, what will come easily, and what will be difficult. However, our earliest predispositions are merely starting points for the movement of personal growth. We could think of this growth using our theatrical metaphor for the psyche.

Someone may be born with an ego oriented more to one of our two audiences than the other—for example, the audience of the world at large. That orientation becomes part of the ego's identity as it enacts the play of individuation on the stage of consciousness. The person is drawn by this ego orientation to lively interaction with the audience of the world. The ego thrives there and plays its part well. From the ego's perspective, the whole play could be enacted from this one conscious role.

But the Self will not have it thus. The play has been written for individuation, not egocentricity. The ego may get comfortable in its predisposed role, and the persona may resist relinquishing its preeminent role; but the aim of this performance is the integration of opposites, not staunch one-sidedness. Only by including the type dispositions harbored in the unconscious, the ones most resisted by ego and persona, will the individual become increasingly whole.

THE VALUE OF INDIVIDUATION

In traversing the experiences of individuation, in becoming increasingly whole, we find that life becomes richer and in many ways easier. The types, formerly less accessible, become increasingly part of life experience. Instead of a one-sided approach to every problem, we can draw on a diverse palette of aptitudes. We experience "flow" more frequently, for we are freer to use the type orientations suited to the need.

What used to be troublesome for us is now less so: if mingling at a party used to be intimidating, it becomes easier; if dealing with logical problems used to be difficult, it becomes easier and even more enjoyable; if meditation used to seem impossible, with individuation it becomes alluring.

We are less troubled by unexpected intrusions from the multiple subpersonalities in the psyche seeking expression.

We gain a more unified, well-poised, and balanced personality—emotionally available *and* thoughtful, imaginative *and* practical, outgoing *and* reflective, prudent *and* generous, sympathetic *and* decisive, spiritually oriented *and* practically grounded.

With individuation, connections to meaning that had previously eluded us become more accessible. The fullness of life is more readily apprehended through the fullness of consciousness. We feel more oriented to what is real and authentic and feel increasingly connected to the purposeful endeavor of *realizing* personality.

CHAPTER SUMMARY

In this chapter we have reviewed the architecture of the psyche as conceived by Jung, illustrating the integral relationships between psychological types and depth psychology. The metaphor of a psychic theater is useful for understanding Jung's architecture of the psyche. It includes some of the fundamental elements of his depth psychology: the collective world, persona, ego, personal unconscious, complexes, shadow, anima/animus, and the archetypes of the collective unconscious. The emphasis of this book will be on the types and individuation, yet Jung's type model is also useful for understanding many other aspects of life. Some of those applications are addressed under "Compass Headings" at the end of the book.

For simplicity, in Chapters 2 through 5, we will consider the types only as modes of *ego* consciousness. However, equally important will be the types as they are oriented on the unconscious side of the theater. Shadow and soul also have type dispositions. Chapters 6 and 7 consider the dynamics of type oppositions and their integration through individuation.

2

The Compass of Consciousness

I would not for anything dispense with this compass on my psychological voyages of discovery. . . . I value the type theory for the objective reason that it provides a system of comparison and orientation which makes possible something that has long been lacking, a critical psychology.

—C. G. Jung speaking of the four functions as a compass

AS A LONG SANDY SHORE is a desert without an ocean, Jung's psychology of consciousness is barren without its complementary psychology of the unconscious. The compass of psychological types is useful for navigating the journey of individuation, for it effectively integrates both conscious and unconscious domains of the psyche with one "critical apparatus."

The metaphor of a circular compass carries much symbolic value as the navigating instrument for a journey to wholeness. The circle is a universal symbol of unity and completion. In ancient Egypt, the circle signified the solar disk—the Sun God—a symbol of divine presence. In Islam, the circle symbolizes heavenly perfection. The Hindu mandala (Sanskrit for *circle*) appears in countless elaborate forms as a symbol for wholeness and the cycles of life. The taijitu, symbol of Taoism in China, is a circle containing the opposites of yin and yang. In alchemy, a circle is used to signify the process of purification. The circular labyrinths of ancient Greece and medieval Europe were containers for a circumambulation to the center.

The four points of the compass also add symbolic significance. Quantities of four constitute some of life's most basic orientations, such as the cardinal directions (north, south, east, and west), the four seasons (spring, summer, autumn, and winter), the phases of the moon (new moon, waxing moon, full moon, waning moon), and the four ages of life (childhood, youth, middle age, and old age).

A compass is useful for establishing orientation and direction. The conceptual compass of psychological types is useful for establishing the ego's orientation and direction.[1] Not simply a compass of ego consciousness, as we will see in later chapters, it also provides insight into the orientation and direction of unconscious actors. With the compass of psychological types, much is uncovered that would otherwise be concealed.

To become better acquainted with the elements of the compass, we return to the theater of individuation already constructed in the previous chapter. Our two audiences—the conscious audience of the world at large (outer object) and the unconscious audience of the collective archetypes (inner object)—create two orientations for ego consciousness that we could call the *great divide*.

THE GREAT DIVIDE

My whole scheme of typology is merely a sort of orientation. –C. G. Jung

The ego is the center of consciousness in this theater. It orients the individual to the experience of life, *on both sides* of the theater, as shown in Figure 2-1. The orientations to the two psychic audiences are so distinctly different that we might liken human consciousness to the Roman god Janus for the ability to attend to each of these audiences together.

The outer audience of the world is subject to temporal and spatial constraints. The ego relates to that audience within a tightly constrained framework of sensual perception and rational judgment. The inner audience of the archetypes is not so constrained by space, time, or practical reason. The ego relates to that audience through loosely constrained, ethereal images, ideas, and ideals. The outer audience, supported by concrete perceptions, is often considered more real than the inner audience, but for Jung, the inner audience is every bit as real and legitimate. Perceptions

---

[1] Jung's type model is useful for understanding dispositions of ego consciousness, yet it does not provide a full and complete model for all facets of human awareness. An awareness of memories, emotions, bodily sensations, personal identity across time, or complexes, for example, is not explicitly included in his type model. Another form of awareness not included in the type model is awareness of consciousness itself. Though Jung does not explicitly address this awareness, either in the type model or in his model of depth psychology, personality itself may have an awareness that transcends ego consciousness and is capable of observing ego and shadow dispositions.

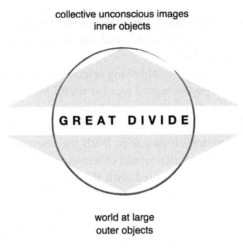

Figure 2.1 The Great Divide in Consciousness

of inspirations, images, and ideas are just as real as perceptions of a DNA molecule, a sunset, or a block of granite.

> In so far as the subjective factor [collective unconscious] has, from the earliest times and among all peoples, remained in large measure constant . . . it is a reality that is just as firmly established as the external object. . . . It is another universal law, and whoever bases himself on it has a foundation as secure, as permanent, and as valid as the man who relies on the object [outer audience]. (CW 6, §622)

Everyone's ego can orient to both audiences, yet each individual is typically drawn to one orientation more than the other. Sometimes the ego, the central actor on our stage of consciousness, has a more engaging relationship with the outer audience of the world and sometimes with the inner archetypal audience.

If the ego's rapport with the inner audience is stronger, the individual will place greater trust in dreams, possibilities, imagination, and inspiration; but if the rapport with the outer audience dominates, the individual will place greater trust in facts, traditions, concrete experience, and practical issues.

We could refer to these two audiences as the first two *orientations* on the compass of psychological types. The inner audience containing the more ethereal dreams, images, ideas, and ideals will be shown to the north. The more tangible, earthbound audience will take its position below to the south.[2] Jung often referred to these orientations as the *inner object* and

---

[2] Orienting the inner object to the north and the outer object to the south is arbitrary. Many stu-

outer object. The term *inner object* refers to the collective unconscious; the term *outer object* refers to the outer world.[3]

With the two orientations on either side of the great divide, we have established our first two cardinal points: the northern orientation to the inner object and the southern orientation to the outer object, as shown in Figure 2-2.

Inner Object

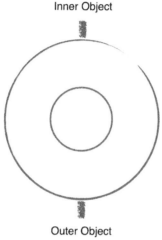

Outer Object

Figure 2.2 Orientations to North and South

These distinctly different orientations are the most significant oppositions on the compass. These oppositions are aptly characterized by Heinrich Heine, as cited in Jung's Introduction to *Psychological Types.*

> Plato and Aristotle! These are not merely two systems, they are types of two distinct human natures, which from time immemorial, under every sort of disguise, stand more or less inimically opposed. The whole medieval world in particular was riven by this conflict, which persists down to the present day, and which forms the most essential content of the history of

---

dents of Analytical Psychology will be accustomed to seeing those orientations reversed, with the unconscious shown below the conscious orientation to the world. However, because orientation to the more ethereal dreams and images is to the inner object, and because orientation to the more concrete earth is to the outer object, orienting the compass as shown in Figure 2-2 may help people who have not studied Jung to better grasp the attributes of these orientations.

[3] Jung often referred to the collective unconscious as the subjective factor. This term is a slippery one because subject can also denote the ego or the individual. Whenever Jung speaks of the *subject* or *subjective factor*, therefore, we must pay close attention. Some have interpreted his use of the term to refer to both the individual and the collective unconscious together. In this book, for the purposes of sorting out these orientations of consciousness, the term *subjective factor* is synonymous with the term *inner object*. See the discussion of *Subject/Subjective Factor* in the section "Terms" at the end of this book for a more detailed analysis.

the Christian Church. Although under other names, it is always of Plato and Aristotle that we speak.[4]

These are orientations, but how does the ego relate to these orientations? Jung used the term *function* to describe the means of consciously relating to an orientation. He noted four functions, two "irrational" and two "rational." The two irrational functions might better be termed *receptive*.

THE TWO RECEPTIVE FUNCTIONS

Jung refers to these two functions as *irrational,* or *non-rational,* because they do not apply any rational judgment. Yet this does not really describe the role of these functions. Saying that they are *not* rational does not allude to what they do, only to what they don't do. We will refer to them as the *receptive* functions, for "they do not proceed selectively, according to principles, but are simply receptive to what happens" (CW 6, §953).

The *sensation* function enables awareness of the outer object. It perceives through the physical senses, creating understanding of those perceptions as coherent experience through a priori time-space frameworks that interpret the flood of sensual stimuli.

The intuition function enables awareness of the images of the inner object. Freed from strict time or space frameworks, the intuition function has more freedom to interpret its intangible perceptions, though its freedom is not absolute. It too is constrained by a priori frameworks of perception.[5]

To add these two functions to our compass of consciousness, we will create an inner compass for the functions themselves (Figure 2-3). On the inner compass, we will represent the function of intuition as N, and the function of sensation as S.[6] Both of the two initial orientations of consciousness, depicted as cardinal points on the outer circle, now have

---

[4] Heinrich Heine, *Deutschland,* Vol. I (Verlag: Diogenes, 2005).

[5] Jung describes intuition as the function of unconscious perception. While he makes it eminently clear that introverted intuition is oriented to the inner object, he is not as explicit about extraverted intuition. In general, and especially for the "crossover types," the functional orientation is subordinated to the directional orientation. Extraverted intuition is one of the crossover types; its directional orientation to the outer object would manifest more clearly than its functional orientation to the inner object.

[6] The use of N for intuition is a convention broadly accepted among analysts and typology professionals alike. It is used here to render the compass of consciousness more readily understandable by those familiar with existing models of psychological types derived from Jung's work, as well as coincidentally being the convention for "North." The initial for sensation (S) is also coincidentally that for "South."

Inner Object

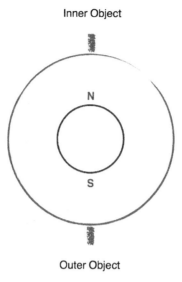

Outer Object

Figure 2.3 North and South Orientations with Corresponding Functions

assigned ego functions that enable awareness of the contents of those orientations.

The sensation function creates awareness of the outer object; it continuously scans for new information through the physical senses. Awareness of the inner object occurs through the function of intuition and is analogous to awareness of the outer object through sensation. The contents of the inner object are just as real to intuition as are the contents of the outer object to sensation.

"The relation of the inner objects to consciousness is entirely analogous to that of outer objects, though their reality is not physical but psychic" (CW 6, §655).

As if through separate windows on experience, each function figuratively gazes out onto worlds in parallel universes. Sensation perceives the physical objective world as real. Perceptions are finite and measurable. Reality consists of discrete and perceivable parts.

Through the opposite window of intuition, the images and ideas emanating from the unconscious are real. The universe of the unconscious is immeasurable, timeless, unpredictable—unbound by gravity or physical laws. Its galaxies of dreams, images, and inspirations are as limitless as the physical universe.

Sensation scans the universe of the outer object, absorbing sensory perceptions, portraying the known; intuition scans the universe of the inner object, absorbing intuitive perceptions, anticipating the unknown.

Sensation attends to concrete definition and rich sensory experience; intuition attends to compelling ideas and possibilities. Sensation perceives

Figure 2.4 Left: Chagall's *I and the Village*. Right: *Vermeer's Girl with a Pearl Earring*. North and South Orientations with Corresponding Functions

distinct and separate pieces; intuition perceives the unified whole. Sensation treasures the tangible sensations of the moment; intuition delights in imagination and possibilities.

These two functions are as different from one another as a Chagall from a Vermeer (Figure 2-4). Chagall's paintings are characterized by dreamy and imprecise qualities. Vermeer's paintings are characterized by their renditions of detail, form, and color.

Like Chagall and Vermeer, intuition and sensation each "paint" the contents of consciousness. What they paint is utterly incongruous, yet in the unified experience of the person, they paint together.

To distinguish between the distinctly different ways the two functions perceive, I will, in this book, refer to the sensation function's mode of perception as *perceiving* and the intuition function's mode of perception as *apprehending*. The sensation function *perceives* the outer object; the intuition function *apprehends* the inner object.

To more fully understand the philosophical grounding for these two functions in particular, let us pause to briefly review some premises of a philosopher from whom Jung drew freely: Immanuel Kant.

Phenomenon and Noumenon

Immanuel Kant's philosophy had a profound influence on Jung. Many of the key terms and ideas in Jung's book *Psychological Types* were derived from Kant's philosophical inquiries. Kant is considered by many to be the most important philosopher of the last thousand years. While Kant's philosophy itself is well beyond the scope of this book, certain elements deserve mention, for they help to illuminate the symmetry of oppositions inherent in Jung's compass of psychological types.

One of the significant epiphanies in Kant's seminal *Critique of Pure Reason*[7] is that we are conditioned in our perceptions and our thinking by a priori frameworks. We are bound by them; they frame our consciousness. Time and space are not necessarily inherent conditions of the world: they are inherent conditions of our *experience* of the world—they are frameworks built into our perceptions that enable us to make sense of experience.

The perceptual function of sensation is conditioned by such frameworks. Sensation does not simply consist of the aggregate perceptions of the senses. Perceptions through the senses alone do not produce understanding; they produce only stimuli. Without a means to sort, organize, and clarify the experience of those sensations, perception would be a cacophony of unintelligible impressions.

Similarly, intuition is also conditioned by frameworks, though Kant's categories of perception apply more readily to the function of sensation.

Another important element of Kant's philosophy distinguishes *phenomenon* from *noumenon*. A phenomenon consists of the representations that are subject to our perceptions; a noumenon is the "thing in itself" (*Ding an sich*) that transcends our perceptual frameworks. What we perceive within our frameworks are only representations of what may actually be present. We are endowed with perceptual equipment to perceive the thing—the "phenomenon"—but not the noumenal *Ding an sich*.

For example, when we place iron filings on a glass table and then place a magnet beneath them, we can see the new form they take on the table, yet we cannot see the magnetic field that has organized them. Jung noted, as an example, that we see colors, not wavelengths. Life, too, is noumenal. No one has ever perceived life itself, only its manifestations as living "things." Similarly, we could consider consciousness to be noumenal; we perceive only the manifestation—the phenomenon—of consciousness, but not consciousness itself.

So the phenomena could be considered representations of the noumena, but not the noumena itself. For Eastern mystics, the world may be *maya*—illusion—but for Kant, it is *representation*. When the tangible objects of the outer object and the intangible objects of the inner object are seen from Kant's perspective, we can better appreciate that the representations of the outer object are no more valid than the representations

---

[7] Immanuel Kant, *Critique of Pure Reason*, trans. Guyer and Wood (Cambridge: Cambridge University Press).

of the inner object. Both are merely representations of an imperceptible noumenal reality.

How does all of this relate to our understanding of psychological types? Our perceptual bias tends to view a block of granite as more "real" than a dream. There's the rub, for in Jung's symmetrical model of consciousness, they are equally real. Each is merely a representation. Granite is a representation of the outer object; a dream is a representation of the inner object. Neither discloses the reality—the noumenon—behind the representation. Each is perceived within our perceptual frameworks, and each is a representation of a reality insufficiently revealed by the representation.

THE TWO RATIONAL FUNCTIONS

The heart has reasons that reason cannot know. —Pascal

The receptive functions apprehend or perceive the perpetual stream of representations of the inner or outer objects, but how shall that ceaseless welter of information be assessed? Two rational governing principles provide frameworks for assessing the contents of ego consciousness: *value* and *logic*.

Each governing principle has a corresponding ego function. The *feeling* function is oriented to the governing principle of value; the *thinking* function is oriented to the governing principle of logic. Each function applies its rational governing principle to assess experience.

The thinking function is usually a bit easier to comprehend because it is rational in the way the term is normally expected to apply. The thinking function uses logic, reasoning, and analysis to assess experience.

The feeling function applies qualitative "feeling values" to assess the contents of consciousness. The feeling function is just as rational as the thinking function, but it can baffle someone oriented to logic. Jung, with an admitted preference for the thinking function, struggled to comprehend the depth and breadth of the feeling function. The intellect, he said, is incapable of grasping the full nature of the feeling function.

The terms *feeling* and *value* do not refer to modes of morality or ethics; nor do they refer to what most people regard as feeling—affect or emotion. The ego's feeling function produces "no physical innervations, i.e., neither more nor less than an ordinary thinking process" (CW 6, §725).

Feeling, as Jung uses the term here, is more oriented to favoring or not favoring, liking or not liking, feeling comfortable or uncomfortable with, related or unrelated to, the object. The aim of feeling is not to establish moral or ethical relationships but to provide subjective evaluations. The

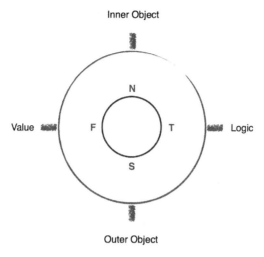

Figure 2.5 Four Orientations with Corresponding Functions

evaluations of the feeling function apply to every content of consciousness, always judging whether something is agreeable or disagreeable.

These then, thinking and feeling, are the two rational functions— rational for they are each predisposed to *assess* rather than simply *receive*. We can expand the ego's compass to include these two new functions, with feeling represented with an F and thinking represented with a T (Figure 2-5). The orientation to value is commensurate with that to logic on the other side of the compass; each is a rational orientation.

These are the four functions of ego consciousness. There might have been more if Jung had been able to discern them empirically, but these were the only four he observed.

> You see, you get your orientation, you get your bearings, in the chaotic abundance of impressions through the four functions, these four aspects of total human orientation. If you can tell me any other aspect by which you get oriented, I am grateful. I haven't found more and I tried.[8]

With the four functions plotted on our compass, corresponding to their accompanying orientations, it is important to now examine more closely two key terms in Jung's lexicon: *attitude* and *orientation*.

---

[8] Richard Evans, *Jung on Elementary Psychology* (Hialeah, FL: Dutton, 1976), pp. 103, 104.

ATTITUDE AND ORIENTATION

Functional Attitude and Orientation

Attitude is a readiness of the psyche to act or react in a certain way. . . . To have an attitude means to be ready for something definite. —C. G. Jung

Each of the four functions is an attitude—an a priori readiness to perform in a certain way. The sensation attitude is ready to perceive the outer object; the intuition attitude is ready to apprehend the inner object. The thinking attitude is ready to apply the governing principle of logic; the feeling attitude is ready to apply the governing principle of value.

The distinction between functional *attitude* and functional *orientation* is subtle but important. Each attitude is oriented by a governing principle—inner object, outer object, logic, or value. The governing principle is the orientation of the attitude. "I use this term to denote the general principle governing an attitude" (CW 6, §780).

We might think of an orientation as a window framing the field of action for the function. The orientation of intuition—its window—is the inner object; that of sensation is the outer object. The window for the thinking function is logic; that of the feeling function is value.

The orienting window frames and governs how the function will take its action. Each of the four functions has a degree of readiness to act (attitude) that is framed by its window (orientation).

If ego consciousness were static, if each of these attitudes could act only in accord with its one window and no other, this exposition would be complete; but the functions alone do not account for the diversity of conscious experience.

One further distinction imbues them with versatility: *libido.*[9] As Jung uses the term, it refers to psychic energy. Psychic energy will direct each of the functional attitudes to either the inner or outer objects. That directional energy is also an attitude.

---

[9] The term libido is used throughout according to this broader Jungian definition, and not Freud's better-known original definition that was narrowly limited to sexual drive. While both Freud and Jung agreed that libido included physical manifestations, they disagreed irreconcilably about its scope.

Directional Attitude and Orientation

An *introverted* attitude is poised to direct a function toward the inner object; an *extraverted* attitude is poised to direct a function to the outer object.

As attitudes, these directional energies have corresponding orientations. Introversion is oriented to the inner object. Extraversion is oriented to the outer object. They are congruent with the functional attitudes, intuition and sensation, because they have common governing principles: introversion, like intuition, is oriented to the inner object; extraversion, like sensation, is oriented to the outer object.

To depict these combinations on our compass of consciousness, we will put the four introverted functions on the northern side of the great divide, directed toward the inner object (Figure 2-6). Each introverted function will be preceded by the letter I. The four extraverted functions will appear on the southern side of the compass, indicating their direction toward the outer object, preceded by the letter E.[10]

For a function to become fully engaged in consciousness, it needs directional energy toward one side or the other of the great divide.

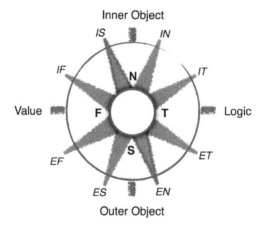

Figure 2.6 The Compass of Consciousnes

---

[10]The location of introverted or extraverted sensation and intuition is somewhat arbitrary. Introverted sensation and introverted intuition, for example, could be interchanged. However, early research with the Gifts Compass Inventory (GCI) suggests that the sensation function may align more frequently with the feeling function than with the thinking function.

COMPOSITE ATTITUDES: THE EIGHT TYPES

When the two directional attitudes merge with the four functional attitudes, they create what we will term eight *composite attitudes*. We will refer to them as *composite* because they combine a functional attitude with a directional attitude.

For example, a thinking attitude is oriented to logic. If the thinking attitude is extraverted, logic will be directed to the outer object, becoming the composite attitude of *extraverted thinking*. Each of the eight composite attitudes will merge a directional attitude with a functional attitude. Because an attitude must have an orientation—a governing principle— each of the eight composite attitudes will have a corresponding *composite orientation*.

We will consider the nature of these composite attitudes and orientations in Chapters 3 and 4. For now, it is important to recognize that they consist of a merger of functional attitude and directional attitude. Extraverted and introverted composite attitudes will be rendered similar and compatible by virtue of a common directional attitude. The directional attitude instills the composite attitude with sensation-like or intuition-like attributes, so each of the extraverted attitudes will gain qualities of *perceiving*, and each of the introverted attitudes will gain qualities of *apprehending*. Even originally opposing functional attitudes will be rendered compatible by the qualities of their common directional attitude.

As Jung uses the term *type*, any of the attitudes or composite attitudes we have discussed so far could be considered "typical" if they are habitually and preeminently relied upon. Someone relying chiefly on extraverted thinking could be said to be a thinking type, an extraverted type, or an extraverted thinking type; each indicates a habitual attitude.

Such shorthand references to types have generated no end of confusion about the nature of psychological types. It is too easy to apply the types reductively, to relegate people to categories, rather than systematically as a fluid framework for understanding diversity.

> It is not the purpose of a psychological typology to classify human beings into categories—this in itself would be pretty pointless. (CW 6, §986) The typological system I have proposed is an attempt, grounded on practical experience, to provide an explanatory basis and theoretical framework for the boundless diversity that has hitherto prevailed in the formation of psychological concepts. (CW 6, §987)

For clarity in this book, we will use the term *type* only when referring to one of these eight composite attitudes. This is a stricter use of the term than Jung's, but it will help to focus his theory on types of consciousness rather than types of people.

Though we will consider each type separately, none of the types ever act alone. They are always acting in concert with or opposition to one another. The dynamics of type interaction will have much to do with navigating the course of individuation, the formation of complexes, and also some of the more practical aspects of life: making career choices, forming teams, teaching children, building relationships, or sorting out marital problems.

But to understand type dynamics, it is first necessary to understand each of the types individually. In Chapter 3 we will examine the extraverted types individually; in Chapter 4, the introverted types.

As a brief introduction to the eight types, and to clarify qualities of the receptive types in particular, in this chapter we will review the types in pairs that share common structural attributes: Crossover Receptive Types; Quintessential Receptive Types; Extraverted Rational Types; and Introverted Rational Types.

The "Crossover" Receptive Types

Extraverted Intuition and Introverted Sensation

Two anomalies highlighted on Figure 2-6 are the way introverted sensa-

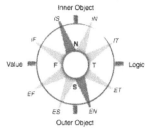

tion and extraverted intuition are positioned on the compass. Their directional positions are on opposite sides of the compass from their original functional positions. "At last," exclaimed Niels Bohr during an especially penetrating study of nuclear physics, "a paradox! Now we are getting somewhere." Bohr would have been pleased with these two types.

The intuition function is oriented to the contents of the inner object, yet when extraverted, it is also directed to the outer object. Extraverted intuition apprehends the contents of the inner object as a background consciousness while simultaneously perceiving the contents of the outer object. Similarly, introverted sensation simultaneously perceives the contents of the outer object while apprehending the contents of the inner object.

It is as though they are moving through the closet doorway in C. S. Lewis's *The Chronicles of Narnia*. They cross through the same closet door, but one (extraverted intuition) brings the possibilities of the magical land of

Narnia to the normal world of objective experience. The other (introverted sensation) brings the contents of the normal world of objective experience into the bedazzling world of Narnia. Each bridges the great psychic divide by engaging *both* the inner and outer objects simultaneously.

If these crossover types could be simplistically personified, introverted sensation would be the "silent type," for he would have much difficulty expressing the bedazzling transformation of his perceptions. The easier of the two to comprehend would be extraverted intuition, for she would figuratively wear her dreams on her sleeve.

Extraverted Intuition

Though functionally oriented to the inner object, the energy of this type is directed to the outer object. With a functional orientation to the inner object, it will apprehend images simultaneously with objective experience in the world. Extraverted intuition will have a quick intuitive grasp of possibilities in the making. With a directional orientation to the outer object, it becomes a close cousin to extraverted sensation.

> The primary function of intuition . . . is simply to transmit images, or perceptions of relations between things, which could not be transmitted by the other functions. . . . But since extraverted intuition is directed predominantly to objects, it actually comes very close to sensation. (CW 6, §611)

Introverted Sensation

With a directional orientation to the inner object, introverted sensation has attributes similar to those of introverted intuition. Yet introverted sensation has a functional orientation to the outer object, so the functional role of this receptive type is to commingle the perceptions of the outer object with images of the inner object—a dazzling transformation.

> We could say that introverted sensation transmits an image which does not so much reproduce the object as spread over it the patina of age-old subjective experience and the shimmer of events still unborn. (CW 6, §649)

The remaining composite attitudes are not so paradoxical, so their nature is easier to grasp. The clearest of the six are the two quintessential receptive types where functional attitudes are amplified by directional attitudes.

The Quintessential Receptive Types

Extraverted Sensation and Introverted Intuition

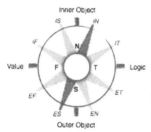

The differences inherent in the two receptive functions, intuition and sensation, are made especially clear by comparing extraverted sensation and introverted intuition, in which the attributes of each function are amplified because their functional and directional orientations align.

Extraverted Sensation

Extraverted sensation is functionally oriented to the outer object and is directed there by its extraverted attitude. The sensation function's orientation to the outer object is amplified by the extraverted attitude, also oriented to the outer object.

Introverted Intuition

Introverted intuition is functionally oriented to the inner object and is directed there by its introverted attitude. It most clearly articulates the nature of the intuition function, for the directional attitude redoubles the functional attitude's orientation.

The two groups of receptive types—crossover and quintessential—illuminate the dynamic relationships of functional and directional attitudes sharing the same or opposite orientations. The rational types never share two orientations that are either the same or opposite one another.

The Extraverted Rational Types

Extraverted Thinking and Extraverted Feeling

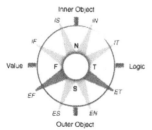

The rational functions have no inherent orientation to either the inner or the outer object; they do not acquire such an orientation until they are endowed with a directional attitude.

The extraverted attitude directs the rational attitudes to the outer object, instilling attributes similar to the sensation function with its orientation to concrete facts and detail.

Extraverted Thinking

Extraverted thinking attends to the established facts in the world: tangible perceptions, standards, established systems, laws, and well-accepted theories. Extraverted thinking is poised to apply logical order to a practical understanding of the world as it is, or as it has been.

Extraverted Feeling

Extraverted feeling also seeks the outer fact, but is oriented to existing social relationships, norms, or traditions. Extraverted feeling seeks to affirm the values already generally accepted by others.

The Introverted Rational Types

Introverted Thinking and Introverted Feeling

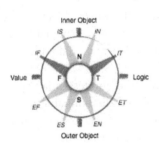

When an introverted attitude orients the rational functions to the inner object, they acquire intuition-like attributes, apprehending images from the collective unconscious. Each of the rational functions is transformed as it turns to the inner object.

Introverted Thinking

Introverted thinking orients to ideas and images—the hazy outline of a felt solution, the vague notion of some clarifying theory that could unite and resolve perplexing incongruities. The functional orientation to logic is directed toward a solution that is only indistinctly perceived.

> Introverted thinking is primarily oriented by the subjective factor [inner object]. At the very least the subjective factor expresses itself as a feeling of guidance which ultimately determines judgment. (CW 6, §628)

External facts may be intertwined in formulating solutions, insights, or ideas; they may be collected as evidence for a theory, but they are never the object of attention for introverted thinking. The inner object, the "initial image hovering darkly before the mind's eye" (CW 6, §628), is of preeminent importance.

Introverted Feeling

Introverted feeling also apprehends vague ideas and images, but they feel more like ideals than philosophical or theoretical ideas.

> The primordial images are, of course, just as much ideas as feelings. Fundamental ideas, ideas like God, freedom, and immortality, are just as much feeling-values as they are significant ideas. Everything, therefore, that we have said about introverted thinking is equally true of introverted feeling, only here everything is felt while there it was thought. (CW 6, §639)

Introverted feeling parallels its introverted cousin oriented to logic. Where introverted thinking would apprehend an image and derive an insightful understanding, introverted feeling apprehends the image and feels a profound ideal. These otherwise opposing functional attitudes are rendered more readily compatible by the introverted attitude.

COMPARATIVE CATEGORIES

To understand the composite qualities of each of the eight types in the chapters that follow, we will use a systematic approach, examining attributes for each type within five "comparative categories." They will provide a framework for understanding the new attributes acquired in the merger of directional and functional attitudes and will also provide much insight about how the types tend to collaborate with or oppose one another. They will help to show that the directional attitudes play a more influential role than the functional attitudes in the merger of composite attitudes, that types with common directional attitudes are more likely to collaborate with one another than types with opposing directional attitudes, and that the attributes of a rational attitude change so markedly after the merger with a directional attitude that it can be a stranger to the same rational attitude merged with the opposite directional attitude.

The categories include *composite orientation* and *composite attitude* discussed in this chapter. While a functional orientation may be clear, and a directional orientation may be clear, the resulting composite orientation, when they merge, may be quite baffling. Introverted sensation, for example, the type that has been most frequently misunderstood, is very hard to grasp without understanding how the new composite orientation and attitude are formed by the merger. Extraverted intuition, the other crossover type, is also difficult to understand, though not as perplexing as introverted sensation. The merger of the rational attitudes with directional attitudes also produces some very interesting combinations. For the rational functions, the introverted and extraverted composite attitudes become so different from one another that they become worthy opponents.

Three other categories will also help to clarify the transformations that occur. The first of these, *new functional role,* describes the newly adopted role of a function. The role of introverted thinking, for example, becomes quite different from extraverted thinking, for one is active with the inner object, and the other with the outer object. The new functional role could also be used to name each type. Introverted thinking, for example, could be considered *conceptual* thinking, and extraverted thinking could be considered *constructive* thinking.

A fourth category, the *composite substance* of the merged attitudes will help to clarify the attributes of the type. How might we describe the new "primary material" of the merged attitudes? The primary material of the thinking attitude, for example, could be "thoughts," but how does that primary material change when introverted or extraverted? We could consider the composite substance, when introverted, as *inner thoughts.* When extraverted, they would be *outer thoughts.*

Finally, we will consider the *composite scope* for each type. A peculiarity of the extraverted attitude is that it sees the parts more readily than the whole, much as sensation focuses on particular detail. Introversion is more holistic; it tends to want to capture the whole picture rather than the individual parts, much as intuition tends to apprehend whole images. This category describes how these attributes of introversion and extraversion affect the resulting types. Using the thinking function again as our example, when extraverted its scope would be to *particular order;* when introverted it would be to *holistic insights.*

The Five Comparative Categories

The five categories we will be using to describe the attributes of the types can be summarized as follows:

1. **Composite Orientation:** the merger of functional and directional orientations

2. **Composite Attitude:** the merger of functional and directional attitudes
3. **New Functional Role (Name):** the revised role of the function as altered by its directional attitude
4. **Composite Substance:** the primary material engaged in the new functional role
5. **Composite Scope:** the composite focus to either the particular or the whole as conditioned by the directional attitude.

CHAPTER SUMMARY

Combining two directional attitudes and four functional attitudes produced eight composite attitudes that we will refer to as the *eight types.* While we may understand functional attitudes and directional attitudes separately, understanding the new composite attitudes born by the merger of functional and directional attitudes can be perplexing. The directional attitude greatly modifies the nature of the underlying functional attitude. To more fully assess the nature of each composite attitude, we created five comparative categories that will be useful for comparing and contrasting the types in the chapters that follow.

In Chapters 3 and 4, we will explore the nature of each of the eight types using the five comparative categories. In Chapter 5, we will use the categories again to examine how the types tend to collaborate. In Chapter 6, they will help to illuminate the dynamics of oppositions among the types.

We will also review the behavioral characteristics associated with each type and relate those characteristics to well-known people. The types are never found in clinical isolation; they combine in lively, complex, and dynamic ways. Any references we make to people are not to typecast the people themselves but simply to illustrate how types of ego consciousness can manifest themselves in human experience.

In Volume 6 of the Collected Works, Jung grouped his descriptions of the types by directional attitudes, reviewing first the types with extraverted attitudes and then those with introverted attitudes. That approach will be helpful because common directional attitudes will organize the types into groups that are rendered more similar than if they were ordered by functional attitudes.

We turn first to the extraverted types.

3

The Extraverted Types

WITH THEIR ATTENTION TO outer experiences, people disposed toward the extraverted types are attuned to participating in and supporting social organizations, sustaining management systems, recognizing social norms, organizing operations, gathering tangible facts, enjoying the moment, perceiving possibilities in existing events and circumstances, improving the world as they find it, and creating order. Their locus of attention starts and ends with the world at large.

Jung compares a few examples of extraverted and introverted types.

> The fact that it is cold outside prompts one man to put on his overcoat [extraverted], while another, who wants to get hardened, finds this superfluous [introverted]. One man admires the latest tenor because everybody else does [extraverted], another refuses to do so, not because he dislikes him, but because in his view the subject of universal admiration is far from having been proved admirable [introverted]. One man resigns himself to circumstances because experience has shown him that nothing else is possible [extraverted], another is convinced that though things have gone the same way a thousand times before, the thousand and first time will be different [introverted]. (CW 6, §563)

Institutions, social organizations, enjoyable parties, gala events, operating rules, social order and norms, the news of the day, titles, recognition, operating systems, fun, action—these are the stock and trade of an extraverted way of life. Current events and circumstances are often sufficiently fascinating in themselves.

His interest and attention are directed to objective happenings, particularly those in his immediate environment. Not only people but things seize and rivet his attention. . . . It is the same with his interests: objective happenings have an almost inexhaustible fascination for him, so that ordinarily he never looks for anything else. (CW 6, §563)

Though "objective happenings" are generally limited to what is, or what has been, only the most innovative of the extraverted types—extraverted intuition—tends to see beyond the palette of practical facts to envision unborn possibilities. People disposed to the extraverted types generally attend to outward expectations—to what is normal, practical, and expected.

His requirements are limited to the objectively possible, for instance to the career that holds out good prospects at this particular moment; he does what is needed of him, or what is expected of him, and refrains from all innovations that are not entirely self-evident or that in any way exceed the expectations of those around him. (CW 6, §564)

We begin our review of the extraverted types, as Jung did, with the types most attentive to creating, affirming, and preserving standards: the extraverted rational types.

EXTRAVERTED RATIONAL TYPES

Though the rational attitudes are opposite, they are rendered similar in many respects by the extraverted orientation to the outer object. Of the two extraverted rational types, extraverted thinking may be easier to grasp, for it has the attributes so commonly regarded as "rational."

Extraverted Thinking

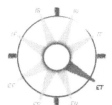

Look at a day when you are supremely satisfied at the end. It's not a day when you lounge around doing nothing; it's when you've had everything to do, and you've done it. —Margaret Thatcher

Composite Orientation: Extensive Order

As the extraverted attitude orients thinking to the outer object, the thinking attitude becomes highly conditioned by external circumstances. Its orientation is still to logic, but a logic that is governed by concrete facts. The extraverted attitude is more influential in shaping the new composite orientation than is the thinking attitude's orientation to logic.

All the logical judgments will be based on factual, tangible, traditional, objective data. Like all the extraverted types, the composite orientation of extraverted thinking is extensive rather than intensive. With the extraverted attitude's orientation to the outer object, coupled with the thinking attitude's orientation to logic, we could say that the composite orientation of extraverted thinking is to *extensive order*.

Composite Attitude: Perceive Order

Extraverted thinking reduces the complexity of many facts by organizing them. The whole is built from an assemblage of the parts. It assembles the facts of experience—data, observations, traditions—into a simplified order. Extraverted thinking is forever poised—ready to act—to reduce the complexity of many facts to the simplicity of ruling formulas. Because the directional attitude has "perceiving-like" attributes, to characterize the composite attitude of this type we could say that it is predisposed to *perceive order* amid a welter of many facts.

Functional Role: Constructive Thinking

Jung described extraverted thinking as constructive.

> Even when it analyses it constructs, because it is always advancing beyond the analysis to a new combination, to a further conception which reunites the analyzed material in a different way. (CW 6, §592)

We could use his term to name the functional role for extraverted thinking and call it *constructive thinking*. Captivated by its orientation to objective data, the new role for thinking as an extraverted functional attitude is to construct order.

Composite Substance: Outer Thoughts

The material being assembled, arranged, and constructed by thinking directed outwardly is the tried-and-true stuff of practical reality. Ideas can also serve as tangible facts, as long as those ideas are already well established and accepted.

Objective facts are the grist for the mill of extraverted thinking. Thinking and concrete facts are united as one. We could characterize the primary substance of extraverted thinking, thoroughly conditioned by the outer object, as *outer thoughts*.

Composite Scope: Particular Order

Extraverted thinking sees the individual trees rather than the forest and constructs its organized conclusions from an assemblage of individual facts. The scope of this thinking could be characterized as *particular order*, for the constructed conclusions are limited by the particular facts being considered.

Behavioral Attributes

People predisposed to extraverted thinking are usually productive, positive, and orderly. They may be found constructing improved standards, policies, procedures, organizations, buildings, or environments—wherever there is a need to create tangible order out of the seeming disorder of many facts. They are concrete thinkers, attentive to details, and confident in the objective substance of their logical conclusions.

They attend to the practical matters of life in the world. They typically have their feet on the ground, know where they are going, and know how to get there. They are familiar with the world as it is: known ideas, traditions, facts, data, things, and people constitute the palette from which they draw conclusions and construct order.

They may be quick to judge, for they always seem to have their ruling formulas at hand. They tend to formulate the "oughts" and "shoulds" that serve as guidelines and rules for themselves and others.

Because their ruling formulas may have broad appeal, they often serve as effective social or commercial reformers. Those people who naturally organize the world are often those who find their way into leadership roles. In every discipline and every arena, if something needs to be organized or accomplished, people who favor extraverted thinking are often the ones either called upon to do it or who take the initiative themselves.

They tend to move, one fact at a time, toward their desired objective order; they arrive at their conclusions deliberately and hold fast to them once attained.

Ideas are merely the byproducts of empirical thinking. Whereas introverted thinking moves from the idea to the outer experience, extraverted thinking moves from the outer experience to the idea. Coming as they do from opposite directions, people disposed to these two modes of thinking may collide like moving trains, much as Freud and Jung eventually did.

People disposed to extraverted thinking tend to scan the external environment for particular facts. As they discover new ones, they may include them with other known facts to construct new combinations; they may improve systems, organize people, or build on accepted theories. They enjoy applying rules, standards, traditions, and operating procedures to construct order. If there is not a suitable organizing formula, they will create one.

As they construct order, they also judge the world by that order. Once a ruling formula is established, it can be used to distinguish right from wrong, correct from incorrect, good from bad, generally accepted practices from untried theories. These ordering formulas are rational frameworks for judgment that can extend into every sphere of life, for example, religion, science, law, medicine, art, morality, commerce, politics, and relationships.

Charles Darwin

When conclusions are being drawn from objective experience, we could expect to find extraverted thinking at work. In scientific or medical research, and among industrialists, business executives, law enforcement officials, attorneys, judges, or military personnel, we find many examples of extraverted thinking.

Though extraverted thinking may often be associated with hard-nosed decision makers like Margaret Thatcher, intent on making decisions and getting things done, the spectrum of biographical examples of extraverted thinking is broad.

Jung suggested Charles Darwin as an example of this type of consciousness; his "ruling formula"—natural selection—was derived from years of assembling many varied observations of flora and fauna.

Later images of Darwin as an older adult suggest a more introverted, dour individual; but in his youth, when type disposition is usually more clearly in evidence, Darwin was adventurous and gregarious. His father was concerned that the boy Darwin, whose favorite pastimes were bird-hunting and rat-catching, would be a disgrace to himself

Charles Darwin 1809–1882

and his whole family, but his five-year adventurous voyage on the survey ship *Beagle* channeled his extraverted energies toward a focused career as a naturalist. He returned to London after his fact-finding voyage with scores of artifacts, notes, mammal pelts, bird skins, pickled reptiles, fish, dried plants, and fossils.

Upon his return, he was commissioned to make sense of his many observations. He found writing tedious, but with the help of other specialists he began to sort out the many forms of life, both extinct and living, that he had retrieved from islands and continents around the world. He took note of the objective clues that indicated a "transmutation" of species.

Decades later, in 1858, after amassing and organizing the many objective facts that would support his theory of evolution, he was almost ready to unveil his theory publicly when he received a letter from fellow naturalist Alfred Russell Wallace, who had been exploring in the East Indies.

With a more introverted disposition to thinking, Wallace had developed a brief outline of some thoughts he had had while lying in a hammock, recovering from an illness. He was not sure if they were important, so he sent his outline to Darwin for review. Shocked and amazed, Darwin saw that Wallace had outlined the very theory that he had been tediously organizing from objective observations.

Wallace, with an orientation to formulating and refining the inner image, was relying on introverted thinking; Darwin, with an orientation to ordering extensive facts, was relying on extraverted thinking. They arrived at the same conclusion from opposite sides of the great divide. Each was credited as cofounder of the theory of evolution, but Darwin's seminal and detailed book, *The Origin of the Species,* was published the following year, establishing him as the preeminent authority on evolutionary theory.

Extraverted Feeling

Composite Orientation: Extensive Norms

Extraverted feeling orients to social conditions. As people, groups, or organizations change, extraverted feeling adjusts to the norms or values discerned in the new situation. For introverted feeling, such a flexible and versatile orientation would be sacrilegious, but nothing could be more natural for extraverted feeling. We could characterize the composite orientation of this type as an orientation to *extensive norms.*

Composite Attitude: Perceive Norms

The aim of extraverted feeling is not to take a stand for personally treasured feeling-values but to empathize with the feeling-values of others. Personal likes or dislikes are less important than what is *already* liked or disliked by others; empathy, not reflection, guides the action of extraverted feeling. As people and social values change, extraverted feeling adapts. We could say that extraverted feeling is ready to *perceive norms*.

Functional Role: Social Feeling

While introverted feeling would seek harmony with the ideas and ideals of the inner object, extraverted feeling seeks harmony in the world, especially the established traditions and values of others. We could characterize the functional role for extraverted feeling as *social feeling*.

Composite Substance: Outer Valuations

The substance of this type could be considered *outer valuations*—perpetual empathy with the values, standards, moods, and loyalties of others.

Composite Scope: Particular Norms

The scope of extraverted feeling, like the scope of all the extraverted types, is to the *particular*. The form of adaptation to one group, circumstance, person, or event may be quite different from that to another. Much would depend on the particular values discerned in each case. For extraverted feeling, this is not hypocrisy but simply adaptation to *particular norms*.

Behavioral Attributes

Jung provides less insight into the behavioral attributes of people favoring this type (likely Jung's own shadow type), but Marie-Louise von Franz, one of Jung's closest associates, provides some helpful commentary, describing them as highly gregarious, empathetic, and self-sacrificing.

They say things like, "What a nice day it is today, I am so glad to see you again, I haven't seen you for a long time!" and they really mean it![1]

They possess the personal qualities that make them highly related. They can move from one social situation to the next, always feeling at ease

---

[1] Marie-Louise von Franz, *Conversations on Aion*. Interview by Claude Drey (Asheville, NC: Chiron Publications, 2004), p. 44.

with the people around them. They are forever adapting to the external conditions, extending their empathy to others and to what those people hold dear.

It is not hard for them to strike up conversations, for there is always so much to share, and they like to share it expressively. They relate easily to many different people and groups because their empathy is so well developed.

They are able to adapt to diverse situations as they find them, sometimes as if to discrete compartments of experience. They could intently empathize with one somber individual in one moment and then swiftly put on a cheerful demeanor for a large and boisterous party in the next. Extending bountiful empathy to people and groups, extraverted feeling weaves the cohesive fabric of social harmony.

People who are predisposed to this type of consciousness are often the standard-bearers of conventional values and harmonious relationships. They affirm and support groups and are often highly oriented to family life. They may sacrifice their own well-being for the benefit of the family, the group, the organization, or the nation.

For major life decisions, they tend to rely on conventional values to guide their choices. A prospective partner's age, position, income, or family status could play a more important role in determining marital choice than personal or romantic feelings.

Hosts to the generally accepted societal or organizational values of the day, they serve as carriers of social traditions and values. "This kind of feeling is very largely responsible for the fact that so many people flock to the theatre or to concerts, or go to church, and do so moreover with their feelings correctly adjusted" (CW 6, §596).

For feeling to have center stage in consciousness, thinking is obliged to wait in the wings. With individuation, thinking may ultimately join the production at center stage, but until it is invited to the play, it will serve as an accessory to feeling, called on only to wait upon the judgments of feeling. What is thought must first be felt.

Queen Elizabeth I

If you think of the people you know who enjoy sustaining harmony in groups, who light up at the thought of people getting together for a party or a meeting, or who are very conscious of social protocol, you are likely recalling people who favor extraverted feeling.

Who could better exemplify the attributes of one who seeks harmony among diverse people, who is mindful of protocol and political correct-

Queen Elizabeth 1533–1603

ness, who affirms traditions and culture, who looks after the well-being of others, and who empathizes with many, than a good monarch?

We could look to the life of "Good Queen Bess"—Queen Elizabeth I of England—for insight and understanding about how this conscious disposition shows up in life experience. Her extraverted feeling was certainly well exercised in her role as sovereign, and she fulfilled her role with ease.

After her coronation, her gracious and compelling speech to the powerful nobility of England inspired loyalty by affirming her commitment to enlist collaboration.

> My lords, the law of nature moves me to sorrow for my sister; the burden that is fallen upon me makes me amazed, and yet, considering I am God's creature, ordained to obey His appointment, I will thereto yield, desiring from the bottom of my heart that I may have assistance of His grace to be the minister of His heavenly will in this office now committed to me. And as I am but one body naturally considered, though by His permission a body politic to govern, so shall I desire you all . . . to be assistant to me, that I with my ruling and you with your service may make a good account to Almighty God and leave some comfort to our posterity on earth. I mean to direct all my actions by good advice and counsel.[2]

She ruled cautiously and collaboratively, relying very much on a close circle of trusted advisors to help her navigate the troublesome waters of political intrigue and foreign aggression. Decisions about war, strategies, conflict, betrayals, and intrigues were not her strong suit. She seemed forever plagued with decisions about conflict and betrayal that painfully stretched her natural feeling attitude.

She sagaciously navigated the religious conflicts of her age—Protestants and Catholics in deadly opposition—and affirmed her loyalty to her father's religion, which was midway between extreme evangelism and papal tradition, to unify a country torn by religious conflicts. She reinstated a revised version of the Book of Common Prayer, first established under the reign of her half-brother, Edward VI.

---

[2] J. A. Froude, *Reign of Elizabeth* (Everyman's Library), p. 11. As quoted in *The Age of Reason Begins*, Will Durant and Ariel Durant (Simon & Schuster, 1961), p. 3.

When not embroiled in stressful strategies, plots, political maneuvering, religious conflicts, and intrigues of monarchy, Elizabeth enjoyed herself, suggesting that her extraverted feeling was well-supported by extraverted sensation. She frequently held extravagant banquets with an abundance of food, wine, music, and dancing. The nobility in her court enjoyed games, sports, riding, and hunting.

Elizabeth was as much a participant as observer; she was an expert rider, a skilled hunter, and an enthusiastic dancer. She danced the difficult and demanding *Galliard* every morning to keep fit and was fond of dancing the *Volta*—an especially energetic dance—with courtiers.

She was patron to musicians and composers and a skilled musician herself. The theatrical arts thrived in her realm, providing receptive audiences for Shakespeare and his contemporaries.

She had a tender heart, though toughened by the contentious demands of monarchy. She fell in love easily, but with the circumspect propriety of one who was already "married" to the people of England. She held herself back from marital commitment, proclaiming herself the "Virgin Queen," for she felt a high calling to be the sovereign ruler of England.

Her forty-four years on the British throne provided welcome stability for her people and forged a sense of common national identity. The years of her reign became England's "Golden Age," and her commitment to "direct all my actions by good advice and counsel" undoubtedly played no small part in this success. She would be remembered affectionately as "Good Queen Bess."

Summary of the Extraverted Rational Types

Both of these types are distinguished by a rational orientation to the outer object. The directional attitude orients the functional attitudes to what is known and accepted.

> The rationality of both types is object-oriented and dependent on objective data. It accords with what is collectively considered to be rational. For them, nothing is rational save what is generally considered as such. (CW 6, §603)

Both of these rational types seek to exclude the chaos of what does not conform to their systems of organization. They are orderly and circumscribed and have their ruling formulas or conventional norms by which to assess experience and order the untidy aspects of life. Everything that fits within their rational order is good; anything else is suspect.

In Table 3-1, which summarizes the resulting comparative categories for each of these otherwise opposing rational attitudes, we can see how similar the extraverted attitude renders them.

Category	Extraverted Thinking	Extraverted Feeling
Composite Orientation	Extensive Order	Extensive Norms
Composite Attitude	Perceive Order	Perceive Norms
Functional Role	Constructive Thinking	Social Feeling
Composite Substance	Outer Thoughts	Outer Valuations
Composite Scope	Particular Order	Particular Norms

Table 3-1 Comparative Categories for Extraverted Rational Types

EXTRAVERTED RECEPTIVE TYPES

The orientation of each of the extraverted receptive types is likewise to the outer object of tangible facts, established traditions, and proven ideas. Even though the intuition attitude is oriented to the inner object, the directional attitude, with its orientation to the outer object, subordinates the functional attitude, rendering extraverted intuition a close cousin to extraverted sensation.

Extraverted sensation is more fully oriented to the concrete facts of the outer object than are any of the other types. It renders a very detailed and accurate understanding of the world.

Extraverted Sensation

Composite Orientation: Extensive Facts

Extraverted sensation is oriented by the factual, concrete, tangible, measurable representations of the outer object—in all the glorious detail that entails. Every fact, every feature, every fine point is of interest, yet some perceptions can be more highly valued than others. "The sole criterion of their value is the intensity of the sensation produced by their objective qualities" (CW 6, §605).

Like scanning radar, the senses are forever at work on behalf of the sensation attitude to detect some new fact or perception. Like all the extraverted types, the orientation is extensive rather than intensive. We could say that the orientation of this type is to *extensive facts*.

Composite Attitude: Perceive Facts

Extraverted sensation is keenly poised to perceive objective facts. The taste, smell, sight, sound, and touch of every individual object perceived may vary enormously. Each nuance, each variation is another fact registered about the reality of that object.

Extraverted sensation has its own predetermined mental structures to frame and make sense of what has been detected. Time, space, duration, sequence, context, form—these are among the preexisting perceptual frameworks necessary for extraverted sensation to interpret what has been perceived. Without them, perception would be an overwhelmingly jumbled and confused mass of colors, forms, textures, tastes, and sounds.

Extraverted sensation is predisposed to *interpret* the outer object just as it is predisposed to detect it. It hears a distant train and registers it as distant. It feels a rough object and registers it as not smooth. It tastes something bitter and registers it in contrast to sweet. It feels a rock and knows that it is hard and not soft.

But people who favor extraverted sensation have no time for such philosophical meanderings, for abstract thinking is not real life. Thinking philosophically that a rock is not actually hard, or a train distant, or a surface rough or smooth would be irrelevant.

Detecting and affirming *real* objective facts is the role of extraverted sensation. If something cannot be perceived as being concretely real, then it simply does not exist. Apprehending the images of the unconscious is outside the bounds of its framework. We could say its composite attitude is poised to *perceive facts.*

Functional Role: Realistic Sensation

"The essential function of sensation is to establish that something exists" (CW 6, §983), and extraverted sensation accomplishes that role masterfully. Oriented *and* directed to the outer object, extraverted sensation accurately affirms what is perceived there. Extraverted sensation perceives with greater clarity and detail than any other type of ego consciousness. "No other human type can equal the extraverted sensation type in realism. His sense for objective facts is extraordinarily developed" (CW 6, §606).

Unlike the rational types that apply rational processes of judgmental filtering and ordering, extraverted sensation merely perceives—detects what is concretely real—and affirms it. There is no shaping or organizing process being applied other than the simple process of perception itself.

The extensive cavalcade of sensations, with their many nuances, varieties, intensities, and details, are sufficient. There is no need for abstracting or subjectively modifying the many experiences of life, for sensation is life itself. We could call this intensification of the sensation function *realistic sensation*.

Composite Substance: Outer Perceptions

Whereas introverted sensation intensively encodes subjective *impressions* of perception, extraverted sensation encodes many accurate and detailed perceptions.

The primary materials for extraverted sensation are the accurate and detailed perceptions of sensory experience. We could refer to its substance as *outer perceptions*.

Composite Scope: Particular Facts

The scope of extraverted sensation is to the particular—the many discrete elements of any perception and their details. The panorama is of less interest than the detail. We could term the composite scope of this type, *particular facts*.

Behavioral Attributes

People primarily disposed to extraverted sensation are often content to experience life as it comes. There is no need to fill a compelling gap between *what is* and *what might be*, for *what is* stimulates them sufficiently. There are few rational judgments to be considered, few intervening intuitions of a larger perspective.

They seem fully content to experience the captivating facts of life as they present themselves, without a need to question, wonder, or judge. Once something has been perceived, nothing more needs to be said or done about it. The perception itself is concretely real for them; philosophical conjectures that go beyond it would be superfluous.

Their lives are perpetually linked to the world as it is, making them very much at home in every new situation. They are remarkably adaptable to circumstances as they find them.[3]

---

[3] Though Jung does not explicitly say this, their perceptions of facts might well include traditions,

Though their aim may be the full sensuous enjoyment of life, this does not necessarily mean that they are devoid of all morality. True enjoyment has its own restraining principles, requiring moderation and sacrifice. Their enjoyment of life can be highly refined and disciplined.

People with this predisposition are often attuned to what constitutes good form or style—dressing well with refined tastes, appreciating the presentation of a well-prepared meal, buoyantly enjoying the company of others. Their enjoyment of life often renders them fun-loving and gregarious. Their love of life is the appreciation of many sensory stimuli; there is no need for idealistic aspirations—to change what exists—for accurately perceiving and enjoying what exists *is* their ideal.

Their attention to detail, to nuance, to variety, and to accurate perception can sometimes present the appearance of highly developed reason, but their appreciation for sensuous experience is the locus of their rationality. The aim is to experience life, and to experience it fully.

Julia Child

Julia Child 1912–2004

Anyone combining a lively appreciation of the sensuous life with a firm grasp of tangible and practical facts could exemplify this type of consciousness.

We could look to the woman whom *Time* magazine called "Our Lady of the Ladle" as our example of extraverted sensation. Julia Child was an American chef, author, and television personality. Educated at San Francisco's elite Katherine Branson School for Girls, she towered above the other students at a height of six feet, two inches. She was adventurous and athletic, enjoying tennis, golf, and basketball.

---

well-accepted theories, conventions, known concepts, laws, and rules, and thus they may be highly aware of political or social nuance. Social norms perceivable via the actions of others, rules that have been explicitly and reliably applied, concepts and theories that have acquired general acceptance, and recognized restrictions and social prohibitions might all be included as facts in their field of perception. They may not be sensitive to the ethos of laws and rules, only to the fact that laws and rules exist and must be reckoned with in the outside world.

Extraverted feeling and thinking, both rational types, also deal with perceived social norms, traditions, and laws. Their extraverted attitudes likewise orient them to these facets of the outer object. Since the rational functions themselves do not technically perceive, the extraverted attitude must carry these perceptual attributes. It might, therefore, reasonably be concluded that extraverted sensation is also capable of the same range of perceptions.

Later, at the prestigious Ivy League Smith College, she still preferred athletics to studies. She was sometimes a prankster who, as one friend recalled, could be "really, really wild." After graduating from Smith College, she took a job with the reputable furnishings company W. & J. Sloane, from which she was eventually fired for "gross insubordination."

During World War II, she served in Asia with the Office of Strategic Services, where she met her lifelong partner, Paul Child. They were married and transferred not long after the war to Paris, where Julia discovered the passion that would engage her for the rest of her life: *food*.

Julia remembered her first meal in Rouen as a culinary revelation; she described one French meal as an "opening up of the soul and spirit for me."

In collaboration with two other "culinary gourmands," she wrote and published the cookbook that introduced French cuisine to the American public: *Mastering the Art of French Cooking*. Julia promoted her book on the Boston public television station near her Cambridge, Massachusetts, home. Forthright, natural, unassuming, and with contagious humor, she prepared an omelet while on the air. The show generated twenty-seven letters and countless phone calls—"a remarkable response," a station executive remembered, "given that station management occasionally wondered if twenty-seven viewers were tuned in."

Though she was not the first television cook, she attracted the broadest audience with her cheery enthusiasm and unaffected *joie de vivre*. Her television program, *The French Chef*, was syndicated to ninety-six stations throughout America. Child was a favorite of audiences and became a familiar personality in American culture. Throughout the 1970s and 1980s, she made regular appearances on the ABC morning show, *Good Morning America*.

Julia Child changed the way Americans related to food, but not everyone was a fan. She was also criticized by more judgmental viewers: "You are quite a revolting chef, the way you snap bones and play with raw meat," one letter read. Others were concerned about the high levels of fat in French cooking. Julia's reply captures the essence of the epicurean aspect of extraverted sensation: "I would rather eat one tablespoon of chocolate russe cake than three bowls of Jell-O!"

In another interview, regarding concerns about nutrition and diet, she said, "Everybody is overreacting. . . . Fortunately, the French don't suffer from the same hysteria we do. We should enjoy food and have fun. It is one of the simplest and nicest pleasures in life."

She exuded warmth, joy, and delight in the sensuous aspects of life. Yet, even with her flamboyant style, she was also detailed, disciplined, hardworking, and determined. She carved a place in American culture by indefatigably promoting the art of French cooking.

In November 2000, following a forty-year career, Julia received France's highest honor: Légion d'Honneur. In August 2002, the Smithsonian's National Museum of American History unveiled an exhibit featuring the kitchen where she filmed three of her popular cooking shows. In 2005, she was lovably portrayed in the movie *Julie and Julia*.

Child died in August 2004, two days before her ninety-second birthday. She hardly slowed down. Even in her final years, she kept at her life's work: "In this line of work . . . you keep right on till you're through. . . . Retired people are boring."

In the life of Julia Child, we can see the lusty, irreverent, impulsive life of a woman who enjoyed extraverted sensation to the fullest, and whose refined sensibilities and discriminating tastes motivated her to introduce America to the fine art of French cooking. Blessed with endless stamina, she was America's gastronomic guru. She taught America to enjoy food and wine as a way of appreciating life's bounty.

The last line in her last book, *My Life in France*, reads: "Thinking back on it now reminds me that the pleasures of the table, and of life, are infinite—toujours bon appétit!"

Extraverted Intuition

Composite Orientation: Extensive Possibilities

 By directional attitude, extraverted intuition is oriented to the outer object; by functional attitude, it is oriented to the inner object. The directional orientation, as always, is more influential than the functional; therefore we could say of extraverted intuition that it is primarily oriented to the extensive outer object.

Yet, with a functional attitude oriented to the inner object, this type continues to apprehend the unseen by way of intuition—the function of unconscious perception. How shall we characterize this extraverted version of intuition, primarily oriented to the outer object yet also oriented to the images of the inner object? The term *possibilities* will be our bridge that connects these oppositions, for the term implies something that is both linked to the outer world *and* imagined. Because the extraverted orientation is always extensive rather than intensive, the composite orientation of this type would be to *extensive possibilities*.

Composite Attitude: Perceive Possibilities

The directional attitude prevails in shaping the composite attitude. While intuition itself might be thought of as *apprehending* the inner image, as introverted intuition does, extraverted intuition is wholly directed to external objects; therefore we will apply the term that is used for perceptions of the world at large—*perceive*.

Yet extraverted intuition does not so much perceive facts as it does the hidden possibilities contained within them. Therefore we could say of this type that its attitude is one of *perceiving possibilities*. Because of the extraverted attitude, intuition and sensation, otherwise complete opposites, become close cousins: "But since extraverted intuition is directed predominantly to objects, it actually comes very close to sensation" (CW 6, §611).

Functional Role: Catalytic Intuition

The next possibility perceived is always the most intriguing one, for only in envisioning possibilities is intuition satisfied. Extraverted intuition, in its perpetual pursuit of external possibilities, serves as a catalyst for change in the world. While introverted intuition may be content to imagine inwardly, extraverted intuition must both imagine *and* create outwardly.

Extraverted intuition applies its imagination to the particular facts of experience to envision new projects, tangible initiatives, and boldly original ventures. It sees around the corner to fresh possibilities and events unborn; it perceives the possibilities inherent in a situation, grasps the practical elements necessary for their realization, and is impelled to make them tangibly real. We could call its composite functional role *catalytic intuition*.

Composite Substance: Outer Imagination

The substance of catalytic intuition is the imagination of possibilities. We could therefore call the primary material of this type *outer imagination*.

Composite Scope: Particular Possibilities

Like introverted intuition that apprehends whole visions and images, extraverted intuition also captures an image of the whole. However, since the composite orientation is extraverted, the focus is on the facts of the world rather than illusive images. The wholeness envisioned by extraverted intuition deals more with the possibilities for particular projects, enterprises, or achievements that are realizable in some physical form. We could refer to its scope as *particular possibilities.*

Behavioral Attributes

People who favor extraverted intuition have boundless enthusiasm for the adventure of making possibilities tangibly real. They are preeminently loyal to their visions of completed projects, but when a new project is sufficiently close to the imagined possibility, they often lose that enthralling creative tension between what is and what could be. The project, once complete or nearly completed, becomes yet another fact that no longer has sufficient unrealized potential to hold their attention.

Facts about current circumstances are useful only as long as they feed imagination directed at change; they are merely stepping-stones to realizing the envisioned possibilities. As long as facts provide a bridge to imagined possibilities, they have value, but once they have served their purpose, they again become merely ordinary and incidental, sacrificed to the next compelling vision of possibilities.

People disposed to extraverted intuition are drawn to the adventure of pursuing new potentialities. Life, as it is, constitutes a banal prison: they must seek and uncover the next possibility. Which is the most exciting of all possibilities? The next one, always the next one.

Their disposition seldom permits staying with one venture long enough to see it through to fruition. "So long as a new possibility is in the offing, the intuitive is bound to it with the shackles of fate" (CW 6, §613). They have no tolerance for the status quo. Stable conditions suffocate them. Nothing—not practicality, not reason, not logical argument, not fear, not wild horses—could keep them from abandoning a former project, now a prison, to pursue the unbridled liberty of a new one. Others more patient with the facts of experience are often the beneficiaries of the discarded ventures of extraverted intuition.

With an orientation to extensive possibilities, people who favor extraverted intuition eagerly seek many projects. They are seldom satisfied by just a few creative possibilities, for they see possibility everywhere and are driven to perceive a wide range of possibilities.

They can often see the future before it arrives, accurately anticipating the outcomes of impending events. They have a knack for knowing what will work, what will turn up, what will prove successful, or how events will conclude. That predictive facility fuels their enthusiasm for creating new projects and ventures. It also provides a prophetic edge to all their interactions with objective data, events, and people.

Because their anticipatory advantage is applied to the external world, it has substantial economic currency. People who favor extraverted intuition are often drawn to those professions where they can materially optimize their capacity for anticipating future events: entrepreneurs, politicians, speculators, or investment analysts, for example. They may play a catalytic role in generating economic growth. They are often innovators, entrepreneurs, and visionaries who apply their imagination creatively to improve the world around them.

Driven by their imaginative intuition, they tend to be far less mindful of commonly accepted norms and social restraints. Every operating rule, every tradition and circumstance considered normal and acceptable, may be inconsequential for them and their passion for innovation.

What will ignite their imagination, and what will not, is unpredictable. Though they are directed to the outer object, the inner object still plays a behind-the-scenes role in selecting which possibilities are most enthralling. "It is not the strongest sensation, in the physiological sense, that is accorded the chief value, but any sensation whatsoever whose value is enhanced by the intuitive's unconscious attitude" (CW 6, §611).

Their morality consists not of obedience to commonly accepted ethics, morality, rules, or norms but of their duty to the creative process of realizing possibilities. They march to a different drummer than do the other extraverted types that are the upholders of the status quo.

Their enthusiasm for transforming facts into their vision of possibilities overflows into all of their relationships. They wear their excitement on their sleeves. They are often convincingly persuasive, readily recruiting others to their favored projects and ventures. They don't just *have* creative inspiration; they *embody* the creative inspiration that drives them.

Their vision often extends to seeing potential in others. They can see hidden possibilities in people and often become enthusiastic champions of their potential.

Those who favor extraverted intuition often bring much value to the world. They have access to the images and dreams of intuition yet direct their energy into the world to encourage people, improve life, and anticipate unborn events.

Andrew Carnegie

Among those engaged in anticipating future events, we find many people predisposed to the extraverted intuition type. Interestingly, some athletes and performing artists have also identified extraverted intuition as their most reliable type. Steve Jobs, Bill Gates, Howard Hughes, and other entre-

Andrew Carnegie 1835–1919

preneurs often represent this type well, for the essence of entrepreneurship is the pursuit of possibilities.

We could look to one of the best-known entrepreneurs in history to see this conscious orientation borne out. Andrew Carnegie started as an impoverished immigrant and pursued his talent for seeing possibilities to become the wealthiest man of his generation. Not content merely to amass enormous wealth, he also felt compelled to give it away for the improvement of the world.

If the unlived life of the parent, as Jung proposed, is the most important influence in a child's development, then perhaps Andrew Carnegie's father would have been more of an impetus for his emboldened life than any of his biographers suspect. His father lacked ambition and persistence. Forced by economic hardship from their home in Dunfermline, Scotland, the family moved to Pittsburgh, Pennsylvania; but even in the "land of opportunity," his father could not make a go of it.

At the age of thirteen, Andrew Carnegie was thrust into the adult world of work to supplement the family income. He started as a bobbin boy, working twelve hours a day, running up and down the aisles of a cotton mill to exchange fresh bobbins for used ones. "The hours hung heavily upon me," he wrote in his autobiography, "and the work itself I took no pleasure in." The work did not last long.

He was soon offered another job for twice the pay as a boiler attendant and soaker of bobbins at a nearby bobbin shop. Before he turned fourteen, he was offered another job as a messenger boy in a telegraph office.

The new work suited him; he delivered messages to Pittsburgh's prominent businessmen and politicians, and he loved it. His aptitude for seeing possibilities thrived among people who were realizing possibilities themselves. He memorized the names of prominent people so that he could acknowledge them when he saw them in public. "Andy" excelled as a messenger and was quickly recognized as one of the best and the most attentive.

Always improving himself, he was not content to remain a messenger boy. He set his sights on becoming a telegraph operator and taught himself to take messages by ear. By the age of fifteen, he was hired as an operator. The telegraph had become the fastest mode of communication between cities, and all the leaders of commerce and industry were using it. Operating the telegraph put him at the epicenter of communications in booming Pittsburgh—in the 1850s, a hub of industrial expansion. He rapidly became the most sought-after telegraph operator in the company.

In his free time, he improved himself ambitiously. The eager lad saw to his own learning, devouring books at the local library. He corresponded with a cousin in Scotland, debating the merits of American democracy, arguing eloquently and enthusiastically for his newly adopted country.

At the age of seventeen, Carnegie was hired by the Pennsylvania Railroad and attached himself to the coattails of his boss, the district manager. As telegraph operator and assistant to the manager, he kept abreast of the news of the day; he was acutely aware of coming events.

His boss recognized his acumen for business and offered him a stake in a "sweetheart" investment virtually guaranteed to pay off. Like many of his subsequent investments, this one generated high financial returns. It delivered his first dividend check. "I shall remember that check as long as I live. . . . It gave me the first penny of revenue from capital—something that I had not worked for with the sweat of my brow. 'Eureka!' I cried. 'Here's the goose that lays the golden egg.'"

With that dividend check, he entered the brave new world of investment capital. Many other opportunities followed; by the time he was in his early thirties, he was a wealthy man, but he did not rest.

He perfected his sales skills as a bond trader, selling investments in American industry to London bankers. He built the Carnegie Steel Company, not from the sweat of his own brow (he worked about four hours a day) but from that of steel workers laboring long days and managers meticulously supervising operations. His managers kept him informed of progress with elaborate operating statements. Carnegie was a remote partner with an office in New York, more than a day's travel from his production facilities. He was an affirming encourager, a big-picture thinker, and an eager deal-broker always sniffing out opportunities to expand, improve, and develop his industrial ventures, but he was not a hands-on manager.

At some reflective point in midlife, he realized that acquiring capital was not in itself enough. It dawned on him that the wealth he was accumulating ought to be applied for the common good. He decided to become a great philanthropist.

With his eventual sale of Carnegie Steel, he became the wealthiest man in the world, and nearly all of his vast wealth, held mostly as fixed production assets, was converted to bonds. He devoted the remainder of his life to channeling his newly liquid capital into worthy causes and projects, among them the creation of public libraries that had been so essential for his own self-education.

He became more extraverted than ever, entertaining, traveling, and counseling monarchs, presidents, and aristocrats. He befriended philosophers and writers, politicians and poets, always glorifying their value and importance to humankind. He had written his *Gospel of Wealth* and *Triumphant Democracy*. In his later years, he wanted to make his indelible mark with the dearest and most important project of his life: *international peace*.

He became the "apostle of peace," lobbying, cajoling, promoting, selling, flattering, and encouraging heads of state to build alliances and establish agreements that would sustain permanent peace in the world. When World War I broke out in August 1914, his vision was shattered. He had become inextricably connected to his vision for peace. The indomitably optimistic Carnegie slipped into silence and depression. He died, despairing of the world's descent into barbarism, in 1919.

Summary of the Extraverted Receptive Types

These are the two extraverted receptive types of consciousness. They are compatible cousins, for the chief duty of each is to perceive something definite in the world at large. Their role is not to organize, evaluate, or rationally judge their experience, only to perceive it fully.

As extraverted types, they share a common orientation to the outer object; all of their experiential perception is directed to the outer world.

Category	Extraverted Thinking	Extraverted Feeling	Extraverted Sensation	Extraverted Intuition
Composite Orientation	Extensive Order	Extensive Norms	Extensive Facts	Extensive Possibilities
Composite Attitude	Perceive Order	Perceive Norms	Perceive Facts	Perceive Possibities
Functional Role	Constructive Thinking	Social Feeling	Realistic Sensation	Catalytic Intuition
Composite Substance	Outer Thoughts	Outer Valuations	Outer Perceptions	Outer Imagination
Composite Scope	Particular Order	Particular Norms	Particular Facts	Particular Possibilities

Table 3-2 Comparative Categories for the Extraverted Types

Extraverted sensation realistically and accurately perceives the world at large, whereas extraverted intuition perceives what is potentially there.

We see the dichotomy between ordering and perception more sharply in the extraverted attitudes than in the less overt introverted attitudes. Yet extending the table we constructed previously for the extraverted rational types, we can see at a glance how all of the extraverted types are remarkably congruent (Table 3-2).

CHAPTER SUMMARY

With this chapter, we have taken a closer look at the extraverted types directed to the southern side of the great divide on our compass of consciousness. They each represent distinct modes of conscious functioning, yet they are also highly congruent because the overriding directional attitude has rendered a common orientation to the outer object. They are each extensively oriented, each focused on particulars more than the whole, and each poised to perceive some aspect of the outer object.

4

The Introverted Types

AN ORIENTATION TO THE INNER OBJECT is the common thread that holds the introverted types together as a group, thus creating a clear divide from the extraverted types.

Both the introverted and the extraverted types can be convinced of the correctness of their views. It is incomprehensible to someone with an introverted disposition why the outer object should be the decisive factor for someone with an extraverted disposition. Similarly, a person disposed to extraversion cannot fathom how the inner life could ever be superior to objective facts.

Orientation to the inner object engenders an extraordinary sense of conviction for those predisposed to introverted attitudes. Therefore, they tend to be stubbornly independent, for they are attuned to a layer of clarity beneath the surface of objective events that is their constant reference.

IMAGE, IDEA, AND IDEAL

The fundamental reference points for the introverted types are the images of the collective unconscious. When the archetypes are made manifest in consciousness, they appear as images. These images are qualitatively different from perceptions in the world.

> When I speak of image in this book, I do not mean the psychic reflection of an external object, but a concept derived from poetic usage, namely, a figure of fancy or fantasy-image, which is related only indirectly to the

perception of an external object. . . . [It] can always be distinguished from sensuous reality by the fact that it is an "inner image." (CW 6, §743)

The image is not isolated from outward experience, but rather it often arrives together with other factors.

The image is a *condensed expression of the psychic situation as a whole*, and not merely, nor even predominately, of unconscious contents pure and simple. . . . Accordingly, the image is an expression of the unconscious as well as the conscious situation of the moment. (CW 6, §745)

The images from the collective unconscious are "archaic," "primordial," and "collective" in character. If an image has personal qualities, then it is likely born from the personal unconscious.

A personal image has neither an archaic character nor a collective significance, but expresses contents of the personal unconscious and a personally conditioned conscious situation. (CW 6, §745)

Images are the progenitors of ideas. Ideas are images that have become intellectually formulated and liberated as independent concepts. They are often the products of one of the two rational functions applied to the inner image.

Though Jung does not make the distinction, in this book we will refer to the images that have been rationally evolved by the thinking function as *ideas,* and by the feeling function as *ideals.* To apprehend images developed into ideas or ideals is the work of the introverted attitudes, and particularly the rational attitudes. The receptive introverted attitudes are more inclined to revel in apprehending the image for its own sake.

We might look to the products of artists, architects, poets, or musicians for concrete examples of these intangible images. Paul McCartney, for example, wrote music that became popular the world over. His song "Yesterday" was written without much effort. He said he woke up one morning and there it was as a hovering image in his inner life. He simply wrote it down and played it on his guitar.

Johann Sebastian Bach was said to have been asked by a student how he was able to come up with so many melodies. His reported response: "My dear boy, I have trouble not tripping over them when I get up in the morning!"

The house called Fallingwater is one of architect Frank Lloyd Wright's most dramatic designs. Wright was known for the ease with which he

Figure 4.1 Frank Lloyd Wright house, "Fallingwater."

generated architectural designs. Most architects need to sketch loosely for days, weeks, or months, developing vague images into more coherent designs, before they ever start hard-line drawings of the emerging design.

Wright was commissioned to design a home on a sloping site with a stream running through it. After his students documented every contour and every tree, Wright just thought about the site for months, arranging and rearranging an emerging image in his imagination. Then one day, a few hours before his client was to arrive, he sat down to draft the hard-line drawings for the home, and Fallingwater was born.

The novelist Vladimir Nabokov, who said, "I don't think in any language. I think in images," artfully described the ineffable experience that images bring when they arrive.

A prefatory glow, not unlike some benign variety of the aura before an epileptic attack, is something the artist learns to perceive very early in life. This feeling of tickly well-being branches through him like the red and the blue in the picture of a skinned man under Circulation. As it spreads, it banishes all awareness of physical discomfort—youth's toothache as well as the neuralgia of old age. The beauty of it is that, while completely intelligible (as if it were connected with a known gland or led to an expected climax), it has neither source nor object. It expands, glows, and subsides without revealing its secret. In the meantime, however, a window has opened, an auroral wind has blown, every exposed nerve has tingled. Presently all dissolves: the familiar worries are back and the eyebrow redescribes its arc of pain; but the artist knows he is ready.[1]

After Goethe began reading *Critique of Pure Reason,* written by his contemporary, Immanuel Kant, Goethe reportedly exclaimed: "Good heavens no!" later explaining to a lady-friend that Kant had omitted the fourth faculty of consciousness, *imagination.* We can thank Jung for including it.

Images are no respecters of vocation. Not only do artists, writers, and musicians turn their attention to them, but so do many others, including scientists. In Charlie Chaplain's autobiography, he recalls a story told by Einstein's second spouse that characterizes how fully images can command the abiding attention of people awake to them.

> The Professor came down in his dressing gown as usual for breakfast but he hardly touched a thing. I thought something was wrong, so I asked him what was troubling him. "Darling," he said, "I have a wonderful idea." And after drinking his coffee, he went to the piano and started playing. Now and again he would stop, making a few notes, then report: "I've got a wonderful idea, a marvelous idea!"
>
> I said: "Then for goodness' sake tell me what it is, don't keep me in suspense."
>
> He said: "It's difficult, I still have to work it out."
>
> She told me that Einstein continued playing the piano and making notes for about half an hour, then went upstairs to his study, telling her that he did not wish to be disturbed, and he remained there for two weeks. "Each day I sent up his meals," she said, "and in the evening he would walk a little for exercise, then return to his work again."
>
> Eventually, she said, he came down from his study looking very pale. "That's it," he told me, wearily putting two sheets of paper on the table. And that was his theory of relativity.[2]

Such is the life of people disposed to an introverted attitude. Image, idea, and ideal—these are the primary "objects" of introverted attention. Not much oriented to extraverted social norms, established traditions, or

[1] Vladimir Nabokov, "Inspiration," *The Saturday Review,* January 6, 1973, pp. 30–32.
[2] Charlie Chaplin, *My Autobiography* (Brooklyn: Melville House, 2011), pp. 320, 321.

known facts, introverted consciousness is more inclined to discern the dream, the vision, the not-yet-born.

INTROVERTED RATIONAL TYPES

The introverted rational types are close cousins to each other. Though they apply different governing principles of rationality, they are oriented by the same images. Of the two, we would more immediately recognize introverted thinking as rational, for it applies intensely intellectual logic.

Introverted Thinking

I think therefore I am. –René Descartes

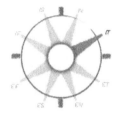

Composite Orientation: Intensive Insights

The orientation of thinking, as modified by the introverted attitude, is to logic and images simultaneously. Insight into the image as idea is the chief orienting factor. Since "intensity is his aim, not extensity" (CW 6, §633), we could say that it is oriented to *intensive insights.*

Composite Attitude: Apprehend Insights

Introverted thinking has an *intuition-like* directional attitude that steers the thinking being applied. The directional attitude, like a magnetic field, draws the thinking back into a dynamic relationship with the inner object, organizing related material that will in some way fill out the luminous idea. Thinking starts with the image and leads back to it, always in pursuit of a clearer understanding of what has been apprehended. Clarifying the inner idea is its aim. This type is poised to *apprehend insights.*

New Functional Role: Conceptual Thinking

Oriented and directed to the archetypal matrix, introverted thinking surveys ideas and images, not for their own sake but to formulate hypotheses, theories, or overarching principles. Facts and concrete experience can lend support to the intense thinking processes at work in the inner life—they can be acquired as supporting material, but the dominant factor influencing their attitude is always the inner object. "Facts are collected as evidence for a theory, never for their own sake."

Introverted thinking does not just add bits and pieces of many facts, as though blending a chemical mixture. It synthesizes new conceptual abstractions that act more like a chemical solution; the many facts dissolve and lose their individual characteristics in service to the whole idea.

The functional role of introverted thinking could therefore be called *conceptual thinking*.

Composite Substance: Inner Thoughts

Recognizing that rational thinking is so thoroughly attached to and conditioned by the inner image, we could call its substance *inner thoughts*.

Composite Scope: Holistic Insights

Introverted thinking sees the whole image and seeks to unify the facts and other insights within its broad and unifying framework. It sees mainly similarities, discounting particular differences, for it is seeking the overarching idea. Broad relationships take precedence over individual features. Its attention is forever directed to the comprehensive and unifying ideas, principles, themes, or theories. We could say that its scope is to *holistic insights*.

Behavioral Attributes

People favoring introverted thinking are drawn to the intensity of the search, first discovering the vague idea and then pursuing their understanding of it with unswerving dedication. They are occupied with the inner world, pursuing luminous ideas and discerning explanatory principles.

Facts and concrete experiences may enhance the intense thinking processes at work in their inner life, but the dominant factor influencing their thinking is always the elusive inner object. (CW 6, §516).

Such people conceive of explanatory principles that may be many steps removed from an empirical base. The focus is on the Gestalt experience—the whole that ineffably engulfs the many parts. The hovering image guides the thinking process.

The new idea or theory comes often as a surprise or epiphany. They resolutely pursue the nature of the image until it emerges as a coherent idea. They strive to continually enhance the clarity and understanding of that inner image. In pursuing insights that closely approximate the inner image, they develop new, original, innovative ideas and theories.

They can unite seemingly unrelated thoughts and sometimes even whole disciplines, applying analogies and metaphors as representations of the inner experience. Everything, from any discipline, is potentially connected to their main idea.

They tend to gather and organize insights to build a hierarchy of logic that explains the whole image. They are like mountain climbers of complex thought who ascend one pitch and then the next, until the summit is finally attained. The summit is the ultimate unifying insight or theory.

Either the inner image itself, or an objective fact that has in some way innervated the image, may be the initial stimulus. The inner image of a potentially insightful idea captivates their attention and they pursue the understanding of that image with fiercely independent resolve. "In his pursuit of ideas he is generally stubborn, headstrong, and quite unamenable to influence" (CW 6, §634).

They may passively accommodate the people and events around them so that they can inwardly continue to untangle some perplexing problem or unify some incongruous theories. Their engagement in solving problems or building theories requires intense concentration.

Vague and nearly unconscious abstractions then become more conscious, but the abstractions are still so conceptual that it is difficult to communicate them to others, let alone discern their practical value for life experience.

Though willing to surmount any obstacle or ignore any danger in the pursuit of a compelling idea, people disposed to this type will have much difficulty opening the curtain of understanding, or promoting their polished idea, to others. It is as though they expect the idea to stand and live on its own. They tend to shy away from the glare of publicity, expecting their idea to essentially speak for itself. They are not self-promoters; their love is the pursuit of the inner image, however impractical it may seem to others.

They are in love with their abstractions and may only be able to explain them awkwardly, if at all. When verbalizing their thoughts, they can appear slow and disorganized, for their thoughts are largely detached from concrete sensory experience. The objective fact is of little consequence unless it contributes in some way to their understanding of the emerging abstract idea.

Unlike their extraverted rational counterparts who may see the trees, the bark, and the insects on the bark, those disposed to introverted thinking will see the forest as the organizing principle for the hierarchy of organic subsets. They see the whole—the unifying themes, relationships, and abstract principles congealed into one organizing idea.

Immanuel Kant

Immanuel Kant 1724-1804

We could certainly consider Carl Jung himself to represent this type of ego consciousness. Undoubtedly oriented to the inner object, his thinking produced the complex yet holistic model of the psyche known as Analytical Psychology. His Collected Works and other writings elaborate that model and its usefulness in scholarly detail. Introverted thinking is readily in evidence among theoretical physicists. Newton, Planck, or Bohr could represent this composite attitude. Philosophers also often illustrate this type of consciousness, and Jung considered the philosopher Immanuel Kant to be a clear representative.

> Just as we might take Darwin as an example of the normal extraverted thinking type, the normal introverted thinking type could be represented by Kant. The one speaks with facts; the other relies on the subjective factor [inner object]. Darwin ranges over the wide field of objective reality. Kant restricts himself to a critique of knowledge. (CW 6, §632)

Immanuel Kant exemplifies not only the intensity of introverted thinking but also the difficulty someone of that disposition may have in articulating the insights that they have assembled. Kant's *Critique of Pure Reason* is virtually unintelligible for the casual reader. "The first hundred pages are tolerably clear; the rest is a philosophical conflagration in which the untutored reader will see nothing but smoke."[3]

Kant was so thoroughly systematic that people said they could set their watches by his afternoon walks. Like others predisposed to introverted thinking, he patiently and steadily built his philosophy, spending years thinking it through, but had little time for the formal explanation. He wrote to Moses Mendelsohn that though the volume was "the result of reflection which occupied me for at least twelve years, I brought it to completion in the greatest haste within four or five months, giving the closest attention to the contents, but with little thought of the exposition."[4]

Immanuel Kant was born in Königsberg, the capital city of the province

---

3 Will Durant and Ariel Durant, *The Story of Civilization*, 11 volumes, Volume 10 (New York: MJF Books, 1993), p. 535.
4 Ibid.

of East Prussia, in 1724; he was a child of the eighteenth-century Age of Enlightenment. Of the eleven children in his family, he was one of only four to live to adulthood. Not an explorer of the world, he traveled no more than ten miles from his native city his whole life. He lived not far from the Baltic Sea but likely never saw it. His exploration of the world of knowledge and ideas was sufficiently adventurous.

Of Scottish and German ancestry, he was brought up by strict Pietist parents. Pietism was a sect within Lutheranism that stressed faith, repentance, and individual piety. In his formative childhood years, he attended a local Pietest Collegium where terror and piety were closely aligned. Kant later said that he recalled those days with fear and trembling.

At the age of sixteen, in 1740, he was liberated to think freely when he enrolled at the University of Königsberg. His interests were in science and philosophy, two subjects that were then virtually inseparable. After six years at the university, he was invited to become a Lutheran minister. He declined, despite the offer of a comfortable post, instead continuing his education. For nine years he lived in poverty as a student, tutoring to make ends meet.

In 1755, he at last received his doctoral degree and was allowed to lecture at the university as a private teacher; he received no formal salary, only what the students chose to pay. For fifteen more years, he continued with that tenuous income, applying for full professorship twice and twice being denied. He moved from one boardinghouse to another, always alone. He never married.

Kant's lectures included the philosophies of Leibniz, Wolff, Newton, Kepler, and Rousseau; he encouraged his students to think beyond the boundaries of dogmatic traditions. One grateful student remembered him fondly: "He encouraged and gently compelled his hearers to think for themselves; despotism was foreign to his disposition."

His earliest scholarly work dealt more with physical science. He uncovered important new insights about the formation of the planets and the constitution of galaxies. He won the Berlin Academy Prize in 1754 for his discovery that the rotation of the earth is retarded by tidal currents. As he progressed, he delved increasingly into philosophy and theology, writing such essays as "The False Subtlety of the Four Syllogistic Figures," "Attempt to Introduce the Concept of Negative Magnitudes into Philosophy," "The Only Possible Argument in Support of a Demonstration of the Existence of God," and "Inquiry Concerning the Distinctness of the Principles of Natural Theology and Morality."

In 1770, at the age of forty-six, he was at last appointed Professor of Logic and Metaphysics at the University of Königsberg, a position that included a modest but steady salary. Custom required newly appointed professors to deliver an inaugural discourse in Latin. Kant's discourse was titled "On the Form and Principles of the Sensible and Intelligible World." In it, he laid down the basic premises for his later magnum opus, *Critique of Pure Reason*:

1. Space and time are not inherent in objects; they are inherent in our perceptual frameworks of objects.
2. The mind is not a passive recipient of sensations; it is an active agent, abiding by inherent categories of operation, transforming sensations into understanding.

Much still needed to be built upon the foundations of that initial dissertation. Kant had been "awakened" from his "dogmatic slumber" by the Scottish philosopher David Hume, who had observed that the presumptions of causality in science were not reliable. To address Hume's observation, Kant set out to expand the premises of his own discourse.

It took him over a decade of intensive thinking. He isolated himself from his normal social events and friendships. Apart from his required lectures, he was an intellectual hermit, obsessively pursuing philosophical answers to perplexing questions well beyond the realm of his prior "dogmatic slumber." In response to a friend's invitation to draw him out, he wrote:

> My great thanks, to my well-wishers and friends, who think so kindly of me as to undertake my welfare, but at the same time a most humble request to protect me in my current condition from any disturbance.[5]

When Kant emerged from his self-imposed isolation in 1781, he had produced his magnum opus, *Critique of Pure Reason*, today broadly recognized as one of the greatest works in the history of philosophy. It radically changed the landscape of our understanding of human consciousness.

Time and space are not inherent in the world, he asserted; they are products of our a priori frameworks for perceiving the world. (Undoubtedly, when the young Einstein read Kant, he took note.) The human mind does not function as an empty container that simply receives data from the world at large; a priori frameworks of recognition and judgment give order to perceptual experience. (Carl Jung, as a young student of philosophy, also took note. Not only is his theory of psychological types aligned with Kant's premises, but his notion of archetypes also parallels Kant's a priori frameworks.)

[5] Letter to Marcus Hertz, April 1778, quoted in Introducing Kant, Christopher Kul-Want and Andrzej Klimowski (Cambridge: Icon Books, 2005).

Kant was disappointed with the reception of the first edition of *Critique*. He published a second edition, heavily revising the first parts of the book to clarify or expand certain themes. In 1788, he published *Critique of Practical Reason,* his treatise on moral philosophy. Two short years later, he published *Critique of Judgment* that considered questions of aesthetics and teleology.

Kant died in Königsberg on February 12, 1804, uttering "Genug" (*enough*). Surely it was enough. The little Prussian professor influenced the course of philosophy, religion, science, psychology, and literature. Fichte, Schelling, and Hegel built upon his philosophy; Schopenhauer acknowledged his debt to Kant. Schiller studied Kant intently; Coleridge and Carlyle were both influenced by his work. The New England Transcendentalists, who included Thoreau and Emerson, owed their name and their philosophy to the intensive, holistic insights of Immanuel Kant.

Introverted Feeling

Composite Orientation: Intensive Ideals

Both introverted feeling and introverted thinking are rationally oriented to the inner object. Both serve the common functional purpose of organizing and evaluating the ineffable images arising from the unconscious.

We may readily grasp introverted thinking by its orientation to logic because logic is readily comprehensible to the intellect; but what can we say, intellectually, about an orientation to *value*? Feeling defies logical description, so the intellect is virtually incapable of formulating its nature; we must *feel* this orientation rather than think about it. The inner images that are the subject of its orientation are *felt through,* not *thought through.*

Rather than referring to the products of felt rationality as emerging ideas, we have called them *ideals,* as mentioned previously, suggesting their immunity from logical analysis. Like the other introverted functions, introverted feeling is intensively oriented. We could say that the composite orientation of introverted feeling is to *intensive ideals.*

Composite Attitude: Apprehend Ideals

While introverted thinking is poised to shape images with analysis into ideas, introverted feeling is poised to shape feeling-toned images into ideals. It is a compelling attraction that forever draws feeling back into a relationship with the inner image. Like all the introverted types, we could describe the attitude of this type with the term *apprehend*. We could say that it is forever poised to *apprehend ideals*.

New Functional Role: Idealistic Feeling

The feeling function undergoes a dramatic transformation when it is directed to the inner object, becoming so different from extraverted feeling that the two scarcely seem related. Introverted feeling is iconoclastic and oblivious to conventional values, whereas extraverted feeling upholds traditions and conforms to norms. One is hard to read and often misunderstood; the other's bountiful expressiveness knows few restraints.

The objective world is only moderately important to introverted feeling. Its new functional role is to stay connected and to grasp the luminous ideals that possess timeless value. The hovering image guides the feeling process. Introverted feeling discerns the value of an idea; it pursues the feeling-toned qualities of the image, shaping it into a deeply felt ideal. Its modified functional role could be said to be *idealistic feeling*.

Composite Substance: Inner Valuations

It might be tempting to call the substance *feelings*, yet the term could be too easily confused with emotional feeling. It has more to do with valuations, so we could refer to the substance of introverted feeling as *inner valuations*.

Composite Scope: Holistic Ideals

Like introverted thinking, introverted feeling is oriented to the vast, the universal, the global, and the enduring, thus transcending the individual elements of any particular situation or experience.

Just as introverted thinking organizes the contents of consciousness according to logic, introverted feeling organizes the contents of consciousness according to their value. Like introverted thinking, it deals with interrelationships and similarities and "puts general characteristics in the place of individual objects" (CW 6, §515).

Broad, holistic abstractions take precedence over particular facts. Introverted feeling begins with the whole and unites things. The scope of introverted feeling could be said to be *holistic ideals*.

Behavioral Attributes

People predisposed to introverted feeling can be difficult to read. With a pre-eminent orientation to the inner life, such people can appear quite aloof and, despite their feeling attitude, can seem cold, abrupt, or arrogant. It seems that they must protect their deeply buried treasures by defending them from the onslaught of comparatively superficial demands from without.

Feeling, and especially deeply introverted feeling, is very difficult to express. Unless they are artistically or poetically endowed, only with great difficulty will people disposed to introverted feeling find a means to express the value and passion of their inner experience.

The phrase "still waters run deep" may best characterize people with this ego disposition. They are drawing from a deep well of images and ideals. They may often be prone to moods of melancholy, for the images apprehended in the inner life are not always sunny and cheerful.

The depth of their feeling may be concealed behind an ironic external mask of innocence, but internally they could be probing the depths of the eternally real. As long as they are protecting their treasured inner experience, they will keep their values to themselves, adapting inconspicuously with little effort to alter or influence the people or events around them. They prefer to avoid unnecessary conflict, for their inner life is already teeming with the angst and storms of ages past and events yet to come.

They are attuned to a side of life that puts all current events in a proportionate perspective. Thus they may appear to be aloof and to possess an air of superiority, deflating those in need of outward affirmation, whereas their functional counterparts, who favor the extraverted feeling type of consciousness, are among the most congenial of people.

The introverted attitude directs feeling intensively inward rather than extensively into the world. Their concentrated but unexpressed feelings build a passionate core that may be channeled privately through art, literature, or poetry; a passionate commitment to a beloved cause; or loyal support for the lives of others.

Those disposed to introverted feeling are guided by images that are forever in need of translation to a more intelligible form. Other people have difficulty understanding what motivates them, and they themselves may not be capable of articulating their inner experience.

They may struggle to find words that capture the feelings and iconic images that are a silent part of their daily experience. They can only approximate their orientation to intensive feeling through language. First they must discern the value of the image for themselves; then they must struggle to convey that value for others.

The titanic force of inner valuations is so deeply and profoundly felt that little energy may remain for superficial expression. They are deeply engaged with the inward images flowing in archetypal currents. Because their deepest feelings remain so effectively concealed, they can possess an almost mysterious power. "This power comes from the deeply felt, unconscious images" (CW 6, §642).

People who favor introverted feeling can be intensely loyal to their inner convictions. They are often content to remain out of the limelight, off in the wings, playing a nearly invisible but vital role in events. They are idealistic to their core. They strive above all else to remain connected to what feels true, beautiful, or good. Their motto could be Goethe's:

> Im Ganzen, Guten, Schönen, resolut zu leben
> (To live resolutely in the whole, the good and the beautiful)

The goal is to stay connected within, and then to *realize,* the underlying ideals and symbols of timeless value. They often seek those events, people, circumstances, and causes in the world that fit with their apprehended inner ideals. Tangible experience lends support to the intense feelings in the inner life. The aim is always to bring the vague images to light through feeling the value they represent and to "approximate more and more to the eternal validity of the primordial images" (CW 6, §637).

Objective social norms are never enough; they look beyond contemporary social standards to discern the abstract ideals that bring enduring value to life. They go deep to discern the overarching feeling-toned images that echo with significance.

Their orientation to intensive ideals could be compared to the keel of a sailboat; it remains fixed, deep in the water of its feeling-values, keeping the conscious life from careening off course. In a sense they live two lives— the life above the surface, managing relationships in the world, and the life beneath the surface that feels more true, enduring, and authentic.

People who favor introverted feeling bear rare gifts for the collective. Sometimes mysterious and aloof, their outward demeanor conceals a rich treasure of values, ideals, passion, and commitment that keeps life in the world true and meaningful.

Anne Frank

People with remarkable reflective insights exemplify the introverted feeling attitude: Lao Tse, Rabindranath Tagore, and Eleanor Roosevelt could rep-

Anne Frank 1929–1945

resent this type of consciousness. John Keats may have spoken for them all when he wrote:

> Thou, silent form! Dost tease us out of thought
> As doth eternity: Cold Pastoral!
> When old age shall this generation waste,
> Thou shalt remain, in midst of other woe
> Than ours, a friend to man, to whom thou say'st,
> "Beauty is truth, truth beauty"—that is all
> Ye know on earth, and all ye need to know.[6]

Many adult poets, artists, writers, or therapists could help to illustrate this type. The diary of a young girl also illustrates it well.

The story of the precocious young girl who, with her family, was forced into exile and then, at the age of thirteen, into hiding as the oppressive Nazi regime gained power in Germany and Europe, is world famous. Through the diary she left behind, Anne Frank has also provided an intimate illustration of many of the attributes of an introverted feeling disposition.

She also exemplifies how type can, and often does, manifest early in life. Type disposition is often evident in the emerging child, and more fully formed in teenagers, irrespective of social conditions. "Ultimately, it must be the individual disposition which decides whether the child will belong to this or that type despite the constancy of external conditions" (CW 6, §560). Certainly Anne Frank's tragic environment was well outside of normal circumstances. Yet, in living under terrible Nazi oppression, she may also illustrate another principle that Jung does not discuss: in trauma,

---

[6] John Keats, "Ode on a Grecian Urn," *Annals of Fine Arts*, no. 15 (January 1820).

people may tend to revert to their "home" type—the lead type disposition that comes most easily to them. Whatever the role of her extraordinary circumstances, introverted feeling is well in evidence in the diary of this precocious teenager.

Born in Frankfurt, Germany, she and her family moved to Holland in the early 1930s when Germany became a dangerous place for Jews; they settled in Amsterdam. When World War II broke out, neutral Holland was forcibly overrun by the Nazis, and the Franks were trapped. The city of Amsterdam and the country of Holland, historically so tolerant of exiled people, quickly became a hostile place under Nazi rule. She remembered in her diary:

> 20 June, 1942 Anti-Jewish decrees followed each other in quick succession. Jews must wear a yellow star, Jews must hand in their bicycles, Jews are banned from trams and are forbidden to drive. Jews are only allowed to do their shopping between three and five o'clock and then only in shops which bear the placard "Jewish shop." Jews must be indoors by eight o'clock and cannot even sit in their own gardens after that hour. Jews are forbidden to visit theaters, cinemas, and other places of entertainment. Jews may not take part in public sports, swimming baths, tennis courts, hockey fields, and other sports grounds are all prohibited to them. Jews may not visit Christians. Jews must go to Jewish schools, and many more restrictions of a similar kind.

Longing for a friend who could understand her deepest and most intimate feelings, she imagined her diary to be a friend named "Kitty." For more than two years she, her parents, her older sister, and four other Jews hid, in a secret annex adjoining her father's former place of business, from the Nazi persecutions and certain death. She found solace in her good friend, Kitty. She could put on a friendly face for her family and for the other occupants of the small annex, but in Kitty, she confided all of her innermost thoughts and feelings.

Her willful independence showed itself early.

> 3 October, 1942 There was another dust-up yesterday. Mummy kicked up a frightful row and told Daddy just what she thought of me. Then she had an awful fit of tears so, of course, off I went too; and I'd got such an awful headache anyway. Finally I told Daddy that I'm much more fond of him than Mummy, to which he replied that I'd get over that. . . . Daddy wishes that I would sometimes volunteer to help Mummy . . . but I shan't.

She held strong opinions about everyone. Her roommate, Mr. Dussel, was a frequent object of her private views.

> 28 November, 1942 It was always said about Mr. Dussel that he could get along wonderfully with children and that he loved them all. Now he shows himself in his true colors; a stodgy, old-fashioned disciplinarian, and preacher of long, drawn-out sermons on manners.

She felt persecuted and misunderstood, evaluated and corrected by the adults in their cramped quarters.

> 28 November, 1942 When I've already had a dose from him [Mr. Dussel] Mummy goes over it all again, so I get a gale aft as well as fore. Then, if I'm really lucky, I'm called on to give an account of myself to Mrs. Van Daan and then I get a veritable hurricane!

> 30 January, 1943 If I talk, everyone thinks I am showing off; when I'm silent they think I'm ridiculous; rude if I answer, sly if I get a good idea, lazy if I'm tired, selfish if I eat a mouthful more than I should, stupid, cowardly, crafty, etc., etc. The whole day long I hear nothing else but that I am an insufferable baby, and although I laugh about it and pretend not to take any notice, I *do* mind.

She felt fortunate to be safely hidden away, but the pain of those she saw outside her window tormented her.

> 13 January, 1943 It is terrible outside. Day and night more of those poor miserable people are being dragged off, with nothing but a rucksack and a little money. On the way they are deprived even of these possessions. Families are torn apart, the men, women, and children all being separated. Children coming home from school find that their parents have disappeared. Women return from shopping to find their homes shut up and their families gone.

Anne saw the beauty in life, sensed it, felt it. Even living in their meager hovel, scrounging for food, arguing about nothing and living on the edge of fear, she found inner security and joy.

> 7 March, 1944 And in the evening, when I lie in bed and end my prayers with the words, "I thank you, God, for all that is good and dear and beautiful," I am filled with joy.

Her values were deeply formed; she was independent and altruistic.

> 11 April, 1944 I am becoming still more independent of my parents, young
> as I am, I face life with more courage than Mummy; my feeling for justice
> is immovable, and truer than hers. I know what I want, I have a goal, an
> opinion, I have a religion and love. Let me be myself and then I am satis-
> fied. I know that I'm a woman, a woman with inward strength and plenty
> of courage. If God lets me live . . . I shall not remain insignificant, I shall
> work in the world and for mankind!

Like her ally in the White House across the Atlantic, Eleanor Roosevelt,
she was ardently devoted to self-improvement.

> 6 July, 1944 How noble and good everyone could be if, every evening before
> falling asleep, they were to recall to their minds the events of the whole day
> and consider exactly what has been good and bad. Then, without realizing
> it, you try to improve yourself at the start of each new day; of course you
> achieve quite a lot in the course of time. . . . Whoever doesn't know it must
> learn and find by experience that: "A quiet conscience makes one strong!"

With ample free time in the annex, she devoted herself to her hobbies, her
interests, and her studies. She was intrigued by mythology, intensely interested in history, and enthralled by family trees. Like many others who are
disposed to introverted feeling, math was not her strong suit.

> 6 April, 1944 Other hobbies are film stars and family photos. Mad on books
> and reading. Have a great liking for history of art, poets, painters. I may
> go in for music later on. I have a great loathing for algebra, geometry, and
> figures.

She loved to write and dreamed of being a writer when they gained their
freedom. Her ideas were already taking shape in her inner life.

> 11 May, 1944 Now, about something else: you've known for a long time that
> my greatest wish is to become a journalist someday and later on a famous
> writer. . . . I want to publish a book entitled *Het Achterhuis* [*The House
> Behind*] after the war. I have other ideas as well, besides *Het Achterhuis*. But
> I will write more fully about them some other time, when they have taken
> clearer form in my mind.

She was an idealist at heart and had a self-awareness that was remarkably advanced. She had a broad and deep insight into her condition.

> 15 July, 1944 "For in its innermost depths youth is lonelier than old age."
> I read this saying in some book and I've always remembered it, and found
> it to be true. . . . It's twice as hard for us young ones to hold our ground,
> and maintain our opinions, in a time when all ideals are being shattered
> and destroyed, when people are showing their worst side, and do not know
> whether to believe in truth and right and God.

She held fast to her steady and trustworthy ideals.

> 15 July, 1944 It's really a wonder that I haven't dropped all my ideals because
> they seem so absurd and impossible to carry out. Yet I keep them, because
> in spite of everything I still believe that people are really good at heart. I
> simply can't build up my hopes on a foundation consisting of confusion,
> misery, and death. I see the world gradually being turned into a wilder-
> ness, I hear the very approaching thunder, which will destroy us too, I can
> feel the sufferings of millions and yet, if I look up into the heavens, I think
> that it will all come right, that this cruelty too will end, and that peace and
> tranquility will return again. In the meantime, I must uphold my ideals, for
> perhaps the time will come when I shall be able to carry them out.

Her self-reflective awareness was remarkable; she recognized in herself
both her persona and a deeper, authentic self.

> 1 August, 1944 I've already told you before that I have, as it were, a dual
> personality. One half embodies my exuberant cheerfulness, making fun of
> everything, my high-spiritedness, and above all, the way I take everything
> lightly. . . . This side is usually lying in wait and pushes away the other,
> which is much better, deeper, and purer. You must realize that no one
> knows Anne's better side and that's why most people find me so insuffer-
> able. . . . I'm awfully scared that everyone who knows me as I always am will
> discover that I have another side, a finer and better side. I'm afraid they'll
> laugh at me, think I'm ridiculous and sentimental, not take me seriously.
> I'm used to not being taken seriously but it's only the "lighthearted" Anne
> that's used to it and can bear it; the "deeper" Anne is too frail for it. I'm
> guided by a pure Anne within but outside I'm nothing but a frolicsome
> little goat who's broken loose.

Tuesday 1 August, 1944 was Anne's last entry. The Allies had crossed the
English Channel and were fighting on land to liberate Western Europe.

With Russians converging on Germany from the east and Allied forces moving from the north, the end of the war was in sight.

On August 4, tipped off by an informer, the Gestapo broke into the secret annex and arrested all eight hideaways. On September 3, the day the Allies liberated Brussels, the eight were on the last freight train to Auschwitz.

Even in the concentration camp, where people moved like walking dead, Anne was acutely sensitive to the misery of others. One survivor remembered Anne:

> I can still see her standing at the door and looking down the camp street as a herd of naked gypsy girls was driven by to the crematory, and Anne watched them go and cried. And she also cried when we marched past the Hungarian children who had already been waiting half a day in the rain in front of the gas chambers because it was not yet their turn. And Anne nudged me and said: "Look, look. Their eyes."

Her mother died at Auschwitz. Anne died in the concentration camp in Belsen, Germany, in March 1945, just after her sister, Margot. The war ended in May 1945. Her father was rescued by the advancing Russian army. Of the eight, he was the only one to survive. He returned to Holland, to their hideaway in the secret annex. Among the articles he collected there was Anne's diary.

Summary of the Introverted Rational Types

People disposed to the introverted rational types are enigmatic because they are so oriented to a "different drummer." They are forever guided by the elusive images of the inner object and therefore may appear less "rational" in the conventional sense.

In a culture that tends to exalt objective, empirical facts, people oriented to the inner object may feel or be undervalued, so they may deny their own predispositions to the inner life in an attempt to fit in. However, by denying their own natures, they would do themselves and the world a disservice.

Individuals who have made some of the most enduring contributions to the advancement of science, philosophy, and culture have often been the ones who have defied the widely accepted norms of their day. Guided by their own inner visions of ideals and ideas not yet born, they have generated radical new insights that have in time become cultural standards. They mine the rich treasures of the inner life.

A review of their comparative categories, shown in Table 4-1, can help to render their attributes succinctly.

Category	Introverted Thinking	Introverted Feeling
Composite Orientation	Intensive Insights	Intensive Ideals
Composite Attitude	Apprehend Insights	Apprehend Ideals
Functional Role	Conceptual Thinking	Idealistic Feeling
Composite Substance	Inner Thoughts	Inner Valuations
Composite Scope	Holistic Insights	Holistic Ideals

Table 4-1 Comparative Categories for the Introverted Types

INTROVERTED RECEPTIVE TYPES

Sensation and intuition may be opposites because of functional attitudes, but the introverted attitude renders them highly compatible. Introversion overrides sensation's functional orientation, and the resulting composite attitude acquires a marked resemblance to introverted intuition. Both of these introverted functions are oriented preeminently to the inner object.

People disposed to each type suffer from the same dilemma: explaining their introverted lives to an extraverted audience. They have no desire to communicate what they have experienced, and they do not have adequate words for it.

> What is going on inside them is so captivating, and of such inexhaustible charm, that they simply do not notice that the little they do manage to communicate contains hardly anything of what they themselves have experienced. (CW 6, §664)

Such people are perceived as reserved, unsympathetic, and secretive. They do not wear their emotions on their sleeves but keep them hidden well behind what may sometimes be mistaken for a rational persona. Their efforts to be forthright may appear clumsy, abrupt, or coarse, for they are relying on their submerged, "inferior" attitudes to do their talking.

Because they conceal so much of the introverted vision that comes so easily to them, they are often underestimated and seen as aloof and quiet.

Yet their surprising access to an overflowing imaginative life within can also endear them to many and endow them with great power.

Introverted Sensation

Still—in a way—nobody sees a flower—really—it is so small—we haven't time— and to see takes time like to have a friend takes time. —Georgia O'Keeffe

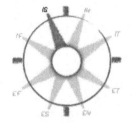

Composite Orientation: Intensive Innervations

Straddling, like a bridge, the great divide in orientation, introverted sensation is constantly attuned to outer objective experience yet is simultaneously oriented to the inner object. It possesses the versatile but unpredictable quality of being oriented in two directions. Accurate perceptions are transformed by the introverted attitude into intense innervations.[7] It is the intensity of experience with the inner object to which introverted sensation is ultimately oriented. We could say of this new orientation for the sensation function that it is oriented to intensive innervations.

Composite Attitude: Apprehend Innervations

Introverted sensation is poised to perceive the detail of the outer object while also ready to apprehend the psychic "mirror world" beneath its surface. Jung artfully articulates the magical nature of this type that perceives both sides of the great divide simultaneously.

> Introverted sensation apprehends the background of the physical world rather than its surface. The decisive thing is not the reality of the object, but the reality of the subjective factor, of the primordial images which, in their totality, constitute a psychic mirror world. It is a mirror with the peculiar faculty of reflecting the existing contents of consciousness not in their known and customary form but, as it were, *sub specie aeternitatis,* somewhat as a million-year-old consciousness might see them. . . . We could say that introverted sensation transmits an image

---

[7] The term *innervation* refers to an enhancement of perceptions; it is not to be confused with the word *enervate* which means "lacking vigor." We use the term *innervate* to indicate how the inner object *adds* vigor to normal perceptions. In a sense, the introverted directional attitude supplies new "nerves" for perceiving the normal outer object as transformed by the dazzling inner object.

which does not so much reproduce the object as spread over it the patina of age-old subjective experience and the shimmer of events still unborn. (CW 6, §649)

This experience is sufficient for introverted sensation. There is no compulsion to change anything, take overt action, or assess these contents. Apprehending the dazzling mirror world beneath the surface of objective experience is quite enough.

Since we are using the term *apprehend* when referring to the ego's perception of the contents of the inner object, and *perceive* when referring to perceptions of the outer object, we could say that the attitude of introverted sensation is transformed from perceiving to apprehending, for the directional attitude prevails over the functional attitude.

Yet what the ego apprehends from the unconscious is dependent on what it perceives. Unlike introverted intuition, it does not apprehend the contents of the inner object directly, but only through its perceptions of the outer object. We could say that the attitude of introverted sensation is *apprehending innervations*—the innervations added to the perceptions of the outer object.

New Functional Role: Aesthetic Sensation

Introverted sensation is the least well understood of the eight types, and some have conflated it with extraverted sensation. Some have thought that introverted sensation renders the outer object precisely, like a photographic plate; others interpreted this type as being sensitively attuned to the body. These misinterpretations may have stemmed from seeing the ego as the object of the introverted attitudes.[8]

Yet, as Jung makes clear, it is not the ego that is the object of the introverted attitude, but the collective unconscious.[9]

But since the introverted attitude is based on the ever-present, extremely real, and absolutely indispensable fact of psychic adaptation, expressions like "philautic," "egocentric," and so on are out of place and objectionable because they arouse the prejudice that it is always a question of the beloved

---

[8] Even someone as close to Jung's work as Marie-Louise von Franz misunderstood this type. In her essay in the book *Jung's Typology*, von Franz presents a diagram of the introverted attitude directed not to the inner object but to the ego. On that premise she built a description of introverted sensation that characterized it as a precise and highly accurate means of perceiving the outer object.

[9] Also see *Subject/Subjective Factor* under "Terms" in the back of this book.

ego. Nothing could be more mistaken than such an assumption. (CW 6, §622)

Introverted sensation, as Jung describes it, is oriented to tangible objective experience, yet its energy is directed to the inner object. In that translation across the psyche's "great divide," objective experience takes on dazzling qualities, essentially re-materializing the object. It is this constant translation from outer object to inner object that constitutes the specific role of introverted sensation.

Outer objective experience is perpetually reinterpreted as inner experience. Certain details, special facts, and particular features discriminatingly acquire heightened qualities; common perceptions elicit deep and intense impressions. Normal sensation is active but embellished by the overlay of the inner object.

> True sense perception certainly exists, but it always looks as though the object did not penetrate into the subject [individual] in its own right, but as though the subject were seeing it quite differently, or saw quite other things than other people see. (CW 6, §647)

The sensation function is adorned with new aesthetic qualities; it takes on an enhanced responsiveness to sensory experience. It does not just perceive a tree, for example; it seems to also figuratively perceive the *soul* of the tree. We could refer to its altered role as *aesthetic sensation*.

Composite Substance: Inner Perceptions

The primary materials for this introverted function are outer perceptions enriched by the inner object. To illustrate the quality of operating on both sides of the great divide, we could refer to its substance as *inner perceptions*.

Composite Scope: Holistic Innervations

The sensation function is generally focused narrowly on the pieces and parts rather than the whole—the trees and their bark rather than the forest. Yet when introverted, the perspective widens to include the "shimmer of events unborn." The images, ideas, visions, and abstractions of the unconscious penetrate the particular sensory experience.

We could say that the scope of introverted sensation is to the special perceptions that resonate with the deeper pattern of primordial images.

The focus is to both the particular and the holistic. Yet "holistic detail" is a contradiction in terms. Because the orientation is transformed from realistic detail to innervation, we could call its scope *holistic innervations*.

Behavioral Attributes

People who favor introverted sensation tend to have a quiet, subdued exterior; they are characteristically difficult for others to read. Their impressions sink to the very depths of the inner life, holding their conscious expressions under a sort of quiescent spell. They show little outward expression, for they are quietly and intensively soaking up the experiences of the moment, processed within as deep, fascinating, lively impressions.

They are capturing vibrant hues and feelings deeply rather than a superficial record of outer experience. The unconscious intervenes as a sort of mystical filter to transform accurate perceptions into innervated impressions that are encoded in memory.

Unlike those who rely on extraverted sensation, people who favor introverted sensation put far less trust in objective facts. The outer world of practical experience is somewhat foreign to them, for their attention is often directed inward to a "mythological world."

They may have difficulty expressing themselves, especially if an auxiliary rational function is not well developed. The images they perceive are so rich that it is difficult to find words for them. Poetry, art, music, photography, and dance may give expression to their inner experience, yet much of what they experience can sink to inexpressible depths.

On the surface, they are often conspicuously calm and may seem rationally self-controlled. They tend to be detached from outward experience, relying predominantly on their lively inner experience. Their personal reaction is not directly correlated with the outward reality; it is correlated with their reality within.

They are intrigued and captivated by perceptual experience, not for its own sake but for the inner experience it excites. Their life experience is painted with the rich and colorful pigments of objective perceptions imbued with the transcendent luminosity of the collective unconscious.

The luminosity renders not only an aesthetic sensitivity but also a larger awareness. They perceive more than persons or objects themselves; they vaguely apprehend a larger sense of history and future—"somewhat as a million-year old consciousness might see them" (CW 6, §622). A walk in a deep forest is more than merely a stroll through nature; it excites far more in the inner life for it also evokes "the patina of age-old subjective experience and the shimmer of events still unborn" (CW 6, §622).

Georgia O'Keeffe

Georgia O'Keeffe 1887–1986

We could look to the lives of many writers, musicians, songwriters, poets, and artists, discovering those people who translate objective experience aesthetically—Vincent Van Gogh or Bob Dylan, for example, could illustrate this mode of consciousness. Jung himself, as evidenced by the imagery in *The Red Book*, might well illustrate this type of consciousness. He could have been one of the century's great artists had he not been devoted to the emerging field of psychiatry. Many Jungian analysts and other therapists have ready access to this type, for it somehow enables them to experience the "soul" of an individual, apprehending much that is beyond pure perception.

Georgia O'Keeffe, the American artist made famous by her sensitive yet bold paintings, will serve as our representative, for she exemplifies both the aesthetic and numinous attributes of this type. Aloof, intense, enthralled with the wonder of perceptions, she experienced life enigmatically through her own mirror world.

She was born on a farm near Sun Prairie, Wisconsin. In her early formative years, she lived in comfortable abundance, surrounded by the security of a nurturing family. Her father was a prosperous, hardworking farmer who played the violin. Her mother was a very sociable woman, attentive to family life and to neighbors, who regularly read to her children at night.

Georgia was largely free to explore and pursue her own interests. She was a solitary child, always busy doing what interested her. With her long slender fingers, she played the piano beautifully, practicing for long hours to get the sound just the way she wanted it. She said that she could have been a musician instead of an artist. As several siblings came along, she became increasingly self-reliant and enjoyed being close to nature.

The blazing sunlight, fertile soil, and clear skies of the Wisconsin farm provided a rich environment for Georgia's early impressions of nature. The beauty of wildflowers, the feel of a cow's tongue or the way it rolled its big eyes, wagons of hay at dusk, apple trees easy to climb, the big round moon as it came up over the woods, endless fields of abundant crops, and the crunch of crisp snow beneath her feet, all left rich and intense memories.

She had a favorite hollow in a meadow where she could go to play alone, and she often went there.

From an early age, she was acutely sensitive to the sights and sounds of her environment. Even a reprimand from her grandmother was fascinating to her.

> "You must not do that a—gain." I was so fascinated by her precise way of speaking that I would do it again just to hear her say it.[10]

Her family moved to Williamsburg, Virginia, in 1901, and Georgia was thrust into a new school and a less rural social culture. A classmate of Georgia's recalled:

> We noticed at once; her absolutely plain suit coat of exceptionally good material, which fitted her loosely, was a contrast to the tiny waists and tight-fitting dresses with ruffles that the rest of us wore.[11]

As in Wisconsin, she was at home and at peace when she was alone with expansive nature.

> The best things during my fifteenth and sixteenth years were my walks in the Virginia hills, with the line of the Blue Ridge Mountains on the horizon calling me, as distances have always called me.[12]

At age seventeen, she began her more concentrated education in fine art. She attended the Art Institute in Chicago and the Art Students League of New York. A friend remembered her from their time together in New York.

> Even in those days O'Keeffe was different. . . . She stood apart, too, in the way she dressed—her coat suit of excellent material and the crisply-starched white blouses that she herself had made.[13]
>
> There was something spartan about her, as direct as an arrow, and completely independent.[14]

Her formal art education had been in the classroom, drawing plaster casts and still lifes. As a scholarship student, she spent a summer at Lake George,

---

[10] Anita Politzer, *A Woman on Paper: Georgia O'Keeffe* (New York: Simon & Schuster, 1988), p. 59.
[11] Ibid., p. 75.
[12] Ibid., p. 77.
[13] Ibid., p. 1.
[14] Ibid., p. 3.

New York, where her affinity for wide-open natural environments was rekindled. There she began to see that her art needed to transcend her training: it needed to be an expression of her life. She began to depict her personal interpretations of what she saw, rather than the accurate renderings encouraged at school.

In 1912 she took a teaching position in Amarillo, Texas. She could have more comfortably stayed on the East Coast, but something within her was calling her to the West and the wide-open spaces. She was captivated by the raw wonder of the West.

> —and the wind blows like mad—and there is nothing after the last house of town as far as you can see—there is something wonderful about the bigness and lonelyness and the windyness of it all—mirages people with all sorts of things at times—sometimes I've seen the most wonderful sunsets over what seemed to be the ocean.[15]

One of her sisters noticed the change in Georgia's work after her time in the West: "Georgia seemed to be drawing just for herself, and her work was like that of no one else." The innervations of her inner life had begun to take hold. She wrote to a close friend about her experience in Texas.

> I've been working like mad all day—had a great time—Anita it seems I never had such a good time—I was just trying to say what I wanted to say—and it is so much fun to say what you want to.... But Anita—I believe I'll have to stop—or risk going crazy.[16]

Returning later to Texas for another teaching position, she wrote again about her observations there; her description sounds dreamlike.

> First plains—then as the sun was lower the canyon—a curious slit in the plains—cattle and little bushes in the bottom pin heads—so small and far away—wonderful color—darker and deeper with the night. Imagination makes you see all sorts of things.[17]

A vacation with one of her sisters brought her to New Mexico. She liked it immediately: "After a few days there, in my mind, I was always on my way back to New Mexico."

---

[15]Ibid., p. 126.
[16]Ibid., p. 128.
[17]Ibid., p. 149.

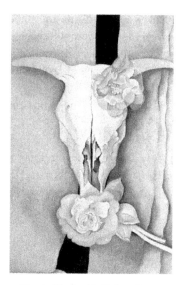

Cow's Skull with Calico Roses
1932

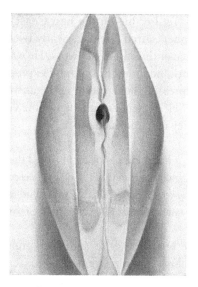

Slightly Opened Clam Shell
1926

Red Tree Yellow Sky
1952

Black Iris
1926

**Four Paintings by
Georgia O'Keefe**

Yet her life on the East Coast was not over. She had met the photographer Alfred Stieglitz, nearly twenty-five years her senior, who became a keen enthusiast of her work. He was the first to exhibit her drawings. In her work, he found a profound expression of life: "Woman is at last on paper expressing her relation to the universe," he said.

He was an animus figure for Georgia, just as she was his anima muse. They inspired each other.

> I had a kind of belief in Alfred that made those days specially fine. I had a need of him that I had never seemed to feel for anyone else before. . . . He would notice shapes and colors different from those I had seen and so delicate that I began to notice more.[18]

He brought her to summer family events at his mother's home on Lake George. His niece remembered Georgia as "so extremely quiet with all of us that she seemed unlike anyone we had ever seen." Meeting new people and hearing much talk drained her and kept her from her more private work.

She married Stieglitz after he divorced his wife. She quickly became recognized as a talented new artist. In 1923 she had a one-woman show featuring one hundred of her paintings and drawings. Said one critic of her work: "Flowers and fruits burn in her conception of them with deep, luminous colors that have no names in spoken or written language."

Art and architecture critic Lewis Mumford saw the unusually authentic brilliance of her work.

> What distinguishes Miss O'Keeffe is the fact that she has discovered a beautiful language, with unsuspected melodies and rhythms, and has created in this language a new set of symbols; by these means she has opened up a whole area of human consciousness which has never, so far as I am aware, been so completely revealed in either literature or in graphic art.[19]

In 1929, she began spending her summers in New Mexico. When her husband died in 1946, she moved there permanently. It was the place where she could see "far away." She called the Southwest "magical," and her paintings began to assimilate its raw and mystical qualities.

She traveled extensively in her later years, with trips to South America, Southeast Asia, India, the Middle East, and Europe. Of Chartres Cathedral she said, "It seemed as beautiful to me as anything made by the hand of man could be. It was like being under great trees." Of Peru, she said, "There

---

[18] Ibid., p. 168.
[19] Ibid., p. 125.

is something dreamlike about it—the days were so wonderful—it was so beautiful one was often left speechless and by night one thought maybe it wasn't real—maybe it was a dream."

She painted till nearly the end of her life and died in 1986 at the age of ninety-eight. Her ashes were scattered to the wind over the beloved land that she called "far away."

Introverted Intuition

If you can swing yourself up for a moment into that in which no creature dwells, then you will hear what God speaks. —Jakob Boehme

Composite Orientation: Intensive Images

 Of all the types, none is more thoroughly saturated with an orientation to the images of the collective unconscious than is introverted intuition. It is both functionally and directionally oriented to the inner object. Recognizing that the introverted attitude prevails with its intensive focus, we could say of its orientation that it is to *intensive images.*

Composite Attitude: Apprehend Images

Of all the composite ego attitudes, none is more detached from the world than introverted intuition, for it is oriented and directed to the inner object. Like its opposite, extraverted sensation that explores the contents of the outer object, introverted intuition explores the images of the inner object.

> This image fascinates the intuitive activity; it is arrested by it, and seeks to explore every detail of it. It holds fast to the vision, observing with the liveliest interest how the picture changes, unfolds, and finally fades. (CW 6, §656)

The images have a mobile and detached life of their own. They appear; they exist apart from the individual consciousness apprehending them. The vision of these images can be as moving and powerful as any objective perception. Images are to introverted intuition what objects are to extraverted sensation.

Introverted intuition, without an auxiliary rational function, could be sufficiently engaged simply observing the visions discovered in the inner object, for the "teeming womb of the unconscious" produces a never-ending display. We could say of its composite attitude that it is poised to *apprehend images.*

New Functional Role: Visionary Intuition

The role, the core purpose, of introverted intuition has a mystical quality. From a conventional perspective, the dreams, reflections, images, and visions of introverted intuition may seem impractical. Though they may have little immediate practical utility, they are the stuff of visionaries and prophets, the outworking of whose lives can alter the course of a civilization.

Introverted intuition provides the insights that inform a way of life that resonates with the archetypal matrix. Architects, writers, artists, poets, prophets, theoretical scientists, composers, and philosophers could all draw inspiration through introverted intuition. Their inspirations are not always necessary from a purely utilitarian standpoint, yet they are necessary if humankind is to rise above a purely utilitarian life. "Without a vision, the people perish."

Introverted intuition grasps a holistic vision of the course of events not yet born. It delivers profound insights, generates sudden leaps of understanding, and connects seemingly unrelated knowledge. We could refer to its modified functional role as *visionary intuition*.

Composite Substance: Subjective Imagination

The inner dreams, images, and visions that appear as representations of the collective unconscious are the primary materials of introverted intuition. We could refer to these primary materials as *inner imagination*.

Composite Scope: Holistic Images

Introverted intuition provides a window to the images and visions of the future as well as the past, which present themselves whole and complete. We could refer to the composite scope of this type as *holistic images*.

Behavioral Attributes

This enthralling private access to inspiring images, visions, and ideas throbbing in the inner life is difficult to overtly conceal; people disposed to introverted intuition often appear to be constant dreamers. They are seldom entirely present to their associates, for their orientation to the inner object relentlessly pulls their attention elsewhere.

They may be preoccupied with the future, for their lucid access to the inner images enables them to see ahead to anticipate the longer-term meanings and implications of events. They see not only beneath the surface of current events and circumstances but also the unborn outworking of those events.

They are forever holding two conversations, one more engaging than the other. Primarily they attend to the inner conversation—the vivifying experience of compelling dreams and visions. Secondarily, the outer conversation—the daily management of practical issues and associations—interrupts the inner conversation. The inner conversation is the preeminent and decisive one; the inner life is the center of their reality. They may seem distant, aloof, and impractical, but the images of the inner life often feel more real to them than any of the down-to-earth experiences in the outer world.

Their experience with the imaginative visions of the inner life may be sufficient for them. If so, they may feel no compulsion to apply their vision; they may be content with the purely imaginative experience of cultivating the alluring, abundant, and altogether fascinating images of the inner life.

If introverted intuition is joined by a rational attitude, these enthralling visions can also be compelling catalysts for directed action. Awakened from their reverie with the inner life, such people often find that they must live an outer life congruent with the visions they have apprehended; they must serve their vision with their whole life, voice, and work; the outworking of their own lives must reflect the dream of life they experience within. Once considered quietly aloof, they now seem irritating or incomprehensible. They still live their lives fully oriented to their vision, but now in a more overt form that others cannot grasp. They must struggle to adapt their vision to the world as they find it. They may seem irrational or "beside themselves," for the eye has not seen nor the ear heard what they have apprehended within.

The way to individuation, as for all of the introverted types, will require living a more extraverted life in community. They may struggle, but if they succeed in that journey, they will also find abundant rewards in a richer and more significant life.

Mahatma Gandhi

Religious mystics could serve as effective examples of this type. Jakob Boehme and Meister Eckhart provide biographical examples. Rufus Jones or George Fox, the profound Quaker mystics with their love of the intangible realities of the spirit, could also exemplify this type. Plato could

Mohandes Gandhi 1869–1948

represent this type when it is joined to introverted thinking. Jung, too, likely relied on this type as an adjunct to introverted thinking. His revolutionary model of the human psyche transcends rational understanding, for it came to him as a series of images and ideas that emerged during his years of a "confrontation with the unconscious."

Jung observed that without introverted intuition there "would have been no prophets in Israel." We can look to a prophet from modern times, Mahatma Gandhi, to see evidence of introverted intuition in life.

Using Gandhi to exemplify introverted intuition may be controversial. Gandhi was an activist; introverted intuition is more meditative. Some might say that introverted feeling was Gandhi's lead type; others, because he was a skillful lawyer, could say it was introverted thinking. Both were probably readily available to him.

Others, because of his overt efforts to realize possibilities, might say of Gandhi "extraverted intuition." Certainly extraverted intuition could have also been at work to some degree, yet Gandhi's vision for the whole of India suggests that he is a better representative of introverted introversion at work. Extraverted intuition tends to focus on material ends to achieve tangible goals. Introverted intuition is attuned to the very big picture of life; it apprehends events for their long-term import. It is oriented to the inner life yet is also inextricably related to life in the world.

Since the unconscious is not just something that lies there like a psychic *caput mortuum,* but coexists with us and is constantly undergoing transformations which are inwardly connected with the general run of events, introverted intuition, through its perception of these inner processes, can supply certain data which may be of the utmost importance for understanding what is going on in the world. It can even foresee new possibilities in more or less clear outline, as well as events which later actually do happen. Its prophetic foresight is explained by its relation to the archetypes, which represent the laws governing the course of all experienceable things. (CW 6, §660)

Introverted intuition, oriented to the inner object, can be utterly unconventional. It finds images and ideas that have little to do with life as it is commonly lived. Extraverted intuition, oriented to the outer object, tends to rely more on conventional methods to achieve its shorter-term vision of possibilities.

Both Gandhi and Andrew Carnegie, our representative for extraverted intuition, sought peace and well-being in the world. Carnegie sought world peace in his time through conventional political agreements. Gandhi sought peace through unconventional, nonviolent resistance and soul-centered *Satyagraha*.

Carnegie, with his extraverted orientation, was very much at home, even as a boy, mingling with the business elite. Gandhi was painfully shy early in life. The world can be a foreign place to one oriented to inner realities.

Carnegie was bold and lived lavishly; Gandhi lived the life of a religious ascetic, a modern-day John the Baptist—suppressing the distractions of the outer world to be more attentive to the inner life.

Anyone who has read his autobiography would acknowledge that introverted intuition played a large role in Gandhi's life, whether it was a lead or an auxiliary type. We can learn much about what was most important to this versatile man from what he wrote about himself. His autobiography confirms that he was a mystic at heart.

My experiments in the political field are now known, not only to India, but to a certain extent to the "civilized" world. For me, they have not much value; and the title of "Mahatma" that they have won for me has, therefore, even less. Often the title has deeply pained me; and there is not a moment I can recall when it may be said to have tickled me. But I should certainly like to narrate my experiments in the spiritual field which are known only to myself, and from which I have derived such power as I possess for working in the political field.

What I want to achieve—what I have been striving and pining to achieve these thirty years—is self-realization, to see God face to face, to attain *Moksha*. I live and move and have my being in pursuit of this goal. All that I do by way of speaking and writing, and all my ventures in the political field, are directed to this same end.

But for me, truth is the sovereign principle, which includes numerous other principles. This truth is not only truthfulness in word, but truthfulness in thought also, and not only the relative truth of conception, but the Absolute Truth, the Eternal Principle, that is God. There are innumerable definitions of God, because his manifestations are innumerable. They overwhelm me with wonder and awe and for a moment stun me. But I worship God as Truth only. I have not yet found Him, but I am seeking after Him. I am prepared to sacrifice the things dearest to me in pursuit of this quest. Even if the sacrifice demanded be my very life, I hope I may be prepared to give it.[20]

His political activism had to be learned; it did not come naturally to him. The religious spirit within him was always his first orientation.

This year's stay in Pretoria was a most valuable experience in my life. Here it was that I had opportunities of learning public work and acquired some measure of my capacity for it. Here it was that the religious spirit within me became a living force.[21]

Jung noted that an orientation to introverted intuition may require an active life in the world.

The moral problem arises when the [introverted] intuitive tries to relate himself to his vision, when he is no longer satisfied with mere perception and its aesthetic configuration and evaluation, when he confronts the questions: What does this mean for me or the world? What emerges from this vision in the way of a duty or a task, for me or the world? . . . His judgment allows him to discern, though often only darkly, that he, as a man and a whole human being, is somehow involved in his vision, that it is not just an object to be perceived, but wants to participate in the life of the subject. Through this realization he feels bound to transform his vision into his own life. (CW 6, §662)

"Be the change you want to see in the world," said Gandhi.

With an understanding of Gandhi as a mystic who was also a lawyer and political activist, we can turn to his life to better understand the nature of introverted intuition. He can help us to understand that highly unconventional orientation, for he was drawn to do more than apprehend visions of possibilities; he also felt compelled to make them real in the world. In

---

[20]From the Introduction to Mohandas K. Gandhi's autobiography, *The Story of My Experiments with Truth* (Boston: Beacon Press, 1993).
[21]Ibid., p. 131.

observing his life in the world, we gain a glimpse of the inner life that was his perpetual guide.

Gandhi was called "Mahatma," the Hindu word meaning "Great Soul." Born Mohandas Karamchand Gandhi, he was married by arrangement at age thirteen. A son was born to him and his wife while they were teenagers; more children arrived later.

Mohandes wanted to become a doctor, but his family insisted that he study law. He was sent off to London in 1888, five years after his marriage, to become an English barrister. Leaving his wife and first child behind, he adapted to British customs. He eagerly read the newspapers and took private lessons in dance, French, elocution, and the violin.

Gandhi had a keen interest in religion. In London, he discovered the Bible, reading the New Testament for the first time. He was deeply moved by the message of tolerance, forgiveness, and love that he found there. He said his reading of the Sermon on the Mount "went straight to my heart." He loved the religion of Christ but was hard-pressed to find Christians who were living it. He resolved to remain a Hindu.

Still, his religious life was imprinted by his reading of Jesus' original teachings. Gandhi also read books by Western writers, including Tolstoy's *The Kingdom of God Is within You,* which left an abiding impression on him.

One of his first commissions as a barrister brought him to South Africa. As a British citizen, trained in the law and confident of his rights, he was shocked and indignant when he was forcibly removed from a first-class cabin on a train in South Africa because his skin was dark. He worked in South Africa for years defending the rights of his compatriots there and organizing their resistance against discrimination.

In South Africa, he developed his soul-based method for revolutionary change: *Satyagraha*—holding fast to truth. For those who took the pledge of Satyagraha, the way was seldom easy. He warned them: "We might be insulted. We might have to go hungry. We might be flogged by rude wardens." In India, many who held to the truth of Satyagraha would be imprisoned, clubbed, or murdered.

The term *truth* for Gandhi did not mean factual accuracy; the word *truth* could be considered interchangeable with the word *God.* Satyagraha was holding fast to the experience of God in the soul. For Gandhi, religion had to be lived to be real.

He forever looked to his own "kingdom within"—his inner voice—for guidance; that voice for him was the voice of Truth. He looked to his inner guidance with a child's trust. His whole life work was fashioned from it. He would make no important decisions without gaining direction or assurance from within. Once he felt that inner assurance, he was immovable.

He had no fear of bodily death. He sought the purity of spiritual experience. He adopted an ascetic way of life: he wore a loin cloth, abandoning Western dress; he ate simple foods; and he had few possessions. He abstained from sex and sought freedom from sexual desire, requiring the same of others who lived with him. He and his wife, Kasturba, lived together amicably; she passionately and daily supported his life work, but, at his request, after their last child was born, they abstained from sexual intimacy. He referred to the practice of abstinence as *Brahmacharya*, seeking not just physical abstinence but also spiritual purity.

When he returned to his native India during World War I, he was a seasoned political organizer and shrewd defender of the oppressed. He led the boycott of British cloth and encouraged everyone in India, no matter of what caste or political standing, to spin cotton to clothe the people of India.

He had an intuitive way of engaging symbols to unite the far-flung and diverse population of India. The spinning wheel became a symbol for revolutionary change. He spun daily. His famous walk to the sea for salt rallied a nation.

He was the defender of the defenseless, insisting on the equal status of the lowly and oppressed untouchable caste. To show his solidarity with them, Gandhi performed all the menial chores, including cleaning chamber pots, that the untouchables were expected to do. He invited untouchables to live with him on his ashram. One of his many fasts to the death was undertaken for them. He lived the humility that Jesus had advocated two millennia before him: "He who would be greatest among you, let him become servant of all."

Gandhi was canny but not devious, honest but not naive, brave but not foolish, and strong-willed but not pigheaded. His patience early in life could be short; later, as the leader of India's liberation, it seemed nearly infinite. He embodied, in human form, the rich spiritual traditions of his people. Everywhere he went he attracted crowds of people. He spoke gently but powerfully and instilled hope and courage. He had no need for the intonations of a powerful orator; his life was his oration.

He easily won the support and admiration of India's National Congress. He acquired more political power than any other Indian during British rule, but he rejected the perquisites of power coveted the world over. He insisted on walking rather than riding to his destinations; when he did ride, he would use only third-class passage. He lived a spartan life, establishing simple communal ashrams in remote villages. No work was beneath him. He lived an ascetic life in prison, the place he called his *temple*, where he sometimes relished the "delicious taste" of fasting. He could be "happy as a bird" when in prison, and he was imprisoned often, as were tens of thousands of his followers.

He became the master of nonviolent civil disobedience. He knew that his method of Satyagraha had applications beyond India, seeing clearly that "an eye for an eye makes the whole world blind." Later crusaders for social change, among them Martin Luther King, Jr., and Nelson Mandela, were inspired by Gandhi's example and employed his methods. Said King, "Christ gave us the goals and Mahatma Gandhi the tactics."

After years of nonviolent resistance, he and his compatriots wore down the British resolve to hold India. On August 15, 1947, depleted by World War II, Great Britain granted India independence. Gandhi was in his seventy-seventh year. He had always confidently prophesied that independence would be gained in his lifetime.

He was heartbroken when his people erupted into violent conflict between Hindus and Moslems at the very inception of their independence. Less than six months later, the gentle but powerful prophet of nonviolence died, as so many prophets before him, as a martyr to his transcendent cause. He was shot three times by an assassin. Albert Einstein took special note of Gandhi's unconventional life: "Generations to come will scarce believe that such a one as this ever in flesh and blood walked upon this earth."

Summary of Introverted Receptive Types

Though these two types are similar, with their common orientations to the inner object, they differ due to their distinctly separate functional orientations. One is directed to the innervated perception, the other to the image behind the innervation.

> Whereas introverted sensation is mainly restricted to the perception, via the unconscious, of the phenomena of innervation and is arrested there, introverted intuition suppresses this side of the subjective factor and perceives the image that caused the innervation. (CW 6, §656)

With these two introverted receptive types, we find people who start the journey of individuation from the inside. In the first half of life, they often learn to rely upon their inner experience preeminently. As individuation progresses, they may be drawn to a more extraverted life with active linkages to the world. Their intoxicating experience with the inner life will often meet with its sobering antidote: practical difficulties.

> Fate itself prepares for them, perhaps even more than for other men, overwhelming external difficulties which have a very sobering effect on those intoxicated by the inner vision. (CW 6, §664)

Category	Introverted Thinking	Introverted Feeling	Introverted Sensation	Introverted Intuition
Composite Orientation	Intensive Insights	Intensive Ideals	Intensive Innervations	Intensive Images
Composite Attitude	Apprehend Insights	Apprehend Ideals	Apprehend Innervations	Apprehend Images
Functional Role	Conceptual Thinking	Idealistic Feeling	Aesthetic Sensation	Visionary Intuition
Composite Substance	Inner Thoughts	Inner Valuations	Inner Perceptions	Inner Imagination
Composite Scope	Holistic Inisights	Holistic Ideals	Holistic Innervations	Holistic Images

Table 4-2 Comparative Categories for the Introverted Types

They complete Table 4-2, our table of comparative categories for the introverted types.

CHAPTER SUMMARY

In this chapter we have more fully amplified the sometimes enigmatic nature of the introverted types of consciousness. Apprehending phenomena unwitnessed by outward perception, they are oriented to the side of the great divide that is intensively oriented to intangible, holistic images.

This completes the review the individual types. We will turn, in Chapters 6 and 7, to the important dynamics of type oppositions and their integration through individuation.

Before moving to that all-important transformational aspect of type dynamics, in Chapter 5 we will review how the types might most readily collaborate. Jung noted briefly that he could frequently observe at least two types working collaboratively as the preeminent dispositions of consciousness. In the next chapter, we will closely examine what he said about those collaborations and derive some conclusions about the likely ways they may tend to support one another. We will again recruit the eight individuals, featured in the previous two chapters as iconic actors, to help illustrate the likely collaborations.

5

Collaborations

HOW SIMPLE PEOPLE WOULD BE if only they would strictly conform to just one of Jung's eight types of consciousness. We would then know others as members of one of eight mutually exclusive cognitive clubs, and everyone in each club would have essentially the same predictable attributes.

Alas, people are not so straightforward. Psychological types are not rigid, "Galtonesque" portraits of personality;[1] there are no homogeneous clubs where everyone is essentially the same. Human nature is much too rich, complex, and nuanced.

It would be presumptuous and simplistic to try to categorize the people whose lives we have briefly summarized in the preceding biographies as belonging exclusively to one psychological type club or another. All we can say is that they exhibited some of the attributes of the psychological type under discussion. Carnegie, for example, quickly saw and seized business opportunities; he exhibited attributes that would be expected from someone engaging extraverted intuition. But he was a fully functioning person; he also engaged the other seven types of ego consciousness.

We have been reviewing each of the types individually, as Jung did, to better understand their individual attributes. To begin to grasp a more robust snapshot of human consciousness, we should also examine how they may tend to support one another, for they are never found isolated and alone but typically act together. As we will see in Chapter 6, they may

---

[1] Galtonesque is a term Jung used, referring to how he had isolated the types in order to describe them. Francis Galton was a prolific English anthropologist, eugenicist, explorer, and statistician. He produced over 340 papers and books on a vast array of subjects, including statistical methods for studying human differences and psychometrics. He died in 1911 at age 88.

also act to oppose one another, but in this chapter, we will be reviewing how they tend to collaborate.

FUNCTIONAL PAIRINGS

In a few brief paragraphs of his seminal work *Psychological Types*, Jung articulated principles that govern the way these eight types would theoretically tend to support one another.[2] We can use those principles to assemble typical pairs of types that might be found together in collaborative roles.

In those paragraphs, Jung addresses the four *functions*. He observes that the "most differentiated function"—the one most often relied upon—plays a leading role (the "dominant" or "lead" function) and is aided by an "auxiliary" or "supporting" function.

> Closer investigation shows with great regularity that, besides the most differentiated function, another less differentiated function of secondary importance is invariably present in consciousness and exerts a codetermining influence. (CW 6, §666)

In the subsequent paragraphs, he established certain principles by which those functions tend to pair up.

1. ***The dominant function must have exclusive sovereignty.***
   This absolute sovereignty always belongs, empirically, to one function alone, and can belong only to one function, because the equally independent intervention of another function would necessarily produce a different orientation which, partially at least, would contradict the first. (CW 6, §667)

2. ***The supporting function must not oppose the lead function.***[3]
   Naturally only those functions can appear as auxiliary whose nature is not opposed to the dominant function. For instance, feeling can never act as the second function alongside thinking, because it is by its very nature too

---

[2] Those guiding paragraphs start with paragraph 666. We might say that "the devil is in the detail" of those few paragraphs, for their contents have been interpreted quite differently by other researchers.

[3] Jung might have been interested to learn that a common directional attitude seems to render the opposing rational functional attitudes more compatible. Using the Gifts Compass Inventory to gauge relative dispositions for the types, sometimes people report a disposition for both introverted thinking and introverted feeling together, or extraverted thinking and extraverted feeling together.

strongly opposed to thinking. Thinking, if it is to be real thinking and true to its own principle, must rigorously exclude feeling. (CW 6, §667)

3. *The supporting function must be different in kind from the lead function.*

Experience shows that the secondary function is always one whose nature is different from, though not antagonistic to, the primary function. Thus thinking as the primary function can readily pair with intuition as the auxiliary, or indeed equally well with sensation, but, as already observed, never with feeling. . . . Hence the auxiliary function is possible and useful only in so far as it serves the dominant function, without making any claim to the autonomy of its own principle. (CW 6, §668)

These are the only paragraphs where Jung makes observations about how the functions (not the types) tend to pair up. In his book of over five hundred pages, he provides scant insight about these kinds of pairings. Because these three paragraphs provide the governing principles for collaborative pairings, we must pay close attention to them. From these few paragraphs, we know that the functional pairings of thinking or feeling with sensation or intuition would be consistent with his principles.

But what about the eight types—the composite attitudes? How might they pair? We could extrapolate these rules about the functions and apply them to the eight types.

TYPE PAIRINGS

The difference between a type and a function is the addition of a directional attitude. Types are functional attitudes modified by either introverted or extraverted attitudes—composite attitudes.

We know, from Jung's principles about pairings, that the supporting functional attitude must not oppose the leading functional attitude. If we apply the same rule to the directional attitudes, then we could begin to draw some conclusions about how the types might pair.

Recalling our discussion from the preceding chapters, we know that an extraverted attitude is always oriented to the outer object; an introverted attitude is always oriented to the inner object. Therefore, an extraverted type would not pair with an introverted type, for they have opposing attitudes. Rather, extraverted types would pair with extraverted types, and introverted types would pair with introverted types. Applying Jung's principles to the eight types produces these potential pairs:

- *Extraverted thinking or extraverted feeling with extraverted sensation or extraverted intuition.*

- *Introverted thinking or introverted feeling with introverted sensation or introverted intuition.*

Jung offered a few examples of the sort of pairings he had in mind.

> For all the types met with in practice, the rule holds good that besides the conscious, primary function there is a relatively unconscious, auxiliary function which is in every respect different from the nature of the primary function. The resulting combinations present the familiar picture of, for instance, practical thinking allied with sensation, speculative thinking forging ahead with intuition, artistic intuition selecting and presenting its images with the help of feeling-values, philosophical intuition systematizing its vision into comprehensible thought by means of a powerful intellect, and so on. (CW 6, §669)

Reviewing each of the examples he offered will help to confirm that we can apply the same governing principles to the types that he described for the functions. To review those examples, we will draw on the understanding from the previous two chapters, enlisting both the comparative categories and the people we chose to illustrate these types.

Though we cannot typecast those people themselves—reduce them to one type or another—we could figuratively cast them on our stage of consciousness as iconic actors playing the roles of the eight types. So, for example, Carnegie could play the role of extraverted intuition; he had a knack for seizing possibilities. Gandhi could play the role of introverted intuition; he sought to align his life with "soul-truth." Kant could play the role of introverted thinking; he spent over a decade intensively seeking the solution to a philosophical conundrum.

Recalling the featured attributes of each of our actors will help us to put "flesh on the bones" of otherwise intellectual concepts. Remembering those attributes will also help us to understand which of the psychological types would tend to collaborate with one another. (In Chapter 6, we will recruit the same company of actors to show which would tend to oppose one another in our theater of individuation.)

Our company of eight actors includes four playing extraverted roles and four playing introverted roles. Let's meet the cast again.

Charles Darwin

Extraverted Thinking

He combed the earth looking for fossils and artifacts and then assembled his ruling formula of natural selection for the theory of evolution.

Elizabeth I

Extraverted Feeling

She presided over the Golden Age of England and sought to conduct her actions "by good advice and counsel."

Julia Child

Extraverted Sensation

She taught America to enjoy French cuisine proclaiming, "The pleasures of the table, and of life, are infinite—toujours bon appétit!"

Andrew Carnegie

Extraverted Intuition

He seized possibilities that made him independently wealthy. Acquiring more wealth than any capitalist before him, he gave it away before he died to make the world a better place.

Immanuel Kant

Introverted Thinking

Awakened from his "dogmatic slumber,"
he isolated himself for ten years to write his
magnum opus, *Critique of Pure Reason.*

Anne Frank

Introverted Feeling

Hiding in a secret annex, she confided to her
diary, "Kitty," reflecting profoundly about life,
people, and relationships.

Georgia O'Keeffe

Introverted Sensation

Private, aloof, and acutely sensitive to the
dreamlike beauty of natural surroundings,
she painted her interpretations in a "beautiful
language, with unsuspected melodies and
rhythms."

Mahatma Gandi

Introverted Intuition

Stubborn yet gentle, profound yet humble, he
lived his life by Satyagraha—holding fast to
soul truth.

Our company of eight actors will help to make each of the eight types of consciousness more memorable. We could imaginatively consider them iconic actors on the conscious stage of *any* individual, perpetually collaborating in dynamic, fluid combinations to navigate life experience. When philosophical investigation is needed, Immanuel Kant, as introverted thinking, may take center stage; when practical awareness of outer circumstances is required, Julia Child, as extraverted sensation, may appear.

We will examine each of Jung's four examples of likely pairings one at a time to consider which of our iconic actors might best represent the examples. His examples were these:

1. Practical thinking allied with sensation

2. Speculative thinking forging ahead with intuition

3. Artistic intuition selecting and presenting its images with the help of feeling-values

4. Philosophical intuition systematizing its vision into comprehensible thought by means of a powerful intellect

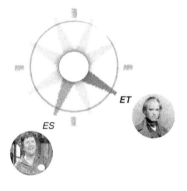

1: Practical Thinking Allied with Sensation

With the term *practical thinking*, we can safely assume that Jung is referring to extraverted thinking. Extraverted thinking is directed to the concrete and tangible. Its directional orientation and attitude are to the outer object—to very practical, particular facts. The question then would be which type of sensation would provide a more supportive role for the leading type—introverted sensation or extraverted sensation? A brief review of the comparative categories (Table 5-1) of those two options shows that extraverted sensation provides a more compatible supporting role.

Our company of actors can help to confirm this conclusion. Our leading role, played by Charles Darwin, could choose either Julia Child or Georgia O'Keeffe as his supporting actor. In his meticulous tour of the world, collecting fossils and artifacts, in pursuit of his ruling formula of natural selection, he would find greater value in Julia Child whose role is realistic sensation: oriented to extensive facts and perceiving facts com-

Category	Extraverted Thinking (ET)	Extraverted Sensation (ES)	Introverted Sensation (IS)	Comments
Composite Orientation	Extensive Order	Extensive Facts	Intensive Innervations	ET and ES oriented extensively; IS intensively
Composite Attitude	Perceive Order	Perceive Facts	Apprehend Innervations	ET and ES are perceiving; IS apprehending
Functional Role	Constructive Thinking	Realistic Sensation	Aesthetic Sensation	Roles for ET and ES related to outer object; IS role is more to inner object
Composite Substance	Outer Thoughts	Outer Perceptions	Inner Perceptions	The substance for both ET and ES is outer; IS is inner
Composite Scope	Particular Order	Particular Facts	Holistic Innervations	Scope for both ET and ES is particular; IS is holistic

Table 5-1 ET Supported by ES

prehensively in meticulous, realistic detail. Georgia O'Keeffe, on the other side of the great divide, would be too captivated by her "far away," holistic innervations of special details.

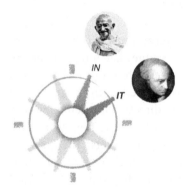

2: Speculative Thinking
Forging Ahead with Intuition

Speculative thinking, unlike practical thinking in the previous example, is oriented to possibilities. It is introverted thinking for sure. Which type of intuition would be more supportive: introverted or extraverted? A brief review of the comparative categories (Table 5-2) for each illustrates that introverted intuition would be more supportive of the sovereignty of introverted thinking.

Jung himself could be a good personal example of someone who was predisposed toward introverted thinking paired with introverted intuition. Jung so ambitiously forged ahead with his ideas and insights that he said he often felt like a man on a battlefield, moving ahead and leaving fallen comrades behind.

From our company of actors, our pensive professor, Immanuel Kant, would choose either Gandhi or Carnegie as his supporting actor. Oriented

Category	Introverted Thinking (IT)	Introverted Intuition (IN)	Extraverted Intuition (EN)	Comments
Composite Orientation	Intensive Images	Intensive Images	Extensive Possibilities	IT and IN are oriented intensively; EN is oriented extensively
Composite Attitude	Apprehend Insights	Apprehend Images	Perceive Possibilities	IT and IN apprehend the inner object; EN perceives outer object
Functional Role	Conceptual Thinking	Visionary Intuition	Catalytic Intuition	IT and IN roles are to the inner object; EN's role is to outer object
Composite Substance	Inner Thoughts	Inner Imagination	Outer Imagination	IT and IN deal with inner substance; EN with outer substance
Composite Scope	Holistic Insights	Holistic Images	Particular Possibilities	IT and IN have holistic scope; EN scope is to the particular

Table 5-2 IT Supported by IN

to intensive insights, he would likely choose Gandhi, oriented intensively to inner images, rather than Carnegie, oriented to extensive possibilities in the world.

3: Artistic Intuition Selecting and Presenting Its Images with the Help of Feeling-Values

By "artistic intuition" we can assume that Jung is referring to an introverted function. Extraverted intuition, with its focus on achievement and initiatives, is not the sort of intuition he is speaking of.

The "help of feeling-values" could refer to either an introverted or extraverted feeling. Introverted feeling, with its intense orientation to the images and ideals of the inner object would more compatibly support "artistic intuition," as illustrated in Table 5-3.

Mahatma Gandhi, representing introverted intuition, would be our leading actor in search of a supporting actor.[4] The artistic temperament in

---

[4] Georgia O'Keeffe, representing introverted sensation, might be a better choice for the lead artistic attitude. We could readily include her here as well, for introverted intuition and introverted sensation are very much alike. Though they are functional opposites, the introverted attitude

Category	Introverted Intuition (IN)	Introverted Feeling (IF)	Extraverted Feeling (EF)	Comments
Composite Orientation	Intensive Images	Intensive Ideals	Extensive Norms	IN and IF are oriented intensively; EF extensively
Composite Attitude	Apprehend Images	Apprehend Ideals	Perceive Norms	IN and IF apprehend; EF perceives
Functional Role	Visionary Intuition	Idealistic Feeling	Social Feeling	IN & IF roles related to inner object; EF outer object
Composite Substance	Inner Imagination	Inner Valuations	Outer Valuations	IN and IF deal with inner substance; EF with outer
Composite Scope	Holistic Images	Holistic Ideals	Particular Norms	IN & IF have holistic scope; EF is to the particular

Table 5-3 IN Supported by IF

search of supporting feeling-values would not look to extraverted feeling, to Queen Elizabeth, for she would be oriented to sustaining the world as it is. To be artistic is to create something new from *inner* inspiration. The better supporting actor would be Anne Frank, representing introverted feeling, oriented to intensive yet holistic ideals and absorbed with inner valuations.

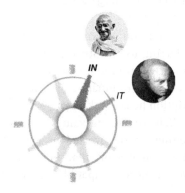

4: Philosophical Intuition Systematizing Its Vision into Comprehensible Thought by Means of a Powerful Intellect

The "philosophical intuition" Jung is speaking of would be introverted intuition. It would not be extraverted intuition, for when extraverted, intuition is directed to the achievement of tangible projects.

The term *powerful intellect* certainly refers to introverted thinking; the qualities of extraverted thinking are more programmatic than intellectual. Because introverted intuition is in the lead now, we should look for those

renders them highly compatible.

Category	Introverted Intuition (IN)	Introverted Thinking (IT)	Extraverted Thinking (ET)	Comments
Composite Orientation	Intensive Images	Intensive Insights	Extensive Order	IN and IT are intensive; ET extensive
Composite Attitude	Apprehend Images	Apprehend Insights	Perceive Order	IN and IT apprehend; ET perceives
Functional Role	Visionary Intuition	Conceptual Thinking	Constructive Thinking	IN & IT roles related to inner object; ET role relates to outer object
Composite Substance	Inner Imagination	Inner Thoughts	Outer Thoughts	IN and IT deal with inner substance; ET with outer substance
Composite Scope	Holistic Images	Holistic Insights	Particular Order	IN and IT have holistic scope; ET is to particular

Table 5-4 IN Supported by IT

representatives who were first highly imaginative and then thoughtful. Einstein (for whom "imagination is everything") or the Indian mathematician Ramanujan could serve as examples of philosophical intuition supported by a powerful intellect.

Our leading actor is Mahatma Gandhi, representing introverted intuition, this time in its more philosophical form. To support the holistic imagination of introverted intuition, Gandhi would certainly choose Kant's powerful intellect with its orientation to intensive insights, its conceptual rather than programmatic thinking, its absorption with inner thoughts, and its scope to holistic insights. Darwin, as extraverted thinking, sorting through his collection of collected specimens to assemble his ruling formula of natural selection, would not be of much help to the holistic, visionary Gandhi.

A review of the comparative categories (Table 5-4) will help to confirm this pairing.

THE 8 PAIRS

We can conclude, from assessing each of Jung's examples, that the three principles regarding functional relationships also apply to relationships among types.

The governing principles are these:

- The dominant type must have exclusive sovereignty.
- The supporting type must not oppose the lead type.
- The supporting type must be different in kind from the lead type.

The pairs that meet those criteria are these:

ET paired with an extraverted receptive type:

1. Extraverted thinking paired with extraverted sensation
2. Extraverted intuition paired with extraverted thinking

EF paired with an extraverted receptive type:

3. Extraverted sensation paired with extraverted feeling
4. Extraverted feeling paired with extraverted intuition

IT paired with an introverted receptive type:

5. Introverted thinking paired with introverted sensation
6. Introverted intuition paired with introverted thinking

IF paired with an introverted receptive type:

7. Introverted sensation paired with introverted feeling
8. Introverted feeling paired with introverted intuition

With the help of our traveling troupe of iconic actors, we can illustrate these eight possible pairings, as shown in Figures 5-1 through 5-4.

THE PRIMARY 16

In any of the preceding pairings, either actor could play the leading role. In the first pair, for example, extraverted thinking (Darwin) could play the lead role, and extraverted sensation (Child) the supporting role; or extraverted sensation (Child) could play the lead role, and extraverted thinking (Darwin) the supporting role.

Acknowledging lead and supporting roles increases the number of pairs to sixteen.[5] They remain very collaborative and supportive, but the lead type weights the attributes of the pair in its favor.

---

[5] None of these sixteen pairs is among the popular "16 personality type" pairs derived by other researchers. The first researcher to recognize the above sixteen likely pairings of Jung's eight types seems to be I. N. Marshall in his article "The Four Functions: A Conceptual Analysis," *Journal of Analytical Psychology* 13(1) 1968: pp. 1–32.

Figure 5.1 ET paired with an extraverted receptive type: Charles Darwin as ET in either a lead or supporting role with Julia Child as ES or Andrew Carnegie as EN

Figure 5.2 EF paired with an extraverted receptive type: Elizabeth I as EF in either lead or supporting role with Julia Child as ES or Andrew Carnegie as EN

Figure 5-3 IT paired with an introverted receptive type: Immanuel Kant as IT in either a leading or a supporting role with Georgia O'Keeffe as IS or Mahatma Gandhi as IN

Figure 5-4 IF paired with an introverted receptive type: Anne Frank as IF in either a leading or supporting role with Georgia O'Keeffe as IS or Mahatma Gandhi as IN

Charles Darwin and Julia Child would appear very different together, depending on who took the lead. If Darwin had the lead, Child would be searching for artifacts and fossils; if Child had the lead, Darwin would be organizing Julia's kitchen. Or, in more technical terms, rational extraverted thinking as the lead, with its preeminent attention to assembling order, would be supported by extraverted sensation in accurately perceiving facts. Extraverted sensation as the lead, with its attention to sensuous experience, would be assisted by extraverted thinking with its penchant for constructing order.

On the other side of the compass, we could imagine the collaboration if Kant were supporting Gandhi: conceptual and intensive analysis would shape the open window to the images of the collective unconscious. When these two types meld in one individual, they engender a threefold orientation to the inner object—two directional orientations and one functional orientation. Imagine the aloof and independent qualities resulting from a combination of these orientations. Jung shared some empirical observations of these two types separately that would become as one if they paired up.

> Not in the least clear where or how [his thoughts] link up with the world of reality (CW 6, §634); oriented neither by immediate experience of objects nor by traditional ideas (CW 6, §578); leaves a feeling of . . . superiority (CW 6, §633); may be polite and amiable . . . but one is constantly aware of a certain uneasiness (CW 6, §633); will shrink from no danger in building up his world of ideas (CW 6, §634); often results in an extraordinary aloofness of the individual from tangible reality (CW 6, §661); may even become a complete enigma to his immediate circle (CW 6, §661); unconscious images acquire the dignity of things. (CW 6, §657)

A preference for these two types together suggests an individual who will be inclined to apply thinking to the imaginative world within. Albert Einstein could serve as an example of this pairing; he freely acknowledged his orientation to the imagination:

> When I examine myself and my methods of thought, I come to the conclusion that the gift of fantasy has meant more to me than my talent for absorbing positive knowledge.[6]

His famous "thought experiments," such as elevators traveling at the speed of light, allowed him to step outside the confines of conventional thinking.

---

[6] Quoted in Ronald W. Clark, *Einstein: The Life and Times* (New York: Random House Value Publishing, 1995).

Without those imaginative, completely impractical exercises, his revolutionary theories of relativity would not have been born.

THE FINAL 24

If we could simply stop here, if the types would always abide by these "Primary 16," we could analyze how their shared attributes might look for each pair, just as we analyzed the composite attributes of the eight types. Then we would have sixteen Galtonesque clubs instead of eight.

But we could go further: we could conceivably create twenty-four pairs from Jung's governing principles. The crossover types, with their dual orientations to both inner and outer objects, provide some possible flexibility in interpreting Jung's rules. We could say that extraverted intuition, for example, with its functional orientation to the inner object, could conceivably be supportive of introverted thinking. If we more liberally interpreted his governing principles, then we could add an additional eight pairs of lead and supporting actors to our group of sixteen.

1. Lead extraverted intuition paired with introverted thinking
2. Lead extraverted intuition paired with introverted feeling
3. Lead introverted sensation paired with extraverted thinking
4. Lead introverted sensation paired with extraverted feeling
5. Lead introverted thinking paired with extraverted intuition
6. Lead introverted feeling paired with extraverted intuition
7. Lead extraverted thinking paired with introverted sensation
8. Lead extraverted feeling paired with introverted sensation

These pairs, illustrated by our iconic actors, would engage Georgia O'Keeffe with Elizabeth I and Darwin, and Andrew Carnegie with Kant and Anne Frank (Figures 5-5 and 5-6). They may be less likely, but there are threads of connections by way of the bilateral orientation of the crossover types.

Knowing these actors as we do, we can begin to imagine the resulting attributes of an individual disposed to any of these pairs. If Kant (IT) played the lead in a role with Carnegie (EN), for example, we can begin to imagine a person with a "powerful intellect" capable of applying that intellect to projects in the world at large.

Figure 5.5 Georgia O'Keeffe as IS in a leading or supporting role with either Charles Darwin as ET or Queen Elizabeth as EF.

Figure 5.6 Carnegie as EN in a leading or supporting role with either Immanuel Kant as IT or Anne Frank as IF.

Adding these additional eight to our sixteen produces twenty-four collaborative pairs. These are the "final" twenty-four. No other pairings are compatible with Jung's governing principles.

Well, we can breathe easily. So we can now create twenty-four Galton-esque clubs and be done with it.

Not so fast.

MIGHT AS WELL SAY 2400!

The twenty-four pairs illustrate the theoretical concepts more than the human reality. Of the fifty-six mathematically possible pairings among the eight types, with one lead and one supporting role, only twenty-four pairings would be consistent with Jung's theoretical construct. Sixteen are quite compatible, and another eight are conceivable. Each of these twenty-four pairings has resulting qualities that further differentiate the ego patterns of consciousness.

That is the theoretical model, but human experience is seldom neat and tidy, so we should be careful not to apply the model rigidly. Primary research with the types suggests that of the fifty-six possible pairings of the eight types, *all* the possible pairings occur.[7] The twenty-four pairs seem to account for a majority of the pairings, but other preferences are also reported that do not conform to the theoretical model.

Complicating the theory of simple pairings, Jung said that he sometimes observed two types supporting the lead. If we assume two supporting types at work, the number of possible combinations grows considerably.

No wonder that, in response to a proposition that there are sixteen type combinations, Jung replied, "You could say 16 but you might as well say 360!"[8] Likewise, we could also say 24, but we might as well say 2400!

---

[7] Initial primary research on pairings with the validated Gifts Compass Inventory suggests that the twenty-four-pair model was congruent with the stated preferences for a majority of the sample population. As expected, incompatible pairs were not nearly as evident as the twenty-four compatible ones, yet of the fifty-six ways that the types could pair as dominant and auxiliary, virtually all of them were in evidence to some degree. One interesting anomaly, however, was the way the feeling function and sensation function seemed symbiotically linked, irrespective of directional attitude. Another anomaly that might have surprised and interested Jung was that opposing functional attitudes were sometimes collaborating dispositions when they shared a common directional attitude.

[8] Evans, *Jung on Elementary Psychology*, p. 104.

Jung would have been the first to say that his model is simply a framework for understanding the dynamics of consciousness. The experience of consciousness is flexible and fluid.

Part of the difficulty in trying to define the preferences for any individual is that those preferences change over time as individuation progresses. Attributes that characterize a person's orientation earlier in life give way to the new attributes that arrive with the personal transformations that individuation brings.

Though the earliest ego dispositions may always be "home," through individuation, all eight types become increasingly conscious and available, and the array of possible combinations becomes more fluid, numerous, and nuanced. The types increasingly *team up* synergistically in groups of three or more, rather than *pair up* as simple sums of two. The varieties of those teams, measured by the number in the team and the degree of disposition for each type, are quite vast.

Rather than attempt to put people in predefined categories, it is actually much more fruitful to "read the melody" of the type variations at work in consciousness. In the work with the Gifts Compass Inventory (GCI) we have learned that there are often from three to five types actively engaged.

And that is on the conscious side of the psyche. To fully understand types in relationship to Jung's depth psychology, and individuation, we must also read the melody of type dispositions playing in the shadow. The oppositions formed by the shadow's type dispositions are as relevant and important to individuation as any occurring in ego consciousness. It is to those oppositions that we now turn.

CHAPTER SUMMARY

So far, in Chapter 1, we reviewed the context for understanding the types—the "theater of individuation." In Chapter 2, we reviewed Jung's important terms *attitude* and *orientation* to systematically derive composite attitudes—the eight types. In Chapter 3, using the five comparative categories and representative individuals, we examined closely each of the four extraverted types. In Chapter 4, we did the same with the four introverted types. In this chapter we reviewed Jung's principles for how the types tend to collaborate. We carefully assessed his scant observations about those collaborations to derive likely pairings compatible with his principles, and we noted that the types collaborate in human experience in fluid and dynamic ways, too numerous to attempt to categorize.

We can now turn to the transformational dynamics of Jung's type model—the integration of opposites through individuation. To do so in the final chapters, we will need to recognize the types as active, not just as the ego's orientations, but also as the shadow's. The persona and soul also have type orientations that correspond to ego and shadow, respectively.

Before moving to a review of these transformational dynamics in the final chapters, let us pause briefly to set the stage with a fairy tale.

The Water of Life

FAIRY TALES ARE LIKE SHORT PLAYS staged in our theater of individuation; they can symbolically portray dynamics occurring within the psyche. Marie-Louise von Franz, one of Jung's closest associates, did much to demonstrate the usefulness of fairy tales for understanding our voyages of psychological discovery.[1]

The classic Grimms' fairy tale "The Water of Life" offers an illuminating introduction to the dynamics of type integration through individuation.

> Long before you or I were born, there reigned, in a country a great way off, a king who had three sons. This king once fell very ill—so ill that nobody thought he could live. His sons were very much grieved at their father's sickness; and as they were walking together very mournfully in the garden of the palace, a little old man met them and asked what was the matter. They told him that their father was very ill, and that they were afraid nothing could save him. "I know what would," said the little old man, "it is the Water of Life. If he could have a draught of it he would be well again; but it is very hard to get." Then the eldest son said, "I will soon find it," and he went to the sick king, and begged that he might go in search of the Water of Life, as it was the only thing that could save him. "No," said the king. "I had rather die than place you in such great danger as you must meet with in your journey." But he begged so hard that the king let him go; and the prince thought to himself, "If I bring my father this water, he will make me sole heir to his kingdom."

1 See, for example, Marie-Louise von Franz, *The Interpretation of Fairy Tales,* rev. ed. (Boston: Shambhala, 1996), p. 19; von Franz, *The Feminine in Fairy Tales,* rev. ed. (Boston: Shambala, 2001); and von Franz, *Shadow and Evil in Fairy Tales* (Boston: Shambala, 1995).

Then he set out. And when he had gone on his way some time he came to a deep valley, overhung with rocks and woods; and as he looked around, he saw standing above him on one of the rocks a little ugly dwarf, with a sugarloaf cap and a scarlet cloak; and the dwarf called to him and said, "Prince, whither so fast?" "What is that to thee, you ugly imp?" said the prince haughtily, and rode on.

But the dwarf was enraged at his behavior, and laid a fairy spell of ill-luck upon him, so that as he rode on, the mountain pass became narrower and narrower, and at last the way was so straitened that he could not go to step forward, and when he thought to have turned his horse round and go back the way he came, he heard a loud laugh ringing round him, and found that the path was closed behind him, so that he was shut in all round. He next tried to get off his horse and make his way on foot, but again the laugh rang in his ears and he found himself unable to move a step, and thus he was forced to abide spellbound.

Meantime the old king was lingering on in daily hope of his son's return, till at last the second son said, "Father, I will go in search of the Water of Life." For he thought to himself, "My brother is surely dead, and the kingdom will fall to me if I find the water." The king was at first very unwilling to let him go, but at last yielded to his wish. So he set out and followed the same road which his brother had done, and met with the same elf, who stopped him at the same spot in the mountains, saying, as before, "Prince, prince, whither so fast?" "Mind your own affairs, busybody!" said the prince scornfully, and rode on.

But the dwarf put the same spell upon him as he put on his elder brother, and he, too, was at last obliged to take up his abode in the heart of the mountains. Thus it is with proud silly people, who think themselves above everyone else, and are too proud to ask or take advice.

When the second prince had thus been gone a long time, the youngest son said he would go and search for the Water of Life, and trusted he should soon be able to make his father well again. So he set out, and the dwarf met him too at the same spot in the valley, among the mountains, and said, "Prince, whither so fast?" And the prince said, "I am going in search of the Water of Life, because my father is ill, and likely to die; can you help me? Pray be kind, and aid me if you can!" "Do you know where it is to be found?" asked the dwarf. "No," said the prince, "I do not. Pray tell me if you know." "Then, as you have spoken to me kindly, and are wise enough to seek for advice, I will tell you how and where to go. The water you seek springs from a well in an enchanted castle and, that you may be able to reach it in safety, I will give you an iron wand and two little loaves of bread. Strike the iron door of the castle three times with the wand, and it will open. Two hungry lions will be lying down inside gaping for their prey, but if you throw them the bread they will let you pass; then hasten on to the well, and take some of the Water of Life before the clock strikes twelve, for, if you tarry longer, the door will shut upon you forever."

Then the prince thanked his little friend with the scarlet cloak for his friendly aid, and took the wand and the bread, and went traveling on and on, over sea and over land, till he came to his journey's end, and found everything to be as the dwarf had told him. The door flew open at the third stroke of the wand, and when the lions were quieted, he went on through the castle and came at length to a beautiful hall. Around it he saw several knights sitting in a trance; then he pulled off their rings and put them on his own fingers. In another room he saw on a table a sword and a loaf of bread, which he also took. Further on he came to a room where a beautiful young lady sat upon a couch; and she welcomed him joyfully, and said: if he would set her free from the spell that bound her, the kingdom should be his if he would come back in a year and marry her. Then she told him that the well that held the Water of Life was in the palace gardens and bade him make haste, and draw what he wanted, before the clock struck twelve.

He walked on and as he walked through the beautiful gardens he came to a delightful shady spot in which stood a couch; and he thought to him-self, as he felt tired, that he would rest himself for a while and gaze on the lovely scenes around him. So he laid himself down and sleep fell upon him unawares, so that he did not wake up till the clock was striking a quarter to twelve. Then he sprang from the couch dreadfully frightened, ran to the well, filled a cup that was standing by him full of water, and hastened to get away in time. Just as he was going out of the iron door, it struck twelve and the door fell so quickly upon him that it snapped off a piece of his heel.

When he found himself safe, he was overjoyed to think that he had got the Water of Life; and as he was going on his way homewards, he passed by the little dwarf, who, when he saw the sword and the loaf, said, "You have made a noble prize; with the sword you can at a blow slay whole armies, and the bread will never fail you." Then the prince thought to himself, "I cannot go home to my father without my brothers"; so he said, "My dear friend, cannot you tell me where my two brothers are, who set out in search of the Water of Life before me, and never came back?" "I have shut them up by a charm between two mountains," said the dwarf, "because they were proud and ill-behaved, and scorned to ask advice." The prince begged so hard for his brothers that the dwarf at last set them free, though unwill-ingly, saying, "Beware of them, for they have bad hearts." Their brother, however, was greatly rejoiced to see them, and told them all that had hap-pened to him: how he had found the Water of Life and had taken a cup full of it; and how he had set a beautiful princess free from a spell that bound her; and how she had engaged to wait a whole year, and then to marry him, and to give him the kingdom.

Then they all three rode on together and on their way home came to a country that was laid waste by war and a dreadful famine, so that it was feared all must die for want. But the prince gave the king of the land the bread, and all his kingdom ate of it. And he lent the king the wonderful sword, and he slew the enemy's army with it; and thus the kingdom was once more in peace and plenty. In the same manner he befriended two other countries through which they passed on their way.

When they came to the sea, they got into a ship and, during their voyage, the two eldest said to themselves, "Our brother has got the water which we could not find, therefore our father will forsake us and give him the kingdom, which is our right"; so they were full of envy and revenge, and agreed together how they could ruin him. Then they waited till he was fast asleep, and poured the Water of Life out of the cup, and took it for themselves, giving him bitter sea-water instead.

When they came to their journey's end, the youngest son brought his cup to the sick king, that he might drink and be healed. Scarcely, however, had he tasted the bitter sea-water when he became worse even than he was before; and then both the elder sons came in, and blamed the youngest for what they had done and said that he wanted to poison their father, but that they had found the Water of Life and had brought it with them. He no sooner began to drink of what they brought him, than he felt his sickness leave him, and was as strong and well as in his younger days. Then they went to their brother, and laughed at him, and said, "Well, brother, you found the Water of Life, did you? You have had the trouble and we shall have the reward. Pray, with all your cleverness, why did not you manage to keep your eyes open? Next year one of us will take away your beautiful princess, if you do not take care. You had better say nothing about this to our father, for he does not believe a word you say; and if you tell tales, you shall lose your life into the bargain: but be quiet, and we will let you off."

The old king was still very angry with his youngest son, and thought that he really meant to have taken away his life; so he called his court together, and asked what should be done, and all agreed that he ought to be put to death. The prince knew nothing of what was going on till one day, when the king's chief huntsmen went a-hunting with him, and they were alone in the wood together, the huntsman looked so sorrowful that the prince said, "My friend, what is the matter with you?" "I cannot and dare not tell you," said he. But the prince begged very hard, and said, "Only tell me what it is, and do not think I shall be angry, for I will forgive you." "Alas!" said the huntsman, "the king has ordered me to shoot you." The prince started at this, and said, "Let me live, and I will change dresses with you; you shall take my royal coat to show to my father, and you give me your shabby one." "With all my heart," said the huntsman, "I am sure I shall be glad to save you, for I could not have shot you." Then he took the prince's coat, and gave him the shabby one, and went away through the wood.

Some time after, three grand embassies came to the old king's court, with rich gifts of gold and precious stones for his youngest son; now all these were sent from the three kings to whom he had lent his sword and loaf of bread, in order to rid them of their enemy and feed their people. This touched the old king's heart, and he thought his son might still be guilt-less, and said to his court, "O that my son were still alive! How it grieves me that I had him killed!" "He is still alive," said the huntsman; "and I am glad that I had pity on him, but let him go in peace, and brought home his royal coat." At this the king was overwhelmed with joy, and made it known throughout all his kingdom, that if his son would come back to his court he would forgive him. Meanwhile the princess was eagerly waiting till her deliverer should come back; and had a road made leading up to her palace all of shining gold; and told her courtiers that whoever came on horseback, and rode straight up to the gate upon it, was her true lover, and that they must let him in; but whoever rode on one side of it, they must be sure was not the right one, and that they must send him away at once.

The time soon came when the eldest brother thought that he would make haste to go to the princess, and say that he was the one who had set her free, and that he should have her for his wife, and the kingdom with her. As he came before the palace and saw the golden road, he stopped to look at it, and he thought to himself, "It is a pity to ride upon this beautiful road"; so he turned aside and rode on the right-hand side of it. But when he came to the gate, the guards, who had seen the road he took, said to him, he could not be what he said he was, and must go about his business.

The second prince set out soon afterwards on the same errand; and when he came to the golden road, and his horse had set one foot upon it, he stopped to look at it, and thought it very beautiful, and said to himself, "What a pity it is that anything should tread here!" Then he too turned aside and rode on the left side of it. But when he came to the gate the guards said he was not the true prince, and that he too must go away about his business; and away he went. Now when the full year was come round, the third brother left the forest in which he had lain hid for fear of his father's anger, and set out in search of his betrothed bride. So he journeyed on, thinking of her all the way, and rode so quickly that he did not even see what the road was made of, but went with his horse straight over it; and as he came to the gate it flew open, and the princess welcomed him with joy, and said he was her deliverer, and should now be her husband and lord of the kingdom. When the first joy at their meeting was over, the princess told him she had heard of his father having forgiven him, and of his wish to have him home again: so, before his wedding with the princess, he went to visit his father, taking her with him. Then he told him everything: how his brothers had cheated and robbed him, and yet that he had borne all those wrongs for the love of his father. And the old king was very angry, and wanted to punish his wicked sons; but they made their escape, and got into a ship and sailed away over the wide sea, and where they went to nobody knew and nobody cared.

And now the old king gathered together his court, and asked all his kingdom to come and celebrate the wedding of his son and the princess. And young and old, noble and squire, gentle and simple, came at once on the summons; and among the rest came the friendly dwarf, with the sugarloaf hat, and a new scarlet cloak.

And the wedding was held, and the merry bells rung. And all the good people they danced and they sung, And feasted and frolick'd, I can't tell how long.

We could use the characters in this tale to represent elements from our theater of individuation, shown in Figure 1.

The King (Self) is ill; the ego has become overly one-sided; and there is a need for revitalizing the psychic kingdom. Early on, we meet three brothers who will go in search of the "Water of Life." We could think of the Water of Life as the collective unconscious that brings vitality and renewed meaning to life.

The first two brothers could be seen as the persona and lead ego type; they are much alike, each with a one-sided, crass, controlling disposition that could be considered extraverted thinking taken to an extreme. As each brother departs, he meets a dwarf. The dwarf could represent the shadow type, the inferior side of the ego that tends to be ignored or demeaned. In this case, as the shadow type to extraverted thinking, it would likely be introverted feeling. The shadow type is a dwarf, for it is smaller in stature than the ego's leading type; it does not have the ego's standing and is often reviled, ignored, or suppressed.

Neither the persona, which is like an actor's mask for the ego's leading role, nor the ego wishes to acknowledge the dwarf in any way, for the dwarf does not "fit" with the ego's lead position. Each of the brothers is in a hurry to accomplish a mission. Each ignores the dwarf and chooses to rush on to his intended destination without heeding the little fellow.

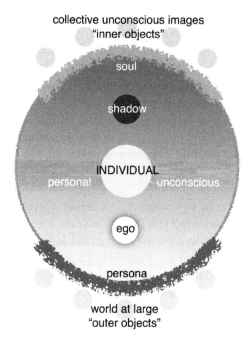

collective unconscious images
"inner objects"

soul

shadow

INDIVIDUAL

personal   unconscious

ego

persona

world at large
"outer objects"

Figure 1 Theater of Individuation

"Prince, whither so fast?" "What is that to thee, you ugly imp?' said the prince haughtily, and rode on.

Each of the two brothers, persona and ego, set out on their one-sided way, only to get stuck, literally in the fairy tale and figuratively in the psyche, between a rock and a hard place. There is no flow in their lives; their progress has been jammed by the oppositional shadow.

The third son is different. He is not so hurried; he is not so haughty. He could be the *individual* at the very center of our psychic stage—midway between the lead ego type on the conscious stage and the shadow type on the unconscious stage. Just as he respects his thinking brothers, he also humbly welcomes this little feeling fellow into his family of relationships.

"Prince, whither so fast?" And the prince said, "I am going in search of the Water of Life, because my father is ill, and likely to die: can you help me? Pray be kind, and aid me if you can!" "Do you know where it is to be found?" asked the dwarf. "No," said the prince, "I do not. Pray tell me if you know." "Then, as you have spoken to me kindly, and are wise enough to seek for advice, I will tell you how and where to go."

The dwarf, as the shadow type, holds the secrets that will guide the individual to the revitalizing Water of Life—the collective unconscious—and to the feminine anima figure who can grant him access.

The prince travels on and finds the castle just as the dwarf had foretold. He also finds the alluring anima figure who gives him access to the well for the water. She is imprisoned by a spell, for she, like the dwarf, has been ignored in this psychic kingdom by the lead ego type. As the persona is an extension of the ego, the anima (soul) could be considered an extension of the shadow type. With the suppression of the shadow type, the anima is also suppressed.

> Further on he came to a room where a beautiful young lady sat upon a couch; and she welcomed him joyfully, and said: if he would set her free from the spell that bound her, the kingdom should be his, if he would come back in a year and marry her. Then she told him that the well that held the Water of Life was in the palace gardens and bade him make haste, and draw what he wanted, before the clock struck twelve.

He does as he is told, but in no great haste, for he nearly sleeps through the appointed hour and must suffer a wound before making away with the water. With the water in hand, he could return to his ailing father, but he will not go back till he has retrieved his lost brothers.

As the individual at the center of the psyche, he seeks wholeness. He has by now accorded respect to the shadow type, the anima, and the lead ego type and its persona. His aim is harmony and honor throughout the whole psychic kingdom. After saving his brothers, he uses his new power to restore other psychic sub-kingdoms—unruly and debilitating complexes.

Yet his inflated brothers are not happy with psychic wholeness; they have one agenda—their own self-promotion. They trick their trusting brother and thrust themselves forward as the real heroes of the journey to well-being. The third brother is temporarily exiled as they again seize an imbalanced center stage in the psychic kingdom.

However, their duplicity cannot succeed, for they again fall victim to their one-sided positions. They go in search of the very soul they have suppressed, but they do not know the way. When they see the street paved with gold—the middle way—they choose not to tread on it, rather choosing to ride on one side or the other. Each is therefore rejected at the threshold of the soul's castle, for neither knows the middle way and the value of individuation.

But the third prince has thoughts only for her. When he arrives at the middle way, paved so preciously in gold, he gives it no conscious thought, for his attention is on his beloved princess. We could call his horse *Wu Wei* ("doing by not doing"), for the horse seems to know instinctively, without effort, that the middle road is the way.

The third son marries the princess and thereby integrates the soul in the consciousness of the individual. Acknowledging both ego and shadow, persona and soul, he restores health in his father's kingdom—the psyche as a whole. The dwarflike shadow type and the representatives of the restored kingdoms (complexes) are welcomed at the wedding, though banished are the *one-sided* ego and persona dispositions that had caused the imbalance in the kingdom.

The disruptive oppositions in the psyche have led, in this tale of a kingdom that has existed since "before you or I were born," to a union that has brought peace and well-being throughout the psychic kingdom. The individual has become more whole, integrating the oppositions.

6

Oppositions

INDIVIDUATION STARTS WITH THE MOST accessible attitude of consciousness. The dominant type charts the initial course of individuation, setting up the necessary oppositions in the psychic theater. A dwarf-like shadow type opposes the ego's lead attitude.[1]

Jung often referred to the oppositions as functional oppositions. If thinking, either extraverted or introverted, were the dominant type, then feeling would be the "inferior" opposing function. The inferior functions could be considered an integral element of the shadow. The inferior function carries many of the discarded or unwanted attributes that the lead does not value, in particular those attributes that could challenge the authority of the established ego and persona.

The term *shadow* in Jung's model is far-reaching, including unwanted moral, ethical, social, and sexual attributes rejected by the conscious ego position. The unsavory character Caliban in Shakespeare's *The Tempest* could serve as a theatrical embodiment of the shadow, for he is ugly, distasteful, odd—thoroughly repugnant in every way. The shadow is "the thing a person has no wish to be" (CW 16, §470).

The shadow is not evil per se; in fact, like the dwarf in the fairy tale, it can provide access to the waters of life.

---

[1] Our research with types using the Gifts Compass Inventory (GCI) has confirmed that usually the shadow type is opposite the ego's lead type. Yet we have also found that sometimes the shadow is not in direct opposition to the conscious attitude. Also, in the case of the crossover receptive types, the shadow type often appears as a rational type, as explained in this chapter.

> If the repressed tendencies, the shadow as I call them, were obviously evil, there would be no problem whatever. But the shadow is merely somewhat inferior, primitive, unadapted, and awkward, not wholly bad. It contains childish or primitive qualities which would in a way vitalize and embellish human existence, but—convention forbids. (CW 11, §134)

The inferior function is hard to disentangle from the shadow as a whole.

> I should only like to point out that the inferior function is practically identical with the dark side of the human personality. (CW 9i, §222)

We could be more specific and think of the shadow as having a *shadow type*—the inferior function modified by a directional attitude. As a compensation for the ego's dominant type, the shadow type assumes an opposing position. If the ego's dominant type were extraverted sensation, for example, the shadow's type would typically be introverted intuition. While the shadow type may not include all the unsavory attributes of the full shadow complex, it too resides in a relatively unconscious state and is often negatively projected onto others.

Functional Alliances and Oppositions

In the seminars he delivered in 1925, Jung discussed the oppositions and alliances that occur as the ego's dominant attitude is established. Considering only alliances and oppositions of the *functions,* excluding reference to their introverted or extraverted attitudes as types, he noted that the ego's dominant function allied with its auxiliary creates an opposition that aligns the inferior function with an auxiliary function of its own.

The inferior function is normally the opposite of the dominant. If the dominant ego function is thinking, for example, the inferior function would be feeling. If sensation is the auxiliary function to thinking, intuition is aligned with feeling.

> Suppose you have sensation strongly developed but are not fanatical about it. Then you can admit about every situation a certain aura of possibilities; that is to say, you permit an intuitive element to come in. Sensation as an auxiliary function would allow intuition to exist. But inasmuch as sensation . . . is a partisan of the intellect [thinking], intuition sides with the feeling, here the inferior function. Therefore the intellect [thinking] will not agree with intuition, in this case, and will vote for its exclusion. Intel-

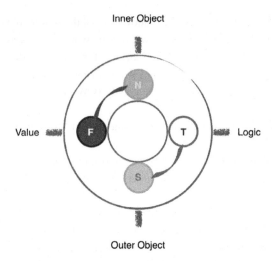

Figure 6.1 Thinking (T) aligned with Sensation (S) vs. Feeling (F) aligned with Intuition (N)

lect [thinking] will not hold together sensation and intuition, rather it will separate them. Such a destructive attempt will be checked by feeling, which backs up intuition. (Jung, *Introduction to Jungian Psychology*, pp. 75, 76)

These oppositions and alliances can be diagrammed on our compass of consciousness. In Figure 6-1, thinking is the dominant function; feeling, the inferior function. Sensation supports thinking, and intuition is similarly aligned with feeling.

The thinking function as the dominant is supported by the sensation function as the auxiliary. Well developed, though not thoroughly, sensation would not be entirely opposed to the possibilities carried by intuition. Yet, because it has aligned with the dominant thinking, its division with intuition is more sharply defined, for thinking would insist on clearer boundaries between sensation and intuition.

Feeling, the opponent of thinking, steps in to defend its ally intuition, and the oppositions within the psyche are more clearly and emphatically drawn: thinking aligns with sensation; feeling, with intuition.

A necessary condition for individuation will be an evolving resolution of the conflict. For psychic wholeness, and for the individuation of the whole person at the center, the oppositions must be resolved and all the functions of consciousness made more readily available. The inferior and dominant must resolve their conflict, but they cannot do so directly because their opposition is too entrenched. They settle their differences first through their allies.

> You cannot get directly to the inferior function from the superior, it must always be via the auxiliary function. It is as though the unconscious were in such antagonism to the superior function that it allowed no direct attack. . . . The way is from the superior to the auxiliary, from the latter to the function opposite to the auxiliary. . . . This may be called the preliminary conflict. The knock-down battle between the superior and inferior functions only takes place in life. (Ibid.)

The knock-down battle between dominant and inferior is circumvented by a less brutal contest between their aides-de-camp. The auxiliary to the dominant is less developed than the dominant function; the auxiliary to the inferior is less repressed than the inferior. Because their positions are more moderate, they can more amiably find resolution to conflict. As they become more compatible, they lead the way for the dominant and inferior to be reconciled.

Alliances and Oppositions for the Types

Though Jung did not develop the oppositions of the types in his 1925 seminars, we could extrapolate to imagine similar oppositions occurring for the types. The types are somewhat more complex because there are eight of them.

If we assume in the previous example that the dominant thinking function is extraverted, then the lead type would be extraverted thinking. Its direct opposite on the compass is introverted feeling (Figure 6-2). If sensation aligns with the lead type, we could assume one of the primary sixteen pairs, rendering sensation, also extraverted.[2] The opposite of extraverted sensation is introverted intuition, which would step up as the auxiliary to introverted feeling. Those alliances would appear on the compass of consciousness as clearly oppositional.

Extraverted thinking and sensation are aligned on the extraverted side of the great divide; on the other side, introverted feeling as the shadow type

---

[2] Note that in Figure 6-2, the position of extraverted sensation has moved to the southeast quadrant of the compass, replacing extraverted intuition. These two types are interchangeable; either can come to the aid of each of the rational types. Extraverted sensation and intuition can each swing right or left, to illustrate the alliances being depicted; the same is true of introverted sensation and intuition.

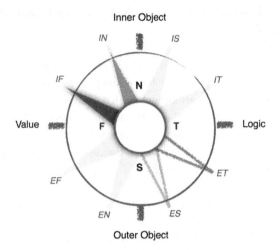

Figure 6.2 Lead and shadow type oppositions and alliances

is aligned with its supporting type: introverted intuition. The first reconciliation would be between extraverted sensation and introverted intuition; the knock-down opposition in the life of the individual would be between the lead—extraverted thinking—and the shadow type—introverted feeling.

Oppositions and Psychic Architecture

As the lead type takes a position in consciousness, the effects on the psychic architecture ripple through the psychic "mirror world" to the threshold of the archetypes. The shadow type plays a compensatory role in the unconscious.

Working from the previous example, in Figure 6-3 the ego's disposition of extraverted thinking with extraverted sensation is depicted with its face toward the outer object; the inferior disposition of introverted feeling supported by introverted intuition is depicted with its face toward the inner object. (If circumstances were reversed in the diagram, and introverted feeling took the lead role, then the shadow type would face the *outer object*, for the lead would be more oriented to the inner object.)

Jung's architecture of the psyche is symmetrical. As the ego is the mediator of conscious experience, the inferior disposition is the gateway to unconscious experience. As the ego's lead type is inextricably related to the persona, the inferior type is inextricably related to the persona's complement—the soul. As the persona is shaped out of the ego's dominant disposition and experience with the outer object, we could imagine a soul shaped out of experience with the inferior disposition and the inner object.

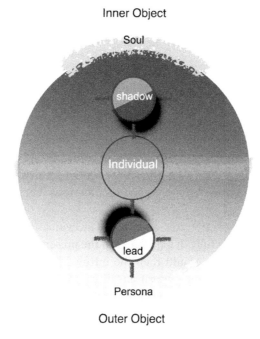

Inner Object

Soul

shadow

Individual

lead

Persona

Outer Object

Figure 6.3 Oppositions of lead and shadow alliances

The tension of opposites established by lead and inferior types is a catalyst for individuation. If the lead type is too much identified with the object of its orientation, if its position becomes extremely one-sided, then the shadow type will rise up to counter the imbalance.

Extreme Oppositions

For extraverted and introverted types alike, the dilemma is the same: the bliss of following the dominant conscious attitude must not become grandiose or extreme. An essential condition of individuation is to bring the shadow to greater consciousness.

The temptation for the extraverted types is to identify too much with the lively world at large. The temptation for the introverted types is to identify too much with the enthralling inner life. As the dominant attitude becomes excessively imbalanced in either direction, the shadow's response destructively interferes with the ego's intentions.

It is an outstanding peculiarity of unconscious impulses that, when deprived of energy by lack of conscious recognition, they take on a destructive character, and this happens as soon as they cease to be compensatory. (CW 6, §574)

If the shadow type is ignored or demeaned as an "ugly imp," "the potentialities repressed by the [conscious] attitude will make themselves indirectly felt by disturbing the conscious conduct of life. When the disturbance reaches a definite pitch, we speak of neurosis" (CW 6, §587). The ensuing neuroses seem purposefully intended to subvert the ego's inflated identity, to return the individual to a more balanced course.

This is the hazard of a superficial application of psychological types. Attending only to one's strengths risks the neuroses that a one-sided attitude can bring.

The integration of opposites is the way of individuation. We will address that integration more fully in Chapter 7. In the present chapter, addressing first the extraverted types and then the introverted types, we will assess more fully the nature of the oppositions themselves.

Jung suggested that the oppositions could be thought of as conversations between the opposites.

> It is exactly as if a dialogue were taking place between two human beings with equal rights, each of whom gives the other credit for a valid argument and considers it worthwhile to modify the conflicting standpoints by means of thorough comparison and discussion or else to distinguish them clearly from one another. (CW 8, §186)

In the tables that follow for both the extraverted and the introverted types, we will engage our company of representative actors to stage a conversation, category by comparative category, to better glean the nature of these oppositions.

OPPOSITIONS FOR THE EXTRAVERTED TYPES

The extraverted types are typically opposed by introverted types. The opposition provides the necessary restraining influence to keep the lead type from getting carried away in excessive one-sidedness.

Should the oppositional shadow fail to inhibit extreme one-sidedness, the shadow will intervene more disruptively on the stage of consciousness to undermine the ego's intentions, generating neurosis. Though neurosis for each of the extraverted types will have its particular attributes, for each of the extraverted types we can expect to see a one-sided, imbalanced identification with its orientation to the world. Jung referred to it as *hysteria*.

> The hallmark of classic hysteria is an exaggerated rapport with persons in the immediate environment and an adjustment to surrounding conditions that amounts to imitation. A constant tendency to make himself interesting and to produce an impression is a basic feature of the hysteric. (CW 6, §566)

The shadow will bring the grand extraverted imbalance to an unceremonious halt.

> This [nervous breakdown] invariably happens when the influence of the unconscious finally paralyzes all conscious action. (CW 6, §573)

For each of the types that follow, we will present the healthy oppositional tension first and then the neurotic condition if the type adopts an excessively one-sided position.

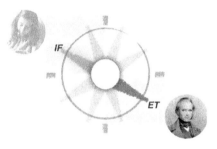

Extraverted Thinking vs. Introverted Feeling

I am fully aware that our age and its most eminent representatives know and acknowledge only the extraverted type of thinking.

—Carl Jung

People disposed to extraverted thinking, with introverted feeling as the shadow type, may only awkwardly express deep feelings and will likely avoid the sentimental and poetic aspects of life. They will be cautious about letting the unpredictable, fledgling feeling side of their nature out, for it is beyond their control and not nearly as finely honed as their thinking. They will tend to dislike showing emotion and may disparage the tearful sentiments of others.

The knock-down battle in their psyche is between Charles Darwin, representing extraverted thinking, and Anne Frank, representing introverted feeling. Anne has the advantage of being apart from the main stage; she can watch the action there, but the lead actor cannot see her. She performs her role as one who whispers from behind the curtain as the lead actor plays his given role, much more attentive to the actors who share the conscious stage with him (Table 6-1).

Extraverted Thinking (ET)	Introverted Feeling (IF)	Comments
Extensive Order	Intensive Ideals	**Orientation:** The lead attends to many particular facts and their logical arrangement; the shadow type urges him to yearn for deep meaning.
Perceive Order	Apprehend Ideals	**Attitude:** The lead is determined to make logical sense of facts; the shadow type would like him to turn his head to lofty ideals.
Constructive Thinking	Idealistic Feeling	**Functional Role:** The lead thinks constantly about practical order; the shadow type urges him to feel his way through life.
Outer Thoughts	Inner Valuations	**Substance:** The lead thinks only about what is out there; the shadow type urges him to feel more "in here."
Particular Order	Holistic Ideals	**Scope:** The lead attends to each of his fossil finds to make sense of it all; the shadow type urges him to feel the overall beauty in it all.

Table 6-1 ET Opposed by IF

To the degree that the shadow is successful in getting through to the lead, she creates a tension that must be resolved. The lead is drawn to reflective soliloquy. He hears a distant voice calling him to another life, but he can't quite make it out. Still, the shadow's voice will not go away, and she holds him in check, keeping him from taking his ruling formulas and constructed order to a one-sided extreme.

Using the comparative categories built in previous chapters, we can better imagine the shadow's subtle but healthy opposition to the lead actor, holding him back from becoming too engrossed in his role, too needy of audience approval, and too much interested in his own acclaim.

If Darwin, as the lead, refuses to listen to Anne Frank's soft voice calling him to remember the beautiful ideals that are also part of life, if she is shut away and forced to live a reclusive life, then the lead has gained full and unrestrained power to dominate the stage with his ruling formulas of right and wrong, good and evil. The stage becomes a desolate place, and the suppressed shadow type is transformed from a helpless kitten into a rampant lioness.

Extreme Extraverted Thinking

Normally accomplished at organizing, forecasting, and synthesizing, extraverted thinking taken to a one-sided extreme can become too identified with and subordinated to the outer object. Engrossed in a multitude of empirical data, it finds few connections amid all of them and seeks a reductive idea to include them all.

> When extraverted thinking is subordinated to the objective data as a result of over-determination by the object, it engrosses itself entirely in the individual experience and accumulates a mass of undigested empirical material. The oppressive weight of individual experiences having little or no connection with one another produces a dissociation of thought which usually requires psychological compensation. This must consist in some simple, general idea that gives coherence to the disordered whole, or at least affords the possibility of such. Ideas like "matter" or "energy" serve this purpose. (CW 6, §583)

The "simple, general idea," the framework for containing many facts, becomes a "ruling formula" that must be applied everywhere. Highly one-sided extraverted thinking relies simplistically and tyrannically on the power of its dogmatic formula. The order conceived attains a dominating power that ignores nuance. The ruling formula, whatever it may be, is never sufficient to fully embody the rich, subtle, and intangible qualities of life to which the complementary shadow is more attuned.

The more the shadow is repressed, the more partial and reductive the conclusions become. With that suppression, the conclusions are adorned in the guise of infallibility and become an intellectual superstition. The repressed shadow rises up with powerful allies from the unconscious. The inferior type attacks everything that extraverted thinking has sought to affirm and does not shrink from secrecy or deception to accomplish its ends.

> There are guardians of public morals who suddenly find themselves in compromising situations, or rescue workers who are themselves in dire need of rescue. . . . In science there are not a few painful examples of highly respected investigators who are so convinced of the truth and general validity of their formula that they have not scrupled to falsify evidence in its favor. Their sanction is: the end justifies the means. Only an inferior feeling function, operating unconsciously and in secret, could seduce otherwise reputable men into such aberrations. (CW 6, §588)

The shadow type's intervention on the conscious stage produces touchy and temperamental suspicions. Traitors seem to lurk behind every curtain. Disagreements quickly devolve into contests of personal retribution. Battle lines are strictly drawn: "Those who are not for us must therefore be against us." Acrimony, resentment, and aggression may reign, for the repressed shadow now screens events and people through a veil of petty mistrust. There is a perpetual tendency to make negative assumptions about other people to invalidate their positions. Those people or those ideas that do not align with the one-sided ruling formula of extraverted thinking are condemned as alien. The individual becomes "petty, mistrustful, crotchety, and conservative" (CW 6, §589).

> His unconscious sensitivity makes him sharp in tone, acrimonious, aggressive. Insinuations multiply. His feelings have a sultry and resentful character—always a mark of the inferior function. (CW 6, §589)

The shadow type, now as an ugly imp, is projected by the lead onto others. The individual withdraws personal sympathy, denigrates critics, and demolishes opposition by any means available, no matter how perverse. The more the ego relies exclusively on extraverted thinking, the more fanatical the individual becomes. He must fend off haunting doubt with tyrannical certainty.

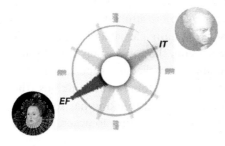

Extraverted Feeling vs. Introverted Thinking

People oriented to extraverted feeling with introverted thinking as the shadow type will tend to avoid philosophical questions and deep thinking. The very meaning of life may ultimately be found there, but extraverted feeling will prefer to find that meaning ready-made in the world of the social order and societal values. They prefer time with others where they gain freedom from the thoughts that periodically alight, often in a critical way, as observations about their own life or others. Being alone with their thoughts can be disconcerting and even frightening sometimes. Their thoughts can too often bring on a melancholic mood. An orientation to others, to the social world of people, norms, values, and expectations, is their safe refuge.

Their primary psychic opposition is between Queen Elizabeth I, representing extraverted feeling, and Immanuel Kant, representing introverted thinking. The Queen on the main stage seeks harmony among her troupe; she is attentive to the norms and standards she finds among them, but her shadow opposite behind stage whispers that she should discard all of that and think for herself. Our table of comparative categories can help us to more fully grasp how Kant could be the Queen's determined antagonist (Table 6-2).

If Elizabeth, as the lead, refuses to listen to the quiet Kant, who is softly reminding her to look to the larger meaning in life, if he is figuratively exiled to her psychic tower of London, then she has gained absolute power to govern consciousness, and a rebellious coup becomes inevitable. Kant will arm himself with mighty weapons from the unconscious and bring her to ignominious defeat.

Extreme Extraverted Feeling

Extraverted feeling carried to a one-sided extreme unduly associates the ego identity with the outer object. When extraverted feeling becomes too attached to the values and social norms of others, feeling is dispossessed of its own most valuable personal qualities. Feeling becomes too closely tied to the objects of its orientation; it loses its own natural validity—its natural charm and warmth.

Extraverted Feeling (EF)	Introverted Thinking (IT)	Comments
Extensive Norms	Intensive Insights	Orientation: The lead attends to many social protocols—she is loathe to transgress tradition; the shadow type urges her to forget all that and to look intently at new ideas.
Perceive Norms	Apprehend Insights	Attitude: The lead is determined to sustain social harmony; the shadow type whispers that she could also be sovereign over new insight.
Social Feeling	Conceptual Thinking	Functional Role: The lead empathizes, feeling her socially harmonious way from one event to another; the shadow type urges her to also find harmony in truth.
Outer Valuations	Inner Thoughts	Substance: The lead feels what she likes or dislikes about her court; the shadow type wants her to think about what is best for her kingdom.
Particular Norms	Holistic Insights	Scope: The lead is oriented to the way people dress and behave; the shadow type urges her to think about their future.

Table 6-2 EF Opposed by IT

> The subject [person] becomes so enmeshed in the network of individual feeling processes that to the observer it seems as though there were merely a feeling process and no longer a subject of feeling. (CW 6, §596)

As the individual is pulled from one empathetic moment to another, the personal identity is lost in the affect of the moment. The identity is lost to collective values, and the individual becomes what Holden Caulfield, the hero of *Catcher in the Rye,* called a "phony."

> It becomes cold, "unfeeling," untrustworthy. It has ulterior motives, or at least makes an impartial observer suspect them. It no longer makes that agreeable and refreshing impression which invariably accompanies genuine feeling; instead, one suspects a pose, or that the person is acting. (CW 6, §596)

The repressed shadow type, introverted thinking, which essentially seeks truth and authenticity, will engender tyranny on the conscious stage. In the repression of the introverted attitudes, the individual loses access to that balance of opposites that only the collective unconscious (inner object) can provide as a counterpoint to the allure of the world at large (outer object.) The ego itself is no match for the power of either the collective unconscious or the manifold world. The shadow attitude will bring its allies from the unconscious to oppose the extreme position.

Rather than the profound intellect of an Immanuel Kant, the repressed and ignored introverted thinking possesses "infantile and archaic" qualities. As conflictive antagonist, it delivers obsessive, intolerant, and shallow thoughts to depreciate everything that extraverted feeling most highly treasures. Shadow projections categorically reduce people to some sterile characterization. "She is nothing but a social gadfly." "He is nothing but a mechanic."

> The unconscious thoughts gravitate round just the most valued objects and mercilessly strip them of their value. The "nothing but" type thinking comes into its own here, since it effectively depotentiates all feelings that are bound to the object. (CW 6, §600)

The individual may be prone to "extravagant displays of feeling, gushing talk, loud expostulations, etc., which ring hollow. . . . It is at once apparent that some kind of resistance is being overcompensated" (CW 6, §599). The obsessively negative thoughts that plague the individual from the unconscious deliver unmanageable fears and emotional excesses.

Extraverted Sensation vs. Introverted Intuition

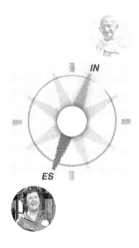

While extraverted sensation is oriented to the concrete, perceivable reality of particular objects, its opposite, introverted intuition, has the largest window to the big and long-distance picture of life as a whole. People oriented to extraverted sensation have a very keenly developed perception of sensuous reality. Naturally the individual will look suspiciously on intuitive hunches. While intuition readily sees three dots and connects twenty-four, sensation will not connect one dot before it's time—before it is fully perceived. If it is not perceived, it does not exist. Apprehending intuitively is a strange and dark art for this orientation. Apprehending the panoramic images of the inner object is a fearful proposition, for the inner object possesses none of the attributes perceivable by extraverted sensation; the inner object is mysterious and suspect. The more that introverted intuition is suppressed as worrisome by the dominant type, the more troublesome it becomes.

Julia Child, as extraverted sensation, who would "rather eat one tablespoon of chocolate russe cake than three bowls of Jell-O!" is opposed by the introverted intuition shadow played by Gandhi, who ate only the simplest foods and found fasting delicious. This could be a yeasty recipe of oppositions. A review of the five comparative categories for each type (Table 6-3) will help to illustrate this dynamic tension of opposites.

Extraverted sensation, fully oriented and directed to the outer object, is more engaged in the pure act of accurate perception than any of the other types. This is both an adaptive advantage and a potential pitfall. The inner life can be too readily devalued in an exclusive absorption with sensory experience.

Extreme Extraverted Sensation

When taken to an extreme, extraverted sensation conflates the ego identity with the outer object. Normally a highly sensitive type that differentiates the qualities of many sensuous experiences, in an extreme mode it is driven to pure pleasure seeking. Extraverted sensation normally carries its own discriminating judgment about sensuous experience. When too one-sided, it loses that restraint, "squeezing dry" sensuous experience, exploiting the outer object merely to further stimulate sensation.

Extraverted Sensation (ES)	Introverted Intuition (IN)	Comments
Extensive Facts	Intensive Images	**Orientation:** The lead attends to the many enjoyable, sensuous facts; the shadow type wants her to look inward to the delicious images that could also captivate her attention.
Perceive Facts	Apprehend Images	**Attitude:** The lead is determined to get her facts just right; the shadow type whispers that God is not in the details, but within.
Realistic Sensation	Visionary Intuition	**Functional Role:** The lead plays her role by savoring all the sensual delights; the shadow type wants her to envision grand possibilities for the future.
Outer Perceptions	Inner Imagination	**Substance:** The lead considers her factual and accurate perceptions, and she kneads them like dough; the shadow type wants her to get her fingers out of the dough and let her imagination rise.
Particular Facts	Holistic Images	**Scope:** The lead enjoys each particular fact for its own sake; the shadow type wants her to relax and also enjoy the whole— the whole cake yes, but even better the whole of life or the whole world.

Table 6-3 ES Opposed by IN

All of life experience is blindly reduced to sensual perception; everything must have a concrete causal connection. "She will unhesitatingly connect a psychogenic symptom with a drop in the barometer (CW 6, §607).

Grandly imaginative introverted intuition asserts itself to actively oppose the conscious position, but in a primitive and disruptive form. It arrives as imagined anxieties, phobias, and magical superstitions. Extraverted sensation, the most practical, realistic, concrete form of ego consciousness, is besieged with preposterous suppositions. The most realistic and practical of all the types turns into a "pathological parody" of imagined troubles. As jealous suspicions and fantasies arise, the individual becomes increasingly petty and sanctimonious.

> A pettifogging captiousness follows, or a grotesquely punctilious morality combined with primitive, "magical" superstitions that fall back on abstruse rights. . . . Reason turns into hair-splitting pedantry, morality into dreary moralizing and blatant Pharisaism, religion into ridiculous superstition, and intuition, the noblest gift of man, into meddlesome officiousness, poking into every corner; instead of gazing into the far distance, it descends to the lowest level of human meanness. (CW 6, §608)

The individual is simultaneously in the grip of an obsessive tie to the outer object and overwhelmed by apparently magical forces from within.

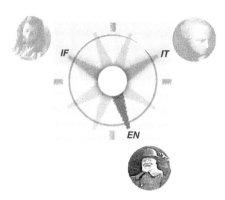

Extraverted Intuition vs. Introverted Feeling or Introverted Thinking

People oriented to extraverted intuition will tend to repress any aspect of consciousness that might obstruct their fascination with possibilities in the making. They don't want to consider practical detail that might impede their vision or to hear the arguments about why their ideas are not feasible. The theoretical opposite of extraverted intuition is introverted sensation, yet introverted sensation, viewing sensory experience through the magical lens of the inner object, may not be a sufficient counterbalance. It is too similar to extraverted intuition: they share a common orientation to the inner object, and they each value imagination. The rational functions are also repressed by extraverted intuition.

> Thinking and feeling, the indispensable components for conviction, are his inferior functions, carrying no weight and hence incapable of effectively withstanding the power of intuition. And yet these functions are the only ones that could compensate its supremacy by supplying judgment which the intuitive type totally lacks. (CW 6, §613)

Though several of the types seem capable of opposing extraverted intuition, for our purposes we will assume that either Anne Frank as introverted feeling, or Immanuel Kant as introverted thinking,[3] will oppose the energetic entrepreneur Andrew Carnegie as extraverted intuition. The nature of their oppositions is made clearer in Table 6-4.

Because intuition is extraverted, the opposing shadow type(s) would be expected to be introverted, but extraverted rational types could also serve as effective inhibitors of extraverted intuition, with their orientation to traditions, norms, and standards. Extraverted sensation might also serve in that oppositional role, with its attention to accurate detail. Yet each of these

---

[3] In our work with the Gifts Compass Inventory (GCI), a rational type, either introverted or extraverted, has most often been recorded as the shadow type for extraverted intuition. Introverted sensation sometimes serves as the shadow type, but it also sometimes serves as the first auxiliary. Extraverted intuition, by virtue of its crossover attributes, has more potential oppositions than the other types.

Extraverted Intuition (EN)	Introverted Feeling or Thinking (IF or IT)	Comments
Extensive Possibilities	Intensive Ideals or Insights	Orientation: The lead is open to new tangible possibilities in the world at large; the shadow type wants him to also consider high ideals or eternally valid insights.
Perceive Possibilities	Apprehend Ideals or Insights	Attitude: The lead moves from one possibility to another; the shadow type urges him to step off the treadmill of chasing possibilities and look to more constant and enduring values or meaning.
Catalytic Intuition	Idealistic Feeling or Conceptual Thinking	Functional Role: The lead is a catalyst for change—current circumstances never satisfy him; the shadow type whispers that his ideals or philosophy will bring him peace of mind.
Outer Imagination	Inner Valuations or Thoughts	Substance: The lead is forever using his imagination to see how the outer world might change; the shadow type wants to direct his imagination to inner valuations or thoughts.
Particular Possibilities	Holistic Ideals or Insights	Scope: The lead enjoys making particular possibilities real; the shadow type wants him to also see how those possibilities relate to the larger meaning of life.

Table 6-4 EN Opposed by IF or IT

extraverted types, as we saw in Chapter 5, could also serve as congenial collaborators with extraverted intuition.

Extreme Extraverted Intuition

With an extreme disposition to extraverted intuition, the ego becomes too identified with unborn possibilities in the world; it is in the grip of the vision of possibilities apprehended there. The inflated ego can run roughshod over other compensating types; it becomes as grand, bold, and important as the possibilities themselves. Less imaginative people are secretly or openly deprecated as contemptible, banal, or timid—only half alive; they are projections of his repressed shadow.

Not prone to patience with the status quo, extraverted intuition thrusts the individual into a pursuit of the next enthralling possibility, each new one seemingly more important and alluring than the one before. He fancies a position of exalted superiority over the outer object. The individual ascends an uplifting spiral of self-importance with the ego conjoined to imagined possibilities. As those possibilities become grander, the ego inflates with them. Never mind that the last possibility was left incomplete and in shambles for lack of attention to practical detail. Life is not lived backward but is always thrust forward into the next imagined project or accomplishment. Like Napoleon abandoning his troops in Egypt, the individual figuratively sails away to pursue more exalted possibilities on the horizon.

The rational shadow type turns hostile and conspires to bring the inflated ego down. The individual may be rattled by attacks of anxiety.

Thinking and feeling, being largely repressed, come up with infantile, archaic thoughts and feelings. . . . They take the form of intense projections . . . and are chiefly concerned with quasi-realities such as sexual suspicion, financial hazards, forebodings of illness, etc. (CW 6, §615)

Absent considered judgment, the individual will often err in the pursuit of new entrepreneurial or romantic possibilities, destined to go awry and retard his intentions, if not bring him to ruin. If he is not undone by his poorly considered possibilities themselves, he may be attacked from within by phobias.

He claims a . . . freedom and exemption from restraint, submitting his decisions to no rational judgment and relying entirely on his nose for the possibilities that chance throws his way. He exempts himself from the restrictions of reason only to fall victim to neurotic compulsions in the form of over-subtle ratiocinations, hair-splitting dialectics, and a compulsive tie to the sensation aroused by objects. His conscious attitude towards both sensation and object is one of ruthless superiority. . . . But sooner or later the object takes revenge in the form of compulsive hypochondriacal ideas, phobias, and every imaginable kind of absurd bodily sensation." (CW 6, §615).

OPPOSITIONS FOR THE INTROVERTED TYPES

When the introverted types go too far, identifying too much with archetypal images, the ego's importance is fancifully inflated, assuming an illusion of secret, almost magical, power or superiority. The dwarf-like extraverted shadow will cast its spell, throwing the introverted ego between the rock and hard spot of the very mundane world it seeks to devalue, enslaving the ego to the facts of life.

The individual's freedom of mind is fettered by the ignominy of his financial dependence, his freedom of action trembles in the face of public opinion, his moral superiority collapses in a morass of inferior relationships, and his desire to dominate ends in a pitiful craving to be loved. (CW 6, §626)

The neuroses generated on this side of the great divide will be in response to a grandiose over-identification with the alluring images of the collective unconscious. Jung referred to it as *psychasthenia*,[4] a form of neurosis characterized by extreme sensitivity, anxiety, phobias, obsessions, and chronic fatigue.

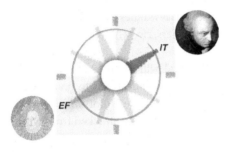

Introverted Thinking vs. Extraverted Feeling

People disposed to introverted thinking with extraverted feeling as the shadow type tend to feel shy, awkward, and ill-equipped for social interaction. The more people present, the less they like it. Social relationships drain their energy. They are strangers to small talk. Though they may get worked up into a passionate fervor discussing, with like-minded associates, some philosophical problem, they will tire of talking too much with others about their lives or the commonplace events of the day. Their feeling side is underdeveloped, so they find empathy difficult. It is easier for them to understand relationships conceptually from the lofty perspective of the head than to either feel or express feelings from the heart.

Queen Elizabeth I, as extraverted feeling, will play the role of compensatory opposite to the lead, played by Immanuel Kant. He is forever lost in thought, only partially aware of the goings-on around him. He just wants people to leave him alone so that he can intensively pursue his unifying ideas and philosophy. Elizabeth would have him spend more time at social gatherings, attend the opera or the theater, and stay in touch with people and with what they value. She would have him be less of a hermit and more of a social butterfly. A review of their attributes, using our comparative categories in Table 6-5, will help to make this tension of opposites clearer.

Extreme Introverted Thinking

With extreme one-sidedness, the ego is unduly commingled with intangible and theoretical ideas and truths. The person's identity is conflated with the inner object. "He begins to confuse his subjective truth with his own personality" (CW 6, §636).

With an exclusive orientation to the inner object, naturally the outer

---

[4] Pierre Janet developed the terms *psychasthenia* and *hysteria* to describe two types of neurosis.

Introverted Thinking (IT)	Extraerted Feeling (EF)	Comments
Intensive Insights	Extensive Norms	Orientation: The lead type is focused intensively on emerging new ideas and insights; the shadow type wants him to cast a broader gaze on people, protocol, norms, and traditions.
Apprehend Insights	Perceive Norms	Attitude: The lead type chases insights all day long; the shadow type wants to affirm tradition and support social harmony.
Conceptual Thinking	Social Feeling	Functional Role: The lead type applies his thinking philosophically, seeking conceptual clarity; the shadow type would have him empathizing and interacting with people.
Inner Thoughts	Outer Valuations	Substance: The lead type thinks analytically about ideas; the shadow type would have him feel what others value.
Holistic Insights	Particular Norms	Scope: The lead type wants to focus on holistic insights; the shadow type would have him focus on norms and traditions.

Table 6-5 IT Opposed by EF

object loses importance and attention. The images and ideas of the inner object are indeed enthralling, but they take on an independent life of their own. No longer do they easily link up with the facts of the world or practical applications; they are sought after for their own sake. The connections between ideas and practical realities get lost. Thoughts, detached from the facts of the outer object, take on mythological qualities.

One-sided thinking taken to an extreme discriminates against all objective facts that do not fit with its treasured truth. The more one-sided the thinking, the more the identity gets lost in the symbolism of the inner object. "It creates theories for their own sake . . . with a distinct tendency to slip over from the world of ideas to mere imagery" (CW 6, §630).

Representations of the archetypal unconscious are indeed enthralling and inspiring; they have an alluring numinous quality. Yet introverted thinking must allow the other complementary attitudes of consciousness to connect those exalted truths to the practical issues of life.

If ignored, the outer object, so coldly rejected, begins to attack from within. They begin to obsess about things that, to others, seem utterly unimportant. They also may lose their social bearings and be prone to troublesome social relationships and to reckless value judgments.

They become increasingly isolated and temperamental. Their touchiness further isolates them from the very people who could help them to compensate for their one-sidedness. Their tone becomes surly. "He will burst out with vicious, personal retorts against every criticism however just. Thus his isolation gradually increases. His originally fertilizing ideas become destructive, poisoned by the sediment of bitterness" (CW 6, §636). They increasingly lose touch with concrete reality as they become plagued with phobias, obsessive compulsions, and anxiety.

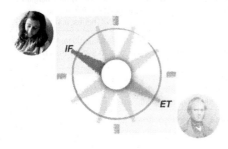

Introverted Feeling vs. Extraverted Thinking

A person disposed to introverted feeling with an extraverted thinking shadow type may feel at a loss to create order, make decisions quickly, or work skillfully with practical problem solving. Imparting tangible order to things, data, processes, or logistics can be difficult. People are the chief interests; an interest in things, data, numbers, facts, or physical systems develops reluctantly, if ever.

The reflective Anne Frank plays the role of introverted feeling; so sensitive, with such poignant observations and personal understanding well beyond her years, she illustrates well the depth of feeling and the stubborn independence that are often the attributes of this type. She is balanced by Charles Darwin, playing the role of extraverted thinking. He assembles many facts to derive his logical conclusions about the world he observes.

The two form a healthy opposition in the psyche, Charles holding Anne in check from too much one-sided identification with the ideals she has apprehended. Her penchant for quietly trusting her ideals, for feeling with deep affect what is most important in life, is balanced by his reliance on outward facts that can be ordered by the power of unaffected logic.

The weak and primitive Darwin will do his best to hold her back, give her second thoughts about this ideal, or hesitations about that lofty pursuit, but he will not oppose her aggressively. Should she not listen to the softly whispered practical admonitions, should she go overboard and identify too much with the powerful images that for her are eternal ideals, then he will become her insidious saboteur, openly undermining all that she holds dear. Their opposition is illustrated in Table 6-6.

Extreme Introverted Feeling

When the ego becomes one with the object of its orientation, it assumes too much power and self-importance. The individual becomes bossy and domineering, for "the mysterious power of the intensive feeling turns into

Introverted Feeling (IF)	Extraverted Thinking (ET)	Comments
Intensive Ideals	Extensive Order	Orientation: The lead attends to images and ideals; the shadow type encourages her to make sense of facts.
Apprehend Ideals	Perceive Order	Attitude: The lead is forever writing to her imaginary friend "Kitty" to share her reflective feelings and observations; the shadow type would have her see to the housework, take care of her things, keep the kitchen in good working order.
Idealistic Feeling	Constructive Thinking	Functional Role: The lead wants to make a contribution in the world, to feel that she is living true to her starry-eyed ideals; the shadow type would rather see her construct an orderly, realistic life than to chase ideals born from the stars.
Inner Valuations	Outer Thoughts	Substance: The lead dwells on inward feeling-toned valuations; the shadow type would have her think about practical matters.
Holistic Ideals	Particular Order	Scope: The lead enjoys basking in very big-picture ideals; the shadow type would have her focus on being orderly.

Table 6-6 IF Opposed by ET

a banal and overweening desire to dominate, into vanity and despotic bossiness" (CW 6, §642).

Now the fool becomes a demon, for it must take extreme measures to subvert an ego position that has gone too far. As introverted feeling is too attached to the inner object, extraverted thinking creates obsessive attachments the other way—in the outer object: "introverted feeling is counterbalanced by a primitive thinking, whose concretism and slavery to facts surpass all bounds" (CW 6, §639).

The otherwise meekly developed thinking turns powerfully negative, demeaning everything and everyone that introverted feeling might normally value; lofty ideals and admirable people are demeaned with thoughts of "nothing but," such as "She is nothing but a social climber." "He is nothing but an obsequious charlatan."

Extraverted thinking is insidiously projected onto others, who are imagined to be thinking all kinds of malignant thoughts and schemes. Such people grow increasingly suspicious; combative rivalries ensue. Soon they believe that no one can be trusted and that they must defend their bitter opinions with every weapon in their arsenal. They may cheapen every ideal and warp every virtue to defeat their wicked imagined enemies. They believe that they, and they alone, represent the true wellspring of eternal ideals with which their lives are now inextricably entangled. Neurosis is the inevitable consequence of their inflated egos and they are subdued with fatigue, anxiety, and depression.

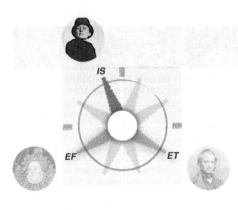

Introverted Sensation vs. Extraverted Thinking or Feeling

People oriented to introverted sensation are often artists, actors, writers, or musicians, for they have a finely honed sense of the drama and beauty of perceptions. Their opposing shadow type could be extraverted intuition but more likely will be one of the extraverted rational types. If extraverted thinking is the repressed type, then they will tend to avoid practical problem solving, much like those too disposed to introverted feeling. If extraverted feeling is the shadow type, then they will struggle with relating to others, much like those too disposed to introverted thinking.

Georgia O'Keeffe, the quiet, aloof, intensive, and mysterious artist, interpreting the lively impressions of nature in bold and engaging art, plays the role of aesthetic sensation—reinterpreting detailed perceptions enigmatically. Extraverted rational types, represented by Darwin and Queen Elizabeth, will play the roles of the shadow's opposition (Table 6-7).

Introverted Sensation (IS)	Extraverted Thinking or Feeling (ET or EF)	Comments
Intensive Innervations	Extensive Order or Norms	**Orientation:** The lead is intensively observant of special perceptions that ignite the archetypal embers; the shadow type wants her to be more oriented to the outward order of things or people.
Apprehend Innervations	Perceive Order or Norms	**Attitude:** The lead inwardly moves from one intensive innervation to the next, seeking to more fully grasp it; the shadow type urges her to come back to the real outer world and to grasp the order of life there.
Aesthetic Sensation	Constructive Thinking or Social Feeling	**Functional Role:** The lead is content to apprehend the innervations, to bask in their aesthetic thrill; the shadow type beckons her to construct some order or affirm some standards.
Inner Perceptions	Outer Thoughts or Valuations	**Substance:** The lead is forever at work with her dreamy inner perceptions; the shadow type wants her to attend to practical thoughts or valuations.
Holistic Innervations	Particular Order of Norms	**Focus:** The lead enjoys seeing her innervations holistically—the enticing images derived from perceptions; the shadow type wants her to focus more objectively on feeling or thinking about those perceptions, without tainting them with her inner patina.

Table 6-7 IS Opposed by EF or ET

Extreme Introverted Sensation

The case of introverted sensation is unusual because it is oriented simultaneously to the inner and outer object. Functionally, it orients to the outer object, but the introverted attitude overrides that orientation, sweeping the libido to the inner object of archetypal images.

Thus the penchant of an extreme introverted sensation attitude, like introverted intuition, is to identify too much with the contents of the collective unconscious. The composite substance—the primary material—consists of the perceptions of the outer object as they are transformed by the enlivened patina of images from the unconscious. In the extreme, the individual loses the ability to differentiate the perceived object from the object in her imagination.

> The subject [individual] has an illusory conception of reality, which in pathological cases goes so far that he is no longer able to distinguish between the real object and subjective perception. (CW 6, §651)

The individual becomes increasingly isolated and alienated from the world as the ego identity aligns with the inner object. The suppression of rational functions gives free rein to the inner life of fantastic innervations. Perceptions of the sensuous reality can be transformed into a divine comedy.

> Actually he lives in a mythological world, where men, animals, locomotives, houses, rivers, and mountains appear either as benevolent deities or as malevolent demons. . . . If he remains faithful to his irrationality, and is ready to grant his sensations reality value, the objective world will appear a mere make-believe and a comedy. (CW 6, §653)

The shadow types that often arise to oppose this extreme attitude engender symptoms of neurosis similar to those for other extreme attitudes. If extraverted thinking plays the role of shadow type, it engages a weakly developed thinking that deprecates everything that the introverted sensation values: "These paintings are nothing but foolishness; no one will ever like your work." If extraverted feeling is suppressed, the weakly developed feeling manifests as a repelling irritability—grumpy, picky, and faultfinding: "I am fed up with the hordes of people admiring my work; they are obtuse and without refined tastes."

Jung assumed that extraverted intuition would be the most suppressed type. If extraverted intuition plays the role of the shadow type, it engenders "shadowy, sordid, dangerous possibilities lurking in the background" (CW

6, §654). It would generate a compulsion neurosis, producing compulsive and perverse ideas. "The snakes may get me if I go out to the canyon tomorrow to paint."

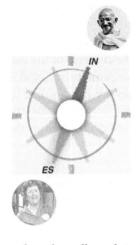

Introverted Intuition vs. Extraverted Sensation

People oriented to introverted intuition with extraverted sensation as the shadow type will usually have much difficulty with concrete, practical reality. So lofty is their vision that they find it difficult to keep their feet on the ground. They are so enthralled with the big picture of life and the long-distance view of the world that their ability to be attentively present here and now is barely developed. Their mind is always elsewhere, in pursuit of imaginative visions in the inner life. Practical reality stumps them; they only awkwardly and timidly make their way in the world. They may forever be misplacing things, forgetting appointments, or running late. They meet the practical requirements of life with great difficulty; they may try to simplify their life in the world to reduce the distractions that keep them from their treasured inner life.

The Indian ascetic Mahatma Gandhi plays the leading role of introverted intuition, the type without which "there would have been no prophets in Israel." Julia Child, so engaged in the sensual pleasures of life, will oppose Gandhi as extraverted sensation. He will strive to keep his head in the archetypal clouds of eternal truths; she will seek to keep her feet planted on the *terra firma* of the concretely real world. A review of the five comparative categories for each type will help to illustrate the tension of opposites at work (Table 6-8).

Extreme Introverted Intuition

Introverted intuition is normally holistic in scope, seeing a vast panorama of events; it is intensively oriented to the inspiring images arising in the inner life. In an extreme position, the ego grows attached to the grand visions apprehended within, thus conflating the person's identity with the archetypal images of the collective unconscious.

Such people, already aloof, become even more isolated as they become more one-sided. Lost in the swirl of alluring archetypal imagery, they

Introverted Intuition (IN)	Extraverted Sensation (ES)	Comments
Intensive Images	Extensive Facts	Orientation: The lead is oriented to intensive images within; the shadow type is oriented to many facts without.
Apprehend Images	Perceive Facts	Attitude: The lead is content to apprehend and fully appreciate the inner images; the shadow type wants him to stick to the facts.
Visionary Intuition	Realistic Sensation	Functional Role: The lead envisions grand possibilities for the future of humanity; the shadow type would have him delight in the pleasures and practical needs of the moment.
Inner Imagination	Outer Perceptions	Substance: The lead works with his inner imagination; the shadow type would have him work with accurate perceptions of the world.
Holistic Images	Particular Facts	Scope: The lead enjoys images of the whole; the shadow type beckons him to focus on each particular fact.

Table 6-8 IN Opposed by ES

become a complete enigma to people well-adapted to the world. The images apprehended from the unconscious may have little connection to daily standards, norms, or practical requirements of life.

They may become content just to apprehend the cavalcade of visions alive in the inner life, losing themselves to archetypal imagery. With the repression of the outer object, they essentially live in a world that others cannot understand.

> He remains uncomprehended. His language is not the one currently spoken—it has become too subjective. His arguments lack the convincing power of reason. He can only profess or proclaim. His is "the voice of one crying in the wilderness." (CW 6, §662)

The extreme imbalance is openly opposed by the renegade shadow type, usually extraverted sensation. It disrupts the conscious focus on the inner life with obsessions about many facts and details, each having exaggerated importance. Such people will often suffer from compulsions and hypochondria.

ONE-SIDED CULTURES

An understanding of the disruptive consequences of extreme types applies not only to individuals but also likely to groups. Just as individuals can generate neuroses and compulsive complexes by taking their type dispositions to an extreme, so too can any association of people organized toward a common end—corporations, associations, societies, faith communities, and so forth; they could generate disruptive strife by becoming typologically one-sided.

A corporation that seeks a unified, one-sided culture congruent with the CEO's dominant type, for example, may bring up disruptive shadow interventions from people who carry his dominant type in their shadow. A society of psychotherapists might generate acrimonious division and conflict by taking its composite introverted feeling orientation too seriously. A superficially friendly church community may develop threads of malicious gossip running under its otherwise pious and ebullient persona. A community of academics, too one-sided toward introverted thinking, might become petty and vindictive as the shadow exacts its revenge.

An organization is only as strong and healthy as the diversely individuated lives of the people who comprise it. The solution for all of these kinds of organizational one-sidedness is always the same: pursuing the unique and authentic middle way of individuation for each person in the organization.

The vitality of organizations depends on the vitality of each individual, and the greater the individuation among them, the more vital, dynamic, balanced, and healthy the organization becomes.

> It is obvious that a social group consisting of stunted individuals cannot be a healthy and viable institution; only a society that can preserve its internal cohesion and collective values, while at the same time granting the individual the greatest possible freedom, has any prospect of enduring vitality. (CW 6, §758)

An extreme emphasis on materialism, individualism, or religious fundamentalism could be considered pathologically one-sided, and any nation or group that embodies such one-sidedness could become embroiled in brutal and self-righteous conflict. Jung noted that "the inability to be anything but one-sided, is a sign of barbarism" (CW 6, §346). The world today is rife with the conflicts arising from extreme one-sidedness, and the twentieth century suffered profoundly from such barbarism.

CHAPTER SUMMARY

With this chapter we have introduced some of the typical oppositions that will be catalysts for individuation. In a normal opposition, the shadow types hold the lead types back from excessive one-sidedness. If the lead types take their position to a one-sided extreme, the shadow types will destructively intervene; neurosis is the consequence of their intervention.

The Self seeks wholeness, and the way of individuation is to neither one extreme nor another but to the middle—the way between the opposites. Individuation progressively moves the seat of personal identity from a one-sided ego to the centered individual, and thus toward becoming increasingly whole. The final chapter is devoted to these transformational dynamics.

7

Becoming Whole

FOR ARISTOTLE, THE MIDDLE WAY was the *golden mean,* the way between extremes to happiness, "the best, noblest, and most pleasant thing in the world."

Buddha, the "awakened one," observed that undue attachments lead to suffering and that the balanced middle way of right living leads to broadened consciousness, emboldened compassion, and a vivified reverence for life.

Lao Tse spoke reverently of the *Tao* (Way) as the source of harmony, a way that includes the complementary opposites yin and yang.

For Confucius, the way was a balanced life of personal growth and communal responsibility.

For Jung, the middle way leads to wholeness—a way between the opposites that integrates and transcends them; the way of individuation; the way to the realization of the whole *personality.*

THE MIDDLE WAY TO UNIQUE PERSONALITY

And so long as you haven't experienced this: to die and so to grow, you are only a troubled guest on the dark earth. —Goethe

We are born predisposed to certain ego attitudes; no tabulae rasae are we. If we are born with introverted attitudes, we are initially oriented to the inner world and the contents of the collective unconscious. If we are born with more extraverted attitudes, we are initially oriented to the outer world and the contents of sensory experience. We do not choose our predispositions; we notice them.

We gain ego strength from our early predispositions. Our ego's dominant attitude becomes that of our persona, and we grow into more complex adults. We acquire our social armor to go out into the world and are more fully equipped to make our way. We are no longer so open and naive; we are streetwise and will not be as easily duped as children. We are on guard. The persona provides a personal mask to adapt and promote ourselves in a challenging world.

Early in adult life, if we have been fortunate, we have discerned our best gifts and applied them successfully in the world.[1] Perhaps we have gained acumen, acclaim, or recognition. We may have found a life partner, someone attracted to us for our best and most natural qualities. As we gain friends with values that reinforce our own, along with familial relationships, we may feel affirmed that we have found our place in the world. As our ego grows in strength, if our favored gifts have met the world successfully, all may seem well.

The first half of the lifelong drama arrives at a sort of intermission in midlife, with the theater fully constructed and oppositions established; the audience has long been seated and the chief actors have polished their roles. A sturdy persona guards the apron of the conscious stage, positioned to defend and supplement the lead actor. A strong and confident ego plays the lead role of consciousness. Numerous complexes lurk behind the scrim in the personal unconscious, where they have been developing since early childhood. A shadowy figure has formed on the unconscious stage as antagonist. The soul (anima or animus) on the apron of the unconscious stage, having been instrumental in life-changing choices in the first half of life, now prepares to facilitate greater access to the illusive treasures that have been largely unconscious.

If transformation is to extend into the second half of life, the persona must lower its defenses. The sturdy armored comrade whose role was to support and defend the ego in the first half of life can become a prison guard in the second half. For the unique individual to find a balanced position midway between both audiences, less dependent on the lead ego attitude, the persona must give up its role, for it is too deeply identified with the one-sided ego.

---

[1] Some people may be required, through family or social pressure, or economic necessity, to develop types that do not come as naturally; they "falsify" their lead types to adapt. Their falsification of type frequently becomes a key developmental issue, and they will often revert to their "natural" lead types later in life.

> The persona is always identical with a typical attitude dominated by a single psychological function, for example, by thinking, feeling or intuition. This one-sidedness necessarily results in the relative repression of the other functions. In consequence, the persona is an obstacle to the individual's development. The dissolution of the persona is therefore an indispensable condition for individuation. (CW 7, §487)

The ego, so long enjoying the limelight as the chief actor, must recognize the aim of the second half of life—the transformation to the true self. It becomes increasingly apparent that the ego/persona identity is a false self that must now make way for the true self at the center. The ego has played its favored roles, and knows them well, but is too one-sided to pilot the way of the emerging personality.

> Hence it is impossible to achieve individuation by conscious intention, for conscious intention leads infallibly to a conscious attitude, which excludes whatever does not fit in with it. (CW 7, §487)

The emerging personality will be forged in the crucible of opposing attitudes. Compensatory shadow attitudes, often opposing the ego's favored orientations, will seek their own integration into the life of the individual. The developing person will gain greater access to both the audience of the manifold world *and* the collective unconscious.

If all goes as scripted, the shadow will be accepted on the conscious stage, the persona's "personality" will relax its social mask, the soul's "personality" will more readily mediate the contents of the unconscious, and the audience of the world will be the beneficiary of a more authentic person, attuned more fully to their collective welfare. These are the essential and recurring themes in the production to ensue. It will be a story of repeated death and rebirth in which the individual grows more whole with each resurrection. Though the elements of the process may be similar for everyone, the path and destination are unique for each individual.

The process of realizing one's true personality defies generalization or full description, for it is an experience beyond the domain of purely ego consciousness. We know when we are caught in the paralyzing tension of opposites, and we know when we have been liberated from that tension, but these are experiences that can hardly be explained objectively.

Analogies, like the ones Jung used, help to describe what the "coming to birth of personality" actually *feels* like: "It is as if a river that had run to waste in sluggish side-streams and marshes suddenly found its way back to its proper bed, or as if a stone lying on a germinating seed were lifted away so that the shoot could begin its natural growth" (CW 17, §317).

Within the human psyche is a latent drive to become whole. Unconscious contents are seeking consciousness as the essential personality seeks realization. It is a teleological movement toward authentic individuality. Jung himself felt this urge intensely:

> My life is a story of the self-realization of the unconscious. Everything in the unconscious seeks outward manifestation, and the personality too desires to evolve out of its unconscious conditions and to experience itself as a whole. (Prologue, *Memories, Dreams, Reflections*)

That path to authentic individuality may at times seem unpredictably erratic, aimless, or even retrogressive. It can be like walking on a labyrinth: the path may not seem to make logical sense or have any purposeful direction, yet in its roundabout way it delivers the individual to the center (Figure 7-1). There are no dead ends on a labyrinth, but there are also no shortcuts. Once on the labyrinthine path, as circuitous and confusing as it may seem, the destination at the center is secure.

Figure 7.1 A Labyrinth

If the ego stubbornly goes its own way, with a one-sided resistance to individuation, the path could become like a maze. Unlike the labyrinth, there may be many shortcuts, but there are also many dead ends (Figure 7-2). Crucially, there is no center.

Jung's close associate Marie-Louise von Franz spoke of the pathway to wholeness as a spiral. As the spiral ascends, the individual becomes more *real*.

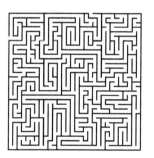

Figure 7.2 A Maze

It is a spiral not a circle. The movement does not go in circles; it goes forward in spirals. This means that you always return to the same point but on a higher level. For instance, if you meet a person who has individuated, you can say: "Oh, this is still old John Smith"—completely, in the true sense of the word. . . . He is still the good old John Smith I once knew, but he is on a higher plane. . . . There is something more mature, more conscious, more calm, and whatever he was is more intensely there and more real. . . . This higher consciousness is something you feel about another person. You have a feeling that this is the same old person but somehow he is more worthy, more intense, more real, more himself. But it is something you can only feel.[2]

The process of individuation, as Jung articulates it, is quite extraordinary: the outcomes are not readily predictable. The spiraling up is not so much an additive process as a process of a transformational integration. The union of opposites in one individual engenders greater "wholeness" and a sense of becoming more *real*, more true to oneself. One may have the feeling that "I used to be different, but now I am the same."

In his book *Transformation: Emergence of the Self*, Jungian analyst Murray Stein likens the process of individuation to the formation of a butterfly that astonishingly transforms from caterpillar, to pupa, to butterfly. Each form is a manifestation of the same creature, but none follows logically from the other or is at all predictable. Yet the latent pattern for the fully formed butterfly is already present in the caterpillar. The final destined form as a butterfly is the *imago*—an underlying pattern of ultimate potential present in each of the creature's manifestations.[3]

Similarly, individuals have a kind of imago—a unique personality that may not begin to emerge until after the "chrysalis" of midlife, when the ego-centered identify defers to the emerging whole personality. In this transformative journey of individuation, the types become progressively engaged, more as a collateral consequence of individuation than as an aim unto themselves.

Attempts to develop and exercise the shadow types build ego strength and may help an individual to become more adaptable and versatile; yet that exercise is like growing the size and strength of the caterpillar. Consciously developing the shadow types is an ego-driven exercise. But the ego does not guide individuation: the unpredictable transformations of individuation are directed by the archetypal Self.

THE SELF

For we are dealing with an eternal image, an archetype, from which man can turn away his mind for a time but never permanently. —C. G. Jung

---

[2] von Franz, *Conversations on Aion*, 2004; p. 164

[3] Adolph Portman, "Metamorphosis in Animals: The Transformations of the Individual and the Type," in *Man and Transformation*, ed. Joseph Campbell (New York: Bollingen Foundation, 1964), p. 299.

Jung provided a window of uncanny insight into the underlying frameworks of human experience. He synthesized many diverse disciplines—religion, philosophy, science, literature, medicine, psychology—to develop coordinated, unifying ideas. The Self[4] is one of the crowning ideas of Jung's remarkably versatile mind.

He referred to the Self as an *Imago Dei*. Literally translated, it means "image of God," but with regard to individuation, it is an image of completed wholeness. Unlike all the other archetypes, which are collectively available to many, the Self alone provides the unique pattern for individuality. It is an imago of completed wholeness, yet it is never perfectly attained, for it is always a destination—a pursuit rather than a final achievement.

> [The Self] expresses the unity of the personality as a whole. But in so far as the total personality, on account of its unconscious component, can be only part conscious, the concept of the self is, in part, only potentially empirical and is to that extent a postulate. In other words, it encompasses both the experienceable and the inexperienceable (or the not yet experienced). (CW 6, §789)

In our psychic theater, the Self could be crudely depicted as a broad field, centered in and including the individual's whole psyche (Figure 7-3).

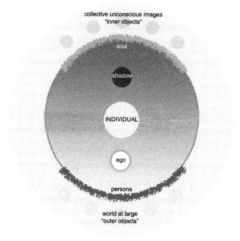

Figure 7.3 The Self

---

[4] Capitalized to differentiate the archetypal Self from the individual self. This convention was introduced post hoc by Erich Neumann, so it does not appear in Jung's original texts. Moreover, Jung wrote mostly in German, in which all nouns are capitalized anyway.

Because the inner and outer objects often seem serendipitously connected, the Self is shown in this figure embracing, in its domain of influence, the collective unconscious, the world at large, *and* the individual's whole psyche. The actualization of full and unique individuality is the destiny to which the Self draws the evolving individual.

> I have called this center the self. . . . It might equally be called the "God within us." The beginnings of our whole psychic life seem to be inextricably rooted in this point, and all our highest and ultimate purposes seem to be striving towards it. (CW 7, §399)

Though he referred to the Self as "God within us," Jung was reluctant to frame the Self in religious terms. He acknowledged that its nature is shrouded in mystery and well beyond the grasp of human cognition.

> Intellectually the self is no more than a psychological concept, a construct that serves to express the unknowable essence which we cannot grasp as such, since by definition it transcends our powers of comprehension. (CW 7, §399)

The Self is both the destined aim of personal transformation and a guide through that transformation. The Self may usher a person through trial, serendipity, storm, struggle, joy, contentment, ambition, patience, generosity, good *and* hard luck, toward a consummate, uniquely differentiated life in community. No one, as Jung was fond of saying, can individuate on Mount Everest. The development of unique individuality requires engagement with others.

> As nobody can become aware of his individuality unless he is closely and responsibly related to his fellow beings, he is not withdrawing to an egoistic desert when he tries to find himself. He only can discover himself when he is deeply and unconditionally related to some, and generally related to a great many, individuals with whom he has a chance to compare, and from whom he is able to discriminate himself. (Jung as quoted in Serrano, *C. G. Jung and Hermann Hesse*, 1968; p. 84)

The aim of individuation is not individualism—an inflated ego/persona identity—but the full expression of the unique personality. To become whole, to more fully express the whole personality, that which is unconscious must be realized in consciousness.

THE SELF-REALIZATION OF THE UNCONSCIOUS

My life is a story of the self-realization of the unconscious. —C. G. Jung

When Jung read Richard Wilhelm's translation of the Taoist text *The Secret of the Golden Flower,* his pioneering insights in psychology over nearly two decades were confirmed. He had unsuccessfully sought some confirmation of his ideas in Western traditions, even searching the Gnostic teachings from the early centuries after Christ. However, in *The Secret of the Golden Flower,* Jung discovered a philosophy from the East that resonated with his empirical experience.

> When I began my lifework in the practice of psychiatry and psychotherapy, I was completely ignorant of Chinese philosophy, and only later did my professional experience show me that in my technique I had been unconsciously led along that secret way which has been the preoccupation of the best minds of the East for centuries . . . and this is the extraordinary thing, in content it is a living parallel to what takes place in the psychic development of my patients, none of whom are Chinese. (C. G. Jung, "Introduction," *The Secret of the Golden Flower*)

The Golden Flower could be considered a symbol. Symbols are pregnant with meaning and with unconscious potentialities seeking realization. The Golden Flower, for example, could be a symbol of wholeness, a symbol of the Self, and of the full expression of vital, living individuality. "If any attain this One, he becomes alive; if he loses it he dies."[5]

Symbols are not signs. A sign indicates unequivocally something that is fully known and can therefore be expressed in words. A stop sign, for example, simply indicates that a vehicle should stop, and everyone recognizes what it represents in the same way.

Some symbols can be universal, holding meaning across cultures. The mandala, for example, is a universal symbol for wholeness. The Golden Flower could be thought of as a mandala image (Figure 7-4).

The term *mandala* is Hindu in origin and derived from the ancient Sanskrit, yet the aesthetic expression of its symmetrical totality is found across centuries and cultures (Figure 7-5).

---

[5] C. J. Jung, "Introduction," *The Secret of the Golden Flower: A Chinese Book of Life,* trans. Richard Wilhelm (New York: Harcourt Brace, 1962), p. 22.

Figure 7.4 A Mandala

Figure 7.5 A mandala from India (left) from Chartres Cathedral
in France (center) and from Japan (right)

The mandala symbolizes the wholeness that embraces the full personality—conscious and unconscious; it is a universal symbol for the Self.

As the mandala is meaningful as a symbol of wholeness for many, some symbols of wholeness speak to a particular individual. Whether universal or individual, these symbols often act in concert with a *transcendent* function, which induces movement toward the hidden imago of the whole personality.

> The transcendent function does not proceed without aim and purpose, but leads to the revelation of the essential man. . . . The meaning and purpose of the process is the realization, in all aspects, of the personality originally hidden away in the embryonic germ-plasm; the production and unfolding of the original, potential wholeness. (CW 7, §186)

Just as the ego has its functions that navigate conscious life, so too the psyche navigates the union of conscious and unconscious attitudes. The transcendent function enables the integration of diverse psychic elements, including the typological dispositions of persona and soul, ego and shadow. Symbols of wholeness are a special subset of symbols generally. They do not represent anything in particular; they transcend attitudes, for they can be both rational *and* irrational, introverted *and* extraverted.

> [The symbol] certainly has a side that accords with reason, but it has another side that does not; for it is composed not only of rational but also of irrational data supplied by pure inner and outer perception. The profundity and pregnant significance of the symbol appeal just as strongly to thinking as to feeling, while its purely plastic imagery, when shaped into sensuous form, stimulates sensation as much as intuition. (CW 6, 823)

Symbols of wholeness cannot represent exclusively the ego's one-sided disposition, for part of their purpose is to integrate the elements that oppose the ego's attitude. They include the primitive, developmentally inferior types lurking behind consciousness and grant them legitimacy. The symbol cannot, once born, be subverted to join one side or the other without losing its potency as a catalyst for transformation. One is obliged to hold the tension, to acknowledge the opposition, to do nothing to take sides in this conflict, if the natural processes of the transcendent function are to ensue.

Holding the tension in this way could be likened to the prince in "The Water of Life" riding the horse *Wu Wei* (doing by not doing.) There is nothing for the individual to do but to relinquish the ego's will to power.

> But when there is full parity of the opposites, attested by the ego's absolute participation in both, this necessarily leads to a suspension of the will, for the will can no longer operate when every motive has an equally strong countermotive. (CW 6, §824)

If the ego's viewpoint can be suspended, if it does not revert to self-righteous justification for its typological position, then transformation may occur. Psychic energy—*libido*—dammed up by the standoff between opposites, is drawn away from the ego's conscious attitude and sinks into the crucible of the unconscious.

> A retrograde movement of libido automatically sets in, i.e., a regression. The libido draws away from the problem of the moment, becomes intro-

verted, and reactivates in the unconscious a more or less primitive ana-
logue of the conscious situation. (CW 6, §314)

The withdrawal of libido leaves the individual off-balance, for the ego is no
longer in control. The tension is reconsidered and reevaluated from within.
The oft-repeated cycle of death and rebirth characteristic of individuation
is underway.

> Hence I regard the loss of balance as purposive, since it replaces a defective
> consciousness by the automatic and instinctive activity of the unconscious,
> which is aiming all the time at the creation of a new balance and will
> moreover achieve this aim, provided that the conscious mind is capable of
> assimilating the contents produced by the unconscious, i.e., of understand-
> ing and digesting them. (CW 7, §253)

With the regression of libido, the transcendent function is given free rein.
Its aim is an integration of the opposites and the emergence of the hitherto
undiscovered third way that transcends and includes the opposites. With
each cycle of movement toward the integration of opposites, the individual
is reborn into a closer and more harmonious relationship with the unconscious. Life becomes richer.

> If we can successfully develop that function which I have called transcen-
> dent, the disharmony ceases and we can then enjoy the favorable side of
> the unconscious. The unconscious then gives us all the encouragement and
> help that a bountiful nature can shower upon man. (CW 7, §196)

Each successful integration of opposites engenders a new "mediatory
product," which enables the movement of individuation. As long as neither
side claims this mediatory product for its own, it aids in the construction
of unique individuality.

> If the mediatory product remains intact, it forms the raw material for a
> process not of dissolution but of construction, in which thesis and antith-
> esis both play their part. In this way it becomes a new content that governs
> the whole attitude, putting an end to the division and forcing the energy of
> the opposites into a common channel. The standstill is overcome and life
> can flow on with renewed power towards new goals. (CW 6, §827)

Not all symbols are holistic and unifying. They may also represent some
element of the psyche. A common symbol for the transcendent function in

dreams, for example, is a bridge or threshold that joins something on one side to something on the other.

Symbols may be compensatory, representing some unconscious aspect of the psyche that could provide balance to the conscious disposition. For example, a Jungian analyst had a shy female client who favored introverted thinking, assisted by introverted intuition. The client had a significant dream. In the dream, a very extraverted, gregarious, fun-loving female friend (extraverted feeling coupled with extraverted sensation) entered the dream; she would be a symbol for the shadow, for she is of the same gender as the dreamer, but with opposing type dispositions.

In the dream, the two friends were at a dance where the shadow figure was flirting with the dreamer's love interest. The love interest would represent the animus—the same type disposition as the shadow but masculine instead of feminine.

The shadow figure ultimately stole the dreamer's boyfriend. The dreamer felt horribly betrayed by her extraverted "friend." But the shadow woman had empathy for her and made up for the betrayal by giving the dreamer her scarf. While the friend is a symbol of unconscious opposition to the ego's position, the scarf would be a unifying symbol—neither rational nor irrational, neither introverted nor extraverted.

In his 1925 seminars, Jung cautioned the attendees not to engage the most inferior type directly, calling the opposition between the conscious dominant and the shadow's dominant a "knock-down battle that occurs in life." Rather, he advised enlisting the conscious and shadow auxiliaries.

For the client above, whose conscious auxiliary was introverted intuition, the analyst might suggest tangibly feeling the fabric of a scarf, playing with it, and imagining many artful ways that it could be used to adorn her. In this way, the imaginative conscious auxiliary, introverted intuition, could assist in integrating the shadow's sensual auxiliary, extraverted sensation.

In the same 1925 seminars, Jung reviewed the case of a young woman who felt inferior, limited, and meager. Her unconscious ushered up compensatory images of ghosts of very important people, creating a tension between her conscious life and the unconscious compensatory images. In the midst of these opposing tensions, a unifying symbol arrived—an image of an older, spiritually beautiful female, who bridged the yawning tension of opposites. Attending to the mediatory symbol, the girl ventured out to effect extraordinary change; she apprenticed to a famous dressmaker and later opened her own shop, generating fame and controversy with her highly original designs.

Jung offered another example of a holistically unifying symbol in a 1939 letter.

Take the classic case of the temptation of Christ, for example. We say that the devil tempted him, but we could just as well say that an unconscious desire for power confronted him in the form of the devil. Both sides appear here: the light side and the dark. The devil wants to tempt Jesus to proclaim himself master of the world. Jesus wants not to succumb to the temptation; then, thanks to the function that results from every conflict, a symbol appears; it is the idea of the Kingdom of Heaven, a spiritual kingdom rather than a material one. Two things are united in this symbol, the spiritual attitude of Christ and the devilish desire for power. (C. G. Jung, *Letters,* Volume I, 1906–51, pp. 267–68)

When symbols serve in a compensatory capacity, they often have their own typological "spin" to oppose the conscious disposition. Marie-Louise von Franz told the story of a client—a very successful businessman, speculator, and entrepreneur; he was oriented more to possibilities than to facts. He could figuratively see around corners and correctly anticipate the future, making a large fortune in the process. But compulsive physical symptoms were interfering with his work.

He had a dream in which a dirty, bad-tempered tramp appeared to him. Through a mode of dialogue with the tramp that Jung called *active imagination,* the tramp explained that he had caused the symptoms that had brought the entrepreneur into therapy. The tramp said that he was not getting enough conscious attention.

Von Franz encouraged her client to work with the figure to bring its meaning to life, and to do as the tramp had suggested. Accordingly, once a week the entrepreneur dressed in simple clothes, went for walks through secluded parts of Switzerland, and stayed in humble inns. Von Franz said that many epiphanies followed.

During this time he had a great number of overwhelming inner experiences which came through contact with nature: the sunrise, and small things like seeing a certain flower in a corner of a rock, and so on. It struck right to the core of his personality and revealed a tremendous number of things. I can only describe it as experiencing, in a very primitive way, the Godhead in nature. He came back very silent and quieted, and one had the feeling that something had moved in him which had never moved before. (von Franz, 1971, p. 39)

The symptoms that had brought him to therapy disappeared. He returned to his native country and continued regular walks for a while, but he soon slipped back into his old habits. He was creating three new companies, and he was swallowed up by the busy and ambitious work of making those possibilities real. His physical symptoms returned.

He started his walks with the tramp again, and again the symptoms went away. He bought a little farm and a horse. He attended to his horse regularly; the horse became a friend of sorts, and he fastidiously looked after it and rode it once a week. The horse replaced the tramp, and his life took a less troubled course.

Von Franz noted that attending to a symbolic image or dream often leads one on a journey of unexpected discoveries, but to make those discoveries usually requires stepping aside from the ego's natural disposition.[6]

In *Man and His Symbols,* Jung recounts the case of a woman who was well-known for stubborn, intransigent prejudices. She could not be dissuaded from her hubris. One night she dreamt that she was attending a very important social event. She was formally greeted by the hostess with the words, "How nice that you could come. All of your friends are here, and they are waiting for you!" The hostess then opened a door and the dreamer stepped through, into a cowshed!

While dreams, fantasies, and inner visions are abundant sources of symbols, the transformative power of a symbol may also be found in the outer world, especially for those highly disposed to introverted types. Certain people, special objects, evocative music, animals, poetry, places, and events can have a compellingly attractive power, figuratively holding an individual in their grasp. They may be described as *numinous* and can be life-transforming catalysts, instrumental in the realization of the unconscious. They may inspire or engender enthusiasm and arrive when least expected.

As a young man, Jung was divided between two interests. He was still reading his beloved philosophy while planning a career in internal medicine. The two interests seemed irreconcilably separate. He had avoided psychiatry as a career because his father, a pastor, had been interested in psychiatry. But he was required to know something of the subject to pass his final exams.

> I got a textbook and started in to investigate this idiotic subject. . . . I said to myself, "Anybody so foolish as to write a textbook on this subject is bound to explain himself in the preface," so I turned to the preface. By the time I had finished the first page I was on edge with interest. By the time

---

[6] For the interested reader, Jung initiated, and contributed to, a book for a more general readership titled *Man and His Symbols.* Carl G. Jung, ed.. (Garden City, NJ: Doubleday/Windfall, 1964). This book explores themes addressed in this chapter in greater detail, and the many examples of symbolism are supplemented by illustrations throughout.

I was halfway down the second page, I had such a beating in my heart I could hardly go on. "By God," I said, "that is what I will be, a psychiatrist." (*Introduction to Jungian Psychology, Notes on the Seminar on Analytical Psychology Given in 1925*, p. 8)

In 1947 at midlife, William Mellon, Jr., a wealthy heir to the Mellon fortune, was casually reading an article in *Life* magazine about Albert Schweitzer, the medical missionary, philosopher, and musician. He was unusually captivated by the story and the image it conjured up for him. He wrote Schweitzer to learn more about setting up a hospital in a Third World country. Schweitzer wrote back, informing Mellon about the importance of medical training.

Mellon's life took an abrupt turn. He applied to medical school and four years later graduated as a physician. He moved, with his wife, to Haiti where they established a hospital on the model of Schweitzer's.[7]

We may project our unconscious contents onto others, a phenomenon called *projection*. When projections render the "other" negatively, the other may become symbolic of our own shadow, just as the tramp for von Franz's client was a symbol for his shadow in his dream. The normal reaction to someone who attracts a shadow projection would be to avoid, dismiss, or denigrate the individual. But where we stumble, noted Joseph Campbell, our treasure lies. Each encounter with one's projected shadow in the world is an opportunity to become more whole. In extending nonjudgmental compassion to the "other," we are also finding a way to extend compassion to ourselves. "For, to the degree that he does not admit the validity of the other person, he denies the 'other' within himself the right to exist, and vice versa" (CW 8, §187).

Positive anima/animus projections can, conversely, hold a compelling transformative power, for they often evoke alluring qualities of destiny and personal potential. The intensely intellectual Catholic theologian Karl Rahner began his academic career as a Jesuit priest and theologian with a doctoral thesis on "knowing." He is considered by many to be the greatest Catholic theologian of the twentieth century and was a driving force for the reforms of the Second Vatican Council. As he began the strenuous intellectual work of guiding the revolutionary reforms of Vatican II, he began a twenty-year intimate and passionate correspondence with the German novelist Luise Rinser.

A sexual union would have been forbidden, but his very personal cor-

---

[7] A summary of the narrative from Murray Stein, *Transformation: Emergence of the Self* (Carolyn and Earnest Fay Series in Analytical Psychology) (Texas A&M University Press; rev. ed., 2004).

respondence with this flesh-and-blood woman, and likely anima projection, enabled a profound psychic union within himself. They both felt the tremor of the unconscious shaking the foundations of their lives. She wrote, "We are both touched in the innermost part of our being by something that is much stronger than we anticipated." He sent her over twenty-two-hundred letters in the last twenty years of his life. As his career flourished, he moved increasingly from intellectual insights about philosophy to impassioned discourses on love.

We may experience, and be impressed by, coincidental events with no apparent causal relationship, events that meaningfully link our conscious experience with the unconscious. Such phenomena, which were investigated for years by Jung in collaboration with the theoretical physicist Wolfgang Pauli, are the manifestations of an acausal connecting principle they termed *synchronicity*. Positive synchronicities seem to occur when we are on a course consistent with the guidance of the Self; negative synchronicities may occur when we are off course, moving in the wrong direction.

In her book *The Tao of Psychology*, Jean Shinoda Bolen tells the story of a woman with an unblemished driving record who, within a few days, had three auto accidents. None were her fault; each accident involved the other driver's failure to apply the brakes. She took the series of accidents to heart, as a negative synchronicity, and "put the brakes" on a relationship that had been quite troublesome for her.

Jung famously related a synchronicity involving a scarab beetle that occurred while meeting with a stubbornly rational patient.

> She had an impressive dream the night before, in which someone had given her a golden scarab—a costly piece of jewelry. While she was still telling me this dream, I heard something behind me gently tapping on the window. I turned round and saw that it was a fairly large flying insect that was knocking against the window-pane from outside in the obvious effort to get into the dark room. This seemed to me very strange. I opened the window immediately and caught the insect in the air as it flew in. It was a scarabaeid beetle, or common rose-chafer (*Cetonia aurata*), whose gold-green colour most nearly resembles that of a golden scarab. I handed the beetle to my patient with the words, "Here is your scarab." This experience punctured the desired hole in her rationalism and broke the ice of her intellectual resistance. The treatment could now be continued with satisfactory results. (CW 8, §982)

Personal transformation—integrating unconscious contents—delivers renewed meaning and purpose for an individual's life. Integrating the unconscious also often awakens broader feelings of connection to others, to the world, and sometimes to the Infinite.

THE UNIVERSAL WAY TO THE CENTER

Personality is Tao. —C. G. Jung

Thanks to its avoidance of religious terms or overt theological bias, Jung's model serves as a unifying conceptual framework for religious and wisdom traditions from both East and West. It provides a psychological language for experiences and teachings that are essentially common to many traditions and cultures.

> The basis of every real understanding is man, and therefore I had to speak of human things. . . . Therefore it seemed to me important above all to emphasize the agreement between the psychic states and symbolisms of East and West. . . . It is rather an atmosphere of suffering, seeking, and striving common to all civilized peoples; it is the tremendous experiment of becoming conscious, which nature has laid upon mankind, and which unites the most diverse cultures in a common task. (Jung, in *The Secret of the Golden Flower,* p. 136)

A few pertinent examples illustrate commonalities among cultures and parallels with Jung's psychology. From China, through the written records of Lao Tse, we learn of the Tao (Way) that integrates the opposites yin and yang.

> He who knows the Always-so [Tao] has room in him for everything; he
> who has room in him for everything is without prejudice.
> To be without prejudice is to be kingly;
> To be kingly is to be of heaven;
> To be of heaven is to be in Tao.[8]

From India, origin of the Upanishads from which Jung derived his term for the archetypal Self, we hear the ancient Hindu scriptures refer to the way that has the Self at its center.

---

[8] Lao Tsu, *The Way and Its Power,* trans. Arthur Waley (New York: Grove Press, 1994), p. 141.

The Self, smaller than small, greater than great, is hidden in the heart of this creature here. Man becomes free from desire and free from sorrow when by the grace of the Creator he beholds the glory of the Self.[9]

From the Middle East, we could liken the words of Jesus of Nazareth to the transformation of moving from the false self to the true self, from the ego/persona invested in some worldly identity to the true personality.

In truth, in very truth I tell you, unless a man has been born over again he cannot see the kingdom of God.[10]

The ancient wisdom of the Hebrew prophets still illuminates the way to an individuated life: "Love thy neighbor as thyself." The charge is really two instructions in one: love yourself—including your shadow; and love others—shadow and all.

In India, the Buddha affirmed that nonjudgmental love is the middle way to wholeness and a well-lived life.

Consider others as yourself.[11]

Hatreds do not ever cease in this world by hating, but by love; this is the eternal truth. . . . Overcome anger by love, overcome evil by good. Overcome the miser by giving; overcome the liar by truth.[12]

Do not look at the faults of others, or what others have done or not done; observe what you yourself have done and have not done.[13]

In China, Confucius advocated self-examination and personal transformation.

Before you embark on a journey of revenge, dig two graves.

Forget injuries; never forget kindnesses. What the superior man seeks is in himself; what the small man seeks is in others.

When we see men of a contrary character, we should turn inwards and examine ourselves.

---

[9] *Katha Upanishad*, 2.20. Cf. Hume, pp. 349ff.

[10] The Bible, John 3:3.

[11] Heartland Sangha American Buddhism, "Parallel Sayings of Buddha and Christ," HeartlandSangha.org, retrieved October 12, 2010.

[12] Dhammapada 1.5 and 17.3.

[13] Dhammapada 4.7.

They must often change who would be constant in happiness or wisdom.[14]

In the Persian Sufi poet and philosopher Rumi, we find the call to individuation through reflective self-awareness.

> Yesterday I was clever, so I wanted to change the world. Today I am wise, so I am changing myself.

In Europe, in about the same era, Meister Eckhart echoed Rumi's thoughts, also with an emphasis on "inward work."

> The outward work will never be great or good if the inward work is small and of little worth. The outward work will never be small if the inward work is great.[15]

INDIVIDUATION AND CIVILIZATION

If people can be educated to see the lowly side of their own natures, it may be hoped that they will also learn to understand and to love their fellow men better.
—C. G. Jung

People committed to the status quo in organizations or states may resist the development of individuality, preferring to impose the conventions of the "herd." Yet the resilience of the social fabric depends on the strength of individuals. The family, the organization, the city, the nation, all flower more fully to the degree that individuation is embraced and promoted as a way of life.

Western culture seems to have deviated from the middle way. Christianity, the dominant religion of the West, has at times been more of a showcase for what ails the world than a living demonstration of the way of its master teacher. The middle way to wholeness has not been well-traveled.

> Unfortunately our Western mind, lacking all culture in this respect, has never yet devised a concept, nor even a name, for the union of opposites through the middle path, that most fundamental item of inward experience, which could respectably be set against the Chinese concept

---

[14] Analects of Confucius.

[15] Meister Eckhart, Sermon VII, "Outward and Inward Morality."

of Tao. It is at once the most individual fact and the most universal, the most legitimate fulfillment of the meaning of the individual's life. (CW 7, §327)

The industrialized West has leaned toward a one-sided rationalism, thus tending to suppress realities that cannot be empirically observed or logically understood.

> Modern man does not understand how much his "rationalism" (which has destroyed his capacity to respond to numinous symbols and ideas) has put him at the mercy of the psychic "underworld." He has freed himself from "superstition" (or so he believes), but in the process he has lost his spiritual values to a positively dangerous degree. His moral and spiritual tradition has disintegrated, and he is now paying the price for this break-up in worldwide disorientation and dissociation. (Jung, *Man and His Symbols*, p. 84)

The antidote for an imbalanced culture rests with the individuals who comprise that culture. Enduring and meaningful cultural change happens one individual at a time. Those who do discover the middle way of the true personality create havens of well-being in the world. It is not the way of the masses that elevates civilization, but the way of individuation.

> In the last analysis, the essential thing is the life of the individual. This alone makes history, here alone do the great transformations take place, and the whole future, the whole history of the world, ultimately springs as a gigantic summation from these hidden sources in individuals. (CW 10, §149)

Paradoxically, the further that one actualizes the potential of individual personality, the more oriented one becomes to contributing to the collective. As Eleanor Roosevelt discovered, the ultimate fulfilling focus of a highly developed person is neither withdrawn self-concern nor selfish ambition but a relationship with the greater community.

> This widened consciousness is no longer the touchy, egotistical bundle of personal wishes, fears, hopes, and ambitions which always has to be compensated or corrected by unconscious counter-tendencies; instead, it is a function of relationship . . . bringing the individual into absolute, binding, and indissoluble communion with the world at large. (CW 7, §275)

THE BIG AND SACRED WORK

The glory of God is the human person fully alive. —Irenaeus of Lyons

We are delivered unannounced from seeming nothingness into a world filled with traditions, standards, and cultures to which we must adapt. In adapting, we may pretend to have control, to know what we are doing or where we are going, but we are groping our way through sheer mystery.

We are the "top animal exiled on a tiny speck of a planet in the Milky Way."[16] None of the other species in our world are intentionally building faith communities, creating constitutional laws, or probing epistemology. We have no one else here with whom to discuss our existential dilemma—to consider our place or purpose in the starry cosmos. Our evolutionary ascent from simple organisms to Homo sapiens may account for our biological *form,* but it does not account for our exponential leap in psychological *kind.* In that context, what separates us from the rest of terrestrial evolution? *Personality.*

Amid much existential uncertainty, it may seem easier to adapt to the conventions of the many. Yet, when our lives are overly devoted to the insignificant or inauthentic, we know that something dies within us. We join the "mass of men," as Thoreau observed, living in "quiet desperation." An alternative is the way of individuation that calls to us from unconscious depths. It is the slow way, neither easy nor expedient, yet it is the way to true personality where we may gain purpose, meaning, and the satisfaction of a life well lived.

> The decisive question for man is: Is he related to something infinite or not? That is the telling question of his life. . . . Only if we know that the thing which truly matters is the infinite can we avoid fixing our interest upon futilities and upon all kinds of goals which are not of real importance. . . . In the final analysis, we count for something only because of the essential we embody, and if we do not embody that, life is wasted. (Jung, *Memories, Dreams, Reflections,* p. 325)

We may travel the world gaining acclaim or notoriety; we may devote our lives to worthy ambitions and particular causes. Yet the outward contribution, as Meister Eckhart observed, "will not be great or good, if the inward one is small or of little worth." Our greatest contribution will issue from pursuing that individuated way that is ours and ours alone to live. The individuated way is the big and sacred work given to each of us.

---

[16]Jung, quoted in Serrano, *C. G. Jung and Hermann Hesse,* p. 84.

Compass Headings

IN THE FINAL THREE CHAPTERS, we saw how the types tend to collaborate, oppose, and integrate for the personal growth that Jung called *individuation*. In this section, we will consider a few of the practical applications of collaborations for navigating life experience.

To take a broad overview of some of these applications, we will be taking some liberties. Jung does not say much about the attributes of collaborations among the types in his book *Psychological Types*. Yet he does make it clear that the types do not act alone; they collaborate with one another in groups of two or more.

It would be impractical to attempt to review all fifty-six possible pairs, and far more impractical to attempt to review the many possible groups formed by three or more types in collaboration. Instead, we will use groups from the "Primary 16" pairings identified in Chapter 5 to provide some reference points regarding practical applications.

We will enlist our traveling troupe again to begin to understand the attributes of these groupings.

Recalling the primary sixteen pairs where rational introverted types pair up with receptive introverted types, we know that Kant, representing introverted thinking (IT), could readily pair with either Gandhi as introverted intuition (IN) or O'Keeffe as introverted sensation (IS). We know that introverted sensation resembles introverted intuition due to their common introverted orientations. These three types could form one group of four pairs.

1. Kant (IT) with Gandhi (IN) in supporting role

2. Kant (IT) with O'Keeffe (IS) in supporting role
3. Gandhi (IN) with Kant (IT) in supporting role
4. O'Keeffe (IS) with Kant (IT) in supporting role

The composite attributes of each of these pairs is different, yet, for the purpose of creating a conceptual framework, we could consider all four in one group. The precise attributes of each of these pairs is not the same, but each is similar enough to the others that we could begin to make *general* comments about them as a group. Each pair is fully introverted; each pair contains the same rational type; each pair has an introverted receptive type that is similar to the other introverted receptive type.

With the understanding that we are creating a framework for making general comments about pairings, we could create a similar group among the pairs formed by Anne Frank (IF), Gandhi (IN), and O'Keeffe (IS). To the southern side of the compass, Julia Child (ES) and Andrew Carnegie (EN) represent two receptive types rendered similar by a common extraverted orientation. They could join either Darwin (ET) or Elizabeth (EF) to form two new groups.

As shown in Figure CH.1, these groups create four quadrants.

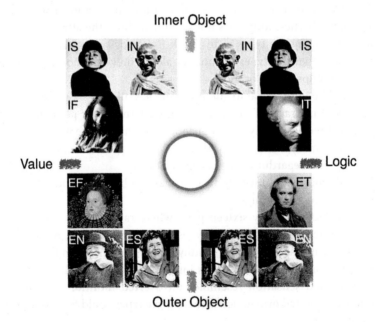

Figure CH.1 Four Compass Quadrants from the Primary 16 Types

Functional Roles

We know the functional role of each type in each quadrant; we could also postulate a general functional role for the whole quadrant. We might think of the role of the northeastern (NE) quadrant, for example, as *formulating*—encompassing the visionary and aesthetic roles in combination, directed by intensive introverted thinking ready to rationally shape ideas, as shown in Figure CH.2.

We could think of the southeastern (SE) quadrant as *producing*, indicating combinations of realistic and catalytic roles, directed by extraverted thinking ready to assemble order in the world at large.

We could think of the northwestern (NW) quadrant as *reflecting*, indicating aesthetic and visionary roles together, directed by introverted feeling ready to apprehend holistic ideals.

The southwestern (SW) quadrant could be thought of as *associating*, suggesting realistic and catalytic roles together, directed by extraverted feeling ready to affirm norms and create harmony.

Figure CH.2 The Four Functional Roles

Masculine Archetypes

Each of the quadrants consists of pairs of rational and receptive types. Whether in the auxiliary or the dominant role, the rational type tends to *direct* the energy of the pair toward some organized conclusion. The receptive types are less inclined to do something with what they have received, so their role can be somewhat less discernible.

The rational types, with their predisposition to apply directed action in some way, possess attributes that are congruent with the archetypal *masculine*. The receptive types, poised to perceive or apprehend, possess attributes congruent with the archetypal *feminine*. In Jung's model, archetypal masculine and feminine[1] are psychic opposites; they do not refer to gender. They are *both* present in every individual, irrespective of gender.[2] Masculine is no more important than feminine, for *being* is just as valuable as *doing*.

In the quadrants as organized on our conceptual compass, the rational types are the only ones that are each found in one quadrant and one quadrant only. We could therefore use them, and their masculine proclivity to direct organizing action, to help differentiate the general characteristics of each quadrant.

In their insightful book *King, Warrior, Magician, Lover,*[3] Robert Moore and Douglas Gillette identified four masculine archetypes and described the characteristics of each. Remembering that their insights could be applied to women as well as men, we could use their four metaphorical descriptors, for their archetypal characterizations are congruent with the functional roles of the quadrants (Figure CH.3).

The NE quadrant could be termed *Magician* for its ability to formulate theories and concepts seemingly from nothing.

Differentiated by extraverted thinking, with its penchant to produce and construct, we could refer to the SE quadrant as *Warrior.*

Differentiated by extraverted feeling and its penchant to seek harmony and to attend to the well-being of others, we could call the SW quadrant *Sovereign* (using *Sovereign* in lieu of *King* to acknowledge that these terms could apply to women or men).

---

[1] We will henceforth refer to them as simply *masculine* and *feminine* (and *archetypal* by default) for brevity.

[2] To reinforce the concept of masculine and feminine transcending gender, I have used both men and women to represent the types in this book, with each representing both masculine (rational) and feminine (receptive) roles.

[3] Robert Moore and Douglas Gillette, *King, Warrior, Magician, Lover* (New York: HarperOne, 1991).

Inner Object

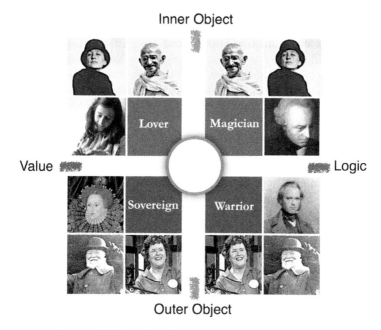

Value

Logic

Outer Object

Figure CH.3 The Four Quadrants as Masculine Archetypes

Finally, differentiated by idealistic feeling, we could refer to the NW quadrant as *Lover* with its penchant for poetry, the arts, and the idealized image.

Each of these quadrants reflects a generalized attitude that broadly includes all the pairs within each quadrant. When we speak of these quadrants, we will call them *compass headings,* for they are each poised to act and direct their aggregate role toward some end.

We should take these compass headings as fluid, generalized indications of dispositions without assigning too much rigid structure to them. If a receptive type is in the lead, it will color the collaboration somewhat differently, reflecting more of the feminine qualities of the receptive type. These nuanced differences are more empirically discernible for the two extraverted headings than they are for the two introverted headings. Empirical observation occurs from the audience of the outer object; therefore the two extraverted headings, Warrior and Sovereign, oriented to the outer object, would more readily exhibit their differences. The introverted headings, Lover and Magician, are oriented to the more quiescent audience of the unconscious, and we are not permitted seats in that audience.

We should remember that individuals are unique: no one will fit neatly or precisely into any of these headings, and all of the headings are available to everyone. Using these headings will merely allow us to make some general comments about practical applications

WORK

In work, do what you enjoy. —Lao Tse

Of the many applications of the compass of psychological types, career choice may be the most straightforward. One's gifts accompany one's type disposition. Each of the types carries particular aptitudes that can bring much enjoyment when engaged. A reliable maxim for career development could be, as Lao Tse said, to "do what you enjoy."

That enjoyment usually comes from exercising one's best gifts—type disposition—at least in the first half of life. In the second half of life, with individuation, other gifts (types) become more enjoyable.

When work is a vocation and not just a job, it engenders individuation.

> What is it, in the end, that induces a man to go his own way and to rise out of unconscious identity with the mass as out of a swathing mist? Not necessity, for necessity comes to many, and they all take refuge in convention. Not moral decision, for nine times out of ten, we decide for convention likewise. What is it, then, that inexorably tips the scales in favor of the extra-ordinary?
>
> It is what is commonly called vocation: an irrational factor that destines a man to emancipate himself from the herd and from its well-worn paths. (CW 17, §299, 300)

Yet few seem to choose, or be able to choose, to follow their vocational calling, for surveys have indicated that many people are unhappy with their work. The compass of psychological types can be a useful resource for identifying one's best and most enjoyable gifts, and for discerning a career path consistent with a vocational calling.

NW: Lover

A disposition for the Lover heading suggests the pursuit of careers that are creative, visionary, and deeply meaningful. The ideal work would provide a connection with the deeper rhythms and sacred aspects of life. Clergy, therapists, teachers, counselors, writers, and composers are among those likely to favor this heading.

NE: Magician

A disposition for the Magician heading suggests the pursuit of careers that are creative, visionary, and rich in complex problem solving. The ideal work would focus on pursuing conceptual possibilities rather than sustaining the status quo. People who prefer this heading often push the envelope of conventional knowledge to develop the next theory, solve the next problem, or find order amid seeming chaos. Architects, engineers, computer programmers, physicists, and philosophers are among the careers consistent with this heading.

SE: Warrior

A disposition for the Warrior heading suggests the pursuit of careers that are practical, dynamic, and productive. The ideal work would include organizing efforts to produce results and solving concrete, practical problems. People who prefer this heading often enjoy adapting to new situations, reorganizing, troubleshooting, defending a position, or managing processes effectively. They like to think and take action. Construction and manufacturing workers, managers, engineers, administrators, pilots, and attorneys are among types of careers consistent with this heading.

SW: Sovereign

A disposition for the Sovereign heading suggests the pursuit of careers that are interactive and attentive to the well-being of others. The ideal work would include much personal interaction and many opportunities for personal expression. People who prefer this heading often enjoy affirming social harmony and empathizing with others. Activity directors, event planners, salespeople, athletic coaches, managers, political leaders, and tour guides are among the kinds of careers consistent with this heading.

TEAMWORK

Effective organizations ultimately rely on capable individuals working cooperatively together. Diverse teams, composed of people whose gifts differ substantially, can be among the most effective "high performance" work groups, but their diversity can also engender conflict. Understanding one's strengths, and the strengths of others, can be helpful in forming teams of people with complementary gifts. People will often work more cooperatively when they realize that different gifts come with different behavioral patterns.

NW: Lover

People who favor the Lover heading can be the soul of a team or organization. They may tend to be quiet, yet they can have a subtle and powerful influence on group interactions. With a quiet bearing of trustworthiness, they tend to become the ethical backbone of the team. They are often creative and able to write effectively, generating perceptive, inspiring, or motivating messages. They tend to dislike mundane, irrelevant, or superficial work, and can be among the first to tune out conversations or meetings that seem to them to be trivial or unnecessary

NE: Magician

People who favor the Magician heading often have a long-distance, big-picture view of the work of the team. They are attuned to systems-thinking—being aware that decisions in one sector can influence and affect others in the organization. They tend to be thorough and thoughtful, some would say analytical, in understanding complexity. When others may want to just get something accomplished, people with a Magician heading may urge caution until decisions are more fully thought through.

SE: Warrior

People who favor the Warrior heading are often catalysts for action. They find practical solutions, troubleshoot concrete issues, and dissolve snags and problems quickly as they rapidly acquire the necessary facts and relevant details. They are seldom content to simply think about the work; they must do it, and do it in a highly directed and organized manner. They provide a grounding influence to team interaction, often considering the practical, concrete aspects of every new idea.

SW: Sovereign

People who favor the Sovereign heading are often inclined to hold groups together. They enjoy generating harmony and camaraderie among people, often seeing the optimistic side of every situation. They affirm the traditions and values that build a sense of community. They are highly attuned to how people are doing and feeling and will go out of their way to make things better for others.

LEADERSHIP

Leaders in organizations often have abundant opportunities to apply their natural gifts and develop new ones. As a person's responsibilities grow in an organization, the need to interact with others usually grows with it. The ability to empathize, relate, affirm, and listen without judgment becomes increasingly important. A leader's effectiveness depends largely on his or her willingness to individuate—to become more balanced and whole. A natural disposition for any of the four compass headings has its own inherent demands.

NW: Lover

People who favor the Lover heading may resist positions of organizational leadership, for they can be so fiercely independent. The daily barrage of questions and problems can be an intrusion on their beloved inner life. Yet people favoring the Lover heading are often natural leaders, for they engender respect and attention from others through their quiet yet profound presence.

They could be more adept at effectively managing an organization if they grew toward the Warrior heading, or, as Eleanor Roosevelt advised, "Do the thing you think you cannot do."

NE: Magician

Leaders who favor a Magician heading are often highly imaginative and insightful. They see the big picture and are forever formulating new and enhanced versions of it. A key strength is their ability to understand complex systems and to perpetually improve upon them. Never content to leave things as they are, they may often be formulating some new approach or project for the organization.

Their task, to become more balanced, is to grow more toward the Sovereign heading, to become increasingly adept in social situations, more easily and casually relating to others. This requires conscientious effort that may often feel odd and uncomfortable; yet developing social graces tends to generate a sense of well-being that puts people at ease. By attending more to the well-being of people in their organization, they will learn that people often do their best work when they feel valued.

SE: Warrior

Leaders who favor the Warrior heading often find their way to positions of management because they tend to have a talent for getting things organized and accomplished; they can be highly goal-oriented, practical, and decisive. They are usually well organized and adept at organizing the work of others.

They could enhance their leadership style by moving toward the Lover heading, where feeling-toned ideals could help them recognize values of deeper import than the bottom line. People want, in their heart of hearts, to be part of something big and sacred. Leaders in touch with deeper values bring the big and sacred to everyday life—to themselves and to those around them.

SW: Sovereign

People often have much affection for leaders who favor the Sovereign heading. These are the leaders who are attentive, socially accomplished, and genuinely interested in the lives of others. They love to meet with people and derive much energy from the many relationships that leadership demands. They support social harmony and enjoy carrying on the established traditions and values of the organization.

Their inclination to maintain harmony would be complemented by moving toward the Magician heading, where strategic thinking, perpetual innovation, and new ideas are generated freely. They, and the organizations they serve, would benefit, for in today's quick-paced economy, it is the responsive, nimble, and innovative organizations that are most likely to thrive.

LEARNING

Rather than applying the same teaching curriculum to everyone and in the same way, educational training could be more closely attuned to each individual's natural aptitudes and orientations. Teachers and students alike could benefit. Teachers could be more effective; students could enjoy learning more.

Extrapolating from Jung's model, we can begin to describe the preferred learning orientations and environments for each of the four compass headings.

NW: Lover

People who enjoy the Lover heading would tend to be deep learners. Like still water, they are often quiet, yet their feelings run deep. If something impresses them, it impresses them intensely and memorably. They often have poetic sensibilities oriented to the values and import of experience. Visionary, imaginative, and artistic, they may need to see a deeper, enduring value for new knowledge for it to be of genuine interest. In learning environments, they would tend to prefer small groups or time alone. They may have little interest in facts that seem unrelated to what they deem important.

NE: Magician

People who enjoy the Magician heading tend to be conceptual learners. They enjoy ideas, imagination, complex problem solving, systems, underlying principles, and overarching theories. They may need to see the whole picture to appreciate the detail. Facts are most useful to them when they contribute to larger insights. In learning environments, they tend to want time alone or focused in small groups. They may get bored with details that seem irrelevant to a big-picture understanding, but they can be enthralled by anything that helps in comprehending a larger systematic framework.

SE: Warrior

People who enjoy the Warrior heading tend to be active learners; they learn by doing—interacting with the world, responding to situations, and accomplishing practical or tangible projects. For them, to *do* is to *learn*. In learning environments, they would want to be physically and actively engaged. They may get bored with anything that is too sedentary, intensive, or conceptual.

SW: Sovereign

People who enjoy the Sovereign heading would tend to be social learners—interactively learning with others. They may learn best from teaching, talking, and enjoying the company of others. They would also appreciate tangible, practical information. They would learn best from social interaction with groups of all sizes and would tend to tire of too much dry, conceptual, or intellectual thinking.

MARRIAGE AND INTIMATE UNIONS

Though modern marriage is a tremendous laboratory, its members are often without preparation for the partnership function. How much agony and remorse and failure could have been avoided if there had been at least some rudimentary learning before they entered the partnership? — Carl Rogers

Marriage is an enthralling crucible of intimate experience potentially conducive to the full development of two individuals. Yet in the developed countries of the world, it is not uncommon to see divorce rates greater than fifty percent, for marriage can also be a crucible of conflict.

Much charged unconscious content is in the mix because "opposites attract." The anima and animus find their projected counterparts in a mate, but the shadow may also be lurking beneath the surface. While anima/animus projections, saturated with alluring expectations, are usually quite positive, shadow projections are typically negative and demeaning. Because the shadow and anima or animus of an individual would carry the same typological "spin," the projections onto the intimate other can become quite complicated and confused.

We can imagine the sort of tension of opposites that might occur from the pairings of the following compass headings.

SW Sovereign and NE Magician

A Sovereign heading suggests someone who is highly gregarious, lively, bold, energetic, and spontaneous. A Magician heading suggests one who is difficult to read, aloof, contemplative, and inexpressive, and who prefers planning to action. A relationship for these two is rich with opportunities for mutual understanding.

One may want time alone to think; the other may yearn for time with others. If they are out with friends, one may withdraw as a detached observer while the other moves eagerly from one conversation to another.

They may be perpetually at odds about outward behavior. One wants what is logical; the other wants what feels valuable. One lives to create elegant ideas; the other lives to create harmonious relationships. One is contemplating a difficult conceptual problem; the other is looking for the next exciting outing.

Yet they are importantly similar in one compelling respect—they complement one another. Each is a personification of the other's unconscious. They have much to learn from each other. If they can learn without judgment, each can become more whole.

NW Lover and SE Warrior

A Lover heading suggests one who is quiet, reflective, idealistic, and deep. A Warrior heading suggests someone who can be efficient, practical, and decisive. They differ in how, and how fast, they make choices. One values the true, the beautiful, and the good and needs time to discern them; the other appreciates efficient progress toward defined goals and concrete objectives.

What one may want to consider slowly, the other may want to decide on the spot. Where shall we eat dinner tonight? For the Lover, this question may involve much reflection about the right mood, ambience, presentation, food quality, and seemingly endless subjective attributes that must *feel* right. For the Warrior, it is simply a matter of choosing a place that fits the right objective criteria—price, distance, and food quality.

One may make no binding decisions until decisions feel right; the other may make binding decisions as soon as they make sense—and they can make sense very quickly. One may aspire to live life deeply and authentically, while the other may aim to live life productively.

This underlying tension of opposing attitudes offers a potentially richer life for each individual. Together, as each learns to more patiently understand the other, they bring balance and wholeness to their lives that would not have been possible without the relationship.

PARENT, CHILD, AND FAMILY

If there is anything that we wish to change in the child, we should first examine it and see whether it is something that could better be changed in ourselves. —C. G. Jung

Family dynamics also have much to do with type dispositions. If parents are oriented to one side of the great divide more than another, children born to the other side of that divide may feel less valued. Their development into secure and confident people may be impaired by conflictive or demeaning early childhood experiences. Research in attachment theory has recognized the vital need to acknowledge and value the emerging identity of children.

Many of the complexes that will influence and shape later life are formed by the relationships and associations of early childhood. The complexes born of these relationships likely get shaped differently, depending on type dispositions. For example, an abusive relationship with a father might embed itself differently in a child reliant on a reflective, imaginative disposition than on a child with a decisive, constructive disposition. The former could suffer from feelings of guilt and responsibility; the latter could respond more aggressively with feelings of anger or revenge. Typological oppositions between father and child could also exacerbate an abusive relationship; the type disposition of the parent's shadow could be the child's natural disposition.

Parents who seek the individuated way are often provided bountiful opportunities to acknowledge their own shadow identities, rather than project shadow complexes on their children. In the dynamic container called *family*, everyone has an opportunity to adjust to other dispositions on the type compass.

NW: Lover

A Lover heading would indicate someone needing time alone, sometimes in deep reflection. Reading may be a favorite pastime, for it allows time to understand and reflect on life more deeply.

People with a preference for this heading are often artistic and, like many others with artistic temperaments, may be very difficult to understand. An inner life of imagination, sacred values, compelling images, and motivating inspirations is often alluring. A quiet but deep commitment to idealistic values may show up as prickly stubbornness if those values are threatened.

NE: Magician

A Magician heading would indicate someone with active inner life where questions are continually pondered. These questions often take the form of scientific or philosophical inquiry. Children with this heading can act like one big question mark, asking seemingly endless questions beginning with the word *Why*. As adults, they may need time away from family to just think and contemplate some perplexing problem or issue.

People with this heading may adapt to family activities or outings, but they may also feel drained by social events unless there is ample opportunity for contemplative thinking. A child with this heading may start out in life feeling painfully shy or awkward, for the opposite Sovereign heading and its accompanying social skills are usually less developed.

SE: Warrior

A Warrior heading would indicate a predisposition for order, organization, and operating rules. People who prefer this heading may have their standard methods for doing everything—from family chores to vacations. They often favor order in every aspect of family life, including appointed meal times, uncluttered rooms, and regular schedules. They are prone to action. Once the facts are known or the idea settled on, they are often the first to get things organized and done.

Living with family disorder might be frustrating for a child with this heading, yet she or he would also be the most likely to take the initiative to address the frustration.

SW: Sovereign

A Sovereign heading would indicate someone interested in family harmony. People who favor this heading are often quick to adapt and empathize with the needs and perspectives of others. Whether as children or adults, their focus is often on people getting along. They may "throw themselves into the breach" to heal disharmony. They are attentive to the practical needs of the people they love, and they enjoy being actively involved with others.

Time spent away from others may feel uncomfortable to them; they may get impatient with the seemingly aloof people favoring either of the northern headings.

FRIENDSHIPS AND COMMUNITY

Of the many relationships formed in community, those of close friends can be among the richest and most vital. Unlike romantic relationships, where "opposites attract," friendships seem to be often formed among people with similar type preferences. The famous friendship between two high school nerds, Steve Jobs and Steve Wozniak, who formed Apple Computer Inc., became fast friends around their common interest in computers. They no doubt had one or two type dispositions in common that drew them to that interest.

As individuation progresses, people are more likely to reach out across the "great divide" to discover the value of others whom they might not have befriended earlier in life. Engaging some common type disposition is often helpful as a bridge to the other side. Two female coworkers in the Netherlands developed a close, congenial friendship, even though they have type dispositions on opposite sides of the compass. One is primarily oriented to the NE Magician heading, the other to the opposite SW Sovereign heading. They share in common an introverted feeling disposition which serves as a kind of bridge connecting their introverted and extraverted orientations. They regularly take walks together to discuss joint projects, each intently seeking to understand the other's viewpoint. As their understanding of one another grows, so too does their understanding of their own shadow types. People favoring different compass headings will tend to form their friendships differently.

NW: Lover

People oriented to the Lover heading can be very particular about who their friends are. Their values and their ideals run deep. Even a hint of violating those values can end a budding friendship. Earlier in life, their closest friends would likely be people who share their preference for the Lover heading. Later, as individuation progresses, people favoring other headings may also come into their trusted circle.

NE: Magician

People oriented to the Magician heading may be the least naturally sociable. Strongly independent and driven by their quest to understand holistic images, they may take longer to discover the riches of personal relationships.

SE: Warrior

People oriented to the Warrior heading readily associate with one another. The common orientation to objective thinking enables them to see the world similarly and to share common objectives. They may also find that friendships come easily with people favoring the Sovereign heading. Both headings are oriented to the practical facts of the world, the Warrior affirming objective standards and the Sovereign affirming social norms.

SW: Sovereign

People oriented to the Sovereign heading are easily drawn to others. They mingle and associate freely, for to associate and relate to others is their stock-in-trade.

Terms

Anima/Animus Terms that refer to the soul at the apron of the unconscious stage. Jung uses a masculine term (*animus*) or a feminine term (*anima*) to refer to the soul. The usage of *soul* in Jung's lexicon is different from its usage in religious applications. The soul is the complement to the persona. If the persona is masculine, the soul is feminine (anima); if the persona is feminine, the soul is masculine (animus). Just as the persona is an extension of the ego's type disposition, the anima or animus is an extension of the shadow's type disposition.

Apprehend In this book, we use the term *apprehend* for the functional attitude of intuition and the composite attitudes of the introverted types. (See *perceive* for the term used for the sensation function and the extraverted types.)

Archetypes were neither invented nor discovered by Jung. They are concepts that have a long history. In one sense, archetypes are much like Kant's categories—frameworks that help to make sense of raw perceptions. The frameworks of time, space, and causality could be considered archetypal frameworks. In another sense, archetypes are much like Plato's forms—prototypical patterns. The term *Tao* from early China and *Logos* from early Greece, each referring to an underlying order to life, might be regarded as expressions of an archetypal order.

Jung observed that much of human experience is founded on predetermined responses to life: a mother nurtures her child; people are drawn to intimacy; social institutions are formed; and traditions are established, not out of thin air but from unconscious, a priori archetypal patterns and energies that underlie and induce them.

The four metaphors used to generalize typical dispositions of consciousness—Lover, Sovereign, Warrior, and Magician—would be expressions of archetypal patterns. They are the phenomenal representations of the noumenal archetypes. The eight types on the compass of consciousness would also be expressions of archetypal patterns.

What the archetypes are of themselves is unknown, for they are beyond the bounds of human consciousness. They are "negative boundary" concepts regarding the unconscious that are derived from conscious experience with the phenomena of human patterns of adaptation.

Attitude "For us, attitude is a readiness of the psyche to act or react in a certain way" (CW 6, §687). In this sense, functions, introversion, and extraversion are each attitudes. When a functional attitude joins a directional attitude, we speak, in this book, of a composite attitude (type). Every attitude has an orientation.

Collective Unconscious The unconscious is both *personal,* where unconscious content is acquired through an individual's experience in the world, and *collective.* The collective unconscious has been built up over millennia and includes the experience of many generations. The collective unconscious provides an archetypal structure for human experience that is akin to instinct; it is home to the unconscious archetypes that engender interactive guidance and a framework for human experience.

The collective unconscious is also home to images, ideas, and ideals that are the orientations of the introverted types.

Complex A complex develops where archetypal patterns meet an individual's experience in the world. The ego could be considered a complex. Other complexes, like mother or father complexes, cluster in the personal unconscious, and are often characterized by emotional affect. Complexes are often autonomous—they seem to have an independent life of their own: "complexes behave like independent beings" (CW 8, 253).

Composite Attitude When any of the four functional attitudes (thinking, feeling, sensation, intuition) is merged with either of the two directional attitudes (introversion or extraversion) we refer to the merger of the two attitudes as a *composite attitude*. There are eight such composite attitudes, and in this book, they are also referred to as the eight *types*.

Composite Orientation The merged orientation of a functional orientation (logic, value, outer object, inner object) with a directional attitude (inner object or outer object).

Composite Scope The focus of merged functional and directional attitudes.

Composite Substance The primary material of merged functional and directional attitudes.

Ego The ego is the center of consciousness and possesses a high degree of identity and continuity. With experience in the world, the ego becomes a complex. The ego is one complex among many embraced by the Self.

> But inasmuch as the ego is only the centre of my field of consciousness, it is not identical with the totality of my psyche, being merely one complex among other complexes. I therefore distinguish between the ego and the self, since the ego is only the subject of my consciousness, while the self is the subject of my total psyche, which also includes the unconscious. (CW 6, §706)

Extraversion Extraversion is an outward turning of libido toward the outer object.

> Everyone in the extraverted state thinks, feels, and acts in relation to the object, and moreover in a direct and clearly observable fashion, so that no doubt can remain about his positive dependence on the object. In a sense, therefore, extraversion is a transfer of interest from subject [individual] to object. If it is an extraversion of thinking, the subject thinks himself into the object; if an extraversion of feeling, he feels himself into it. In extraversion there is a strong, if not exclusive, determination by the object. (CW 6, §710)

Extreme Types The term *extreme* is used in this book to refer to conditions when the ego identifies with its object of orientation to a pathologically one-sided degree, excessively repressing the normally compensatory shadow.

Feeling Jung offers various definitions and descriptions of feeling while also acknowledging that it is impossible to provide the essence of feeling with intellectual descriptions. The intellect (thinking) is incapable of understanding feeling in conceptual terms; feeling must be experienced to be truly known.

> Feeling is primarily a process that takes place between the ego and a given content, a process, moreover, that imparts to the content a definite *value* in the sense of acceptance or rejection ("like" or "dislike"). (CW 6, §724)
> Feeling is distinguished from affect by the fact that it produces no perceptible physical innervations, i.e., neither more nor less than an ordinary thinking process. (CW 6, §725)
> Feeling, like thinking, is a rational function, since values in general are assigned according to the laws of reason, just as concepts in general are formed according to these laws. (CW 6, §724)

Function Functions enable the ego complex to become experientially *functional*. They are modes of psychic activity that are always oriented by certain governing principles. Each of the four functions of consciousness is distinctly different; none can fully grasp the nature of the other.

Great Divide In this book, we use the term *great divide* to characterize the vast difference between the two primary orientations of consciousness: an orientation to the outer object versus an orientation to the inner object.

Individual/Individuality The differentiation of the unique individual is the very purpose of individuation. It is bringing to consciousness the individuality that has an a priori unconscious existence. Individuality is brought to consciousness as the person is differentiated from the collective at large.

Individuation The very centerpiece of Analytical Psychology, individuation plays a large role in Jung's model.

> In general, it is the process by which individual beings are formed and differentiated; in particular, it is the development of the psychological individual as a being distinct from the general, collective psychology. Individuation, therefore, is a process of differentiation, having for its goal the development of the individual personality. (CW 6, §724)

Individuation is distinct from individualism, a mode of egocentricity that can engender isolation. Individuation engenders deeper, broader, and more meaningful relationships with others.

> As the individual is not just a single, separate being, but by his very existence presupposes a collective relationship, it follows that the process of individuation must lead to more intense and broader collective relationships and not to isolation. (CW 6, §758)

Inner Object The term *inner object* refers to one of the two orienting objects of consciousness: the collective unconscious.

Intuition Intuition is one of the four basic ego functions; like sensation, it mediates perceptions, but it mediates perceptions of what is outside the frameworks of sensual perception.

Its mode of perception may be directed to either the inner object or the outer object. If intuition is directed to the inner object, it apprehends images; if directed to the outer object, it perceives possibilities. In either case contents appear holistically.

Like sensation, the contents are given rather than derived; therefore it is considered a receptive function, for it derives or produces nothing on its own. Its sole purpose is to receive what is presented to it.

Intuition possesses an intrinsic certainty about what it has apprehended. In the same way that sensation may be certain about its perception of a rock or a fragrance, there is also certainty for intuition about apprehending a possibility or an idea.

In this book, we have portrayed intuition with an orientation to the inner object, that is, the images of the collective unconscious. Merged with the introverted attitude, intuition apprehends those images directly. In the extraverted attitude, where the directional attitude overrides the functional attitude, intuition's orientation to the collective unconscious is secondary, therefore engendering images that seem more closely tied to the outer object. In the extraverted attitude, the images become imagined possibilities.

Introversion Introversion is an inward turning of libido toward the inner object—the images of the collective unconscious.

Irrational Jung used the term *rational* to refer to the two functions of judgment—thinking and feeling. He used the term *irrational* to refer to the two functions that perceive rather than judge. The term *irrational* describes what the functions *do not do*, not what they *do*. In this book, we have coined the term *receptive* to refer to the two functions—sensation and intuition—that Jung termed the *irrational functions*.

Libido Jung uses the term *libido* synonymously with psychic energy. Related to the types, the term refers to introverted or extraverted energy, but the term has a broader meaning in Analytical Psychology as a whole.

> By libido, I mean psychic energy. Psychic energy is the intensity of a psychic process, its psychological value.... I often use "libido" promiscuously with "energy." (CW 6, §778)

New Functional Role The new role of a functional attitude when it merges with a directional attitude.

Orientation *Orientation* and *attitude* are two fundamental terms that must be distinguished to fully understand Jung's conceptual model of psychological types. Every attitude has some governing principle to which it is oriented. The governing principle constitutes its orientation.

> Every attitude is oriented by a certain viewpoint, no matter whether this viewpoint is conscious or not. A power attitude is oriented by the power of the ego to hold its own against unfavorable influences and conditions. A thinking attitude is oriented by the principle of logic as its supreme law; a sensation attitude is oriented by the sensuous perception of given facts. (CW 6, §780)

Outer Object The term *outer object* is equivalent to the term *object* as used in philosophical dialogue. It refers to the manifold world at large, everything that is outside of the experiencing person. We use the term *outer object* in this book to distinguish it from the object on the other side of the "great divide": the *inner object*.

Perceive In this book, we use the term *perceive* for the functional attitude of sensation and the composite attitudes of the extraverted types. (See *apprehend* for the term used for the intuition function and the introverted types.)

Persona A kind of social mask useful for adapting to and navigating life in the social world. The persona is usually the extension of the ego's typical disposition. It is also complementary to the anima/animus. What the anima/animus is, the persona is not.

> As to the character of the anima, my experience confirms the rule that it is, by and large, complementary to the character of the persona. The anima usually contains all those common human qualities which the conscious attitude lacks. . . . If the persona is intellectual, the anima will quite certainly be sentimental. (CW 6, §804)

Personal Unconscious While people are born with a collective unconscious that is generally common to all, the personal unconscious develops with the individual's unique personal experience in the world. The personal unconscious contains the memories and complexes that grow with experience.

Personality/Person The term *personality,* as Jung uses it, is multifaceted. For Jung, many of the psychic identities have personality—a distinctive identity. Neither the term *person* nor the term *personality* found a place among the many definitions included in Volume 6. Jung's definition of the term *individual* comes the closest to a definition of the term *person.*

  Personality, as used in this book, refers to the state of being a person. A person is the unique individual that is the central subject of individuation; a person includes an ego, a shadow, a persona, and a soul and unifies them all within one individual. Personality may be endowed with a consciousness of consciousness, an objective awareness of ego consciousness. A personality awareness that transcends ego consciousness could be consistent with Jung's model but would add a dimension that probably exceeds the explicit premises he articulated. Jung's psychological types pertain to types of ego consciousness rather than types of persons, though much might be learned about a person by understanding preferred psychological types.

Projections A projection is the transfer of unwanted or repressed psychic content onto others.

Receptive In this book, we use the term *receptive* for the functions of sensation and intuition that Jung termed *irrational.* The term is more descriptive of what the functions actually do, rather than what they do not do, and carry none of the negative connotations of the word *irrational.*

Self The term *Self*, when capitalized, refers to an a priori archetypal pattern of potentiality. The Self is the chief orchestrating archetype and is the behind-the-scenes producer of the drama of individuation.

The term *self*, when not capitalized, refers to the individual or personality. The full expression and development of the self—the unique person—is the aim of individuation.

The individual is depicted on the psychic theater in Chapter 1 at the center of the theater. With individuation, in that conceptual theater the ego and shadow are increasingly united within one individual whose awareness and vitality grow. Functions of relationship become increasingly available with both the world at large and the collective unconscious.

Sensation "Sensation is the psychological function that mediates the perception of a physical stimulus. It is therefore identical with perception" (CW 6, §792). Sensation is more than merely the five senses, for Jung recognizes with Kant that certain a priori perceptual frameworks are built into the raw perceptions of sensation (e.g., time, space, and causality). In its perceptions of the external world (outer object), it conveys to the mind a perceptual image of external objects—representations of them. In its perceptions of the body, it conveys bodily changes to consciousness—representations of physiological impulses.

Empirical experience with the Gifts Compass Inventory (GCI) suggests that the sensation function may be unusually aligned with the feeling function, sometimes even crossing over the "great divide" of inner and outer orientations to unite a feeling type with a sensation type, even though their orientations might be opposite one another (e.g., ES with IF).

> It is, on the one hand, an element of ideation, since it conveys to the mind the perceptual image of the external object; and on the other hand, it is an element of feeling, since through the perception of bodily changes it gives feeling the character of an affect. (CW 6, §793)

Shadow Generally, as Jung uses the term, the shadow is "the thing a person has no wish to be" (CW 16, §470). In this broader sense, we might think of the unsavory character Caliban in Shakespeare's *The Tempest* as a living embodiment of the shadow. In this more general sense, the shadow includes far more than merely the least developed ego functions; it includes, for example, unacceptable social and moral attributes.

As the term is being used with the compass of consciousness—psychological types—it refers primarily to the ego type that is least available to consciousness. Jung and von Franz refer to the "inferior function" as the function that is least accessible. The terms *shadow* and *shadow type* are used in this book to more precisely refer to the type that is least accessible.

As the persona is an extension of the ego type, so too is the anima/animus theoretically an extension of the shadow's type. Knowing the ego disposition therefore theoretically arranges the typical orientations of the psyche from persona to anima/animus. In practice, the dispositions do not appear to be so readily predictable, for the shadow's type is not always the diametric opposite of the ego's disposition.

Whether using the more general use of the term or the more narrowly contained usage referring to type disposition, the aim of individuation is to bring the shadow to light in a union with conscious dispositions.

> Everyone carries a shadow, and the less it is embodied in the individual's conscious life, the blacker and denser it is. If an inferiority is conscious, one always has a chance to correct it. Furthermore, it is constantly in contact with other interests, so that it is continually subjected to modifications. But if it is repressed and isolated from consciousness, it never gets corrected, and is liable to burst forth suddenly in a moment of unawareness[;] . . . it forms an unconscious snag, thwarting our most well-meant intentions. (CW 11, §131)

Soul *Soul,* as Jung uses the term, refers specifically to either the masculine animus or the feminine anima. (See Animus/Anima.) His use of the term is more precise than the conventional uses referring to intangible human attributes like spiritual depth, compassion, or heart; or to the religious use of the term referring to a spiritual entity that survives death; or to references that might interchange soul with psyche.

Subject/Subjective Factor The terms *subject* and *subjective* are traditionally associated with either the ego or the individual, and Jung also uses the term in this sense. In response to a question in the 1925 seminar, Jung said, "'Subjective' denotes in the first place just what you know it does, that is, the view of a given individual which is special to him and different from that of any other individual" (*Introduction to Jungian Psychology, Notes on the Seminar Given in 1925, 2012*; p. 63). In that sense, both the extraverted and the introverted attitudes would be conditioned by the subjectivity of the individual. He amplified that use of the term in *Psychological Types*:

> But what is the subject? The subject is man himself—we are the subject. Only a sick mind could forget that cognition must have a subject, and that there is no knowledge whatever and therefore no world at all unless "I know" has been said, though with this statement one has already expressed the subjective limitation of all knowledge. (CW 6, §621)

In response to a question in the 1925 seminar, Jung posited a second meaning for the term *subjective*:

> Then the term "subjective" also means an argument coming from the subject, but nonetheless an object. In every person there are certain collective ideas—such, for example, as the Darwinian Theory—which are quite objective. They in no sense belong to the subject simply because they are to be found in his mind. Again there are certain unconscious products which people like to think of as establishing forever the uniqueness of their individualities, but which in reality are shared by all and are, by reason of this collective quality, objects vis-a-vis the subject's mind. (*Introduction to Jungian Psychology, Notes on the Seminar Given in 1925, 2012*; p. 63)

He elaborated, to further clarify what he meant by the term *subjective factor*:

> Thus the images in our mind tend to form prejudices from which we can never be wholly free. These preexisting mental images into contact with which the stream of our personal experience comes, I call the subjective factor. . . . The subjective factor, then, in this second sense, is held to be made up of objective material, namely ancestral views. The artist returns to these ancestral views. He leaves the outer object and returns to the object as seen by his mind rather than as seen by his senses. (Ibid., p. 64)

Again in *Psychological Types,* he elaborated also on this use of the term.

> In so far as the subjective factor has, from the earliest times and among all peoples, remained in large measure constant, elementary perceptions and cognitions being almost universally the same, it is a reality that is just as firmly established as the external object. . . . It is another universal

law, and whoever bases himself on it has a foundation as secure, as permanent, and as valid as the man who relies on the object. (CW 6, §622)

Each of the introverted types is oriented by subjective factors.

As I have already explained in the previous section, the introvert is distinguished from the extravert by the fact that he does not, like the latter, orient himself by the object and by objective data, but by subjective factors. (CW 6, §620)

Along with the term *subjective factor,* Jung refers to the orientation of the introverted attitudes as the *collective unconscious, psychic structure,* and *inner object.*

The introverted attitude is normally oriented by the psychic structure, which is in principle hereditary and is inborn in the subject. (CW 6, §624)

The psychic structure is the same as what Semon calls "mneme" and what I call the "collective unconscious." (CW 6, §624)

The extravert bases himself on the value of the outer object, the introvert on that of the inner object. (*Analytical Psychology,* p. 59)

The contents of the collective unconscious are represented in consciousness in the form of pronounced preferences and definite ways of looking at things. These subjective tendencies and views are generally regarded by the individual as being determined by the object—incorrectly, since they have their source in the unconscious structure of the psyche and are merely released by the effect of the object. . . . Thus, just as it seems incomprehensible to the introvert that the object should always be the decisive factor, it remains an enigma to the extravert how a subjective standpoint can be superior to the objective situation. He invariably comes to the conclusion that the introvert is either a conceited egoist or a crack-brained bigot. (CW 6, §625)

To distinguish between the term *subject* as a reference to the individual, and the term *subject* as a reference to the orientation of an introverted consciousness, we have substituted the term *inner object* for *subject* or *subjective factor* when referring to the orientation of the introverted attitudes.

The term *subject* in this book would typically refer to the individual, and the term *subjective* would refer to a person's individual experience of either the inner or outer object.

Thinking Thinking is one of the four basic psychological functions. The thinking function is oriented to the governing principle of logic; it functions to impart order through the principle of logic. Jung considers this form of thinking to be *directed* thinking. It is a rational function conditioned by the conscious will.

Transcendent Function The transcendent function intervenes to resolve a tension of opposites in the psyche. The transcendent function enters, often by way of a *symbol,* to unite the two, offering a "mediatory product" or middle ground that accommodates both sides of the opposition.

> If the mediatory product remains intact, it forms the raw material for a process not of dissolution but of construction, in which thesis and antithesis both play their part. In this way it becomes a new content that governs the whole attitude, putting an end to the division and forcing the energy of the opposites into a common channel. The standstill is overcome and life can flow on with renewed power towards new goals. (CW 6, §827)

The term *transcendent* does not imply a metaphysical quality: it is used to denote a transition or bridge to an emerging attitude. It is transcendent in the sense that it rises above a tension of opposites, transcending each with a new metaphor or symbol that unites them. With each intervention of the transcendent function, *individuation* incrementally progresses.

The use of the term *function* here refers to a more complex process than any of the four conscious functions. If the four functions are the handmaidens of the ego, we might think of the transcendent function as the handmaiden of the Self.

> The raw material shaped by thesis and antithesis, and in the shaping of which the opposites are united, is the living symbol. Its profundity of meaning is inherent in the raw material itself, the very stuff of the psyche, transcending time and dissolution; and its configuration by the opposites ensures its sovereign power over all the psychic functions. (CW 6, §828)

Types As the term is used by Jung, *type* refers to any disposition of psychological types that is habitually relied upon: a thinking type, an extraverted type, or an extraverted thinking type could exemplify the term *type* as used by Jung.

It is too easy, in using the term this way, to begin to think of people as the types rather than the dispositions themselves as types. On the one hand, Jung railed against using psychological types to put labels on people; on the other, he freely used the term *type* when referring to people in his text. Though he opposed the use of the term as a means of categorizing people, he inadvertently used it that way himself.

A person's habitual type disposition is not stationary; with individuation, a person gains greater access to all the types, even the "shadow type" that is the least accessible and the compensatory attitude to the preferred type. To refer to people as a "type," as Jung sometimes did, only characterizes their natural habitual preferences; it says nothing about the more complex preferences being acquired through individuation.

In this book, *type* is used to refer only to one of the eight composite attitudes where a functional attitude has merged with a directional attitude. The term *type* refers to types of consciousness and not to persons predisposed to them.

Bibliography

From *The Collected Works of C. G. Jung*

Note: References to (CW, Volume #, §#) *in the text refer to volume number and paragraph number from the Collected Works.*

Jung, Carl. *Psychological Types; The Collected Works of C. G. Jung*, Vol. 6 (Princeton: Princeton University Press, 1971).

———. *Two Essays on Analytical Psychology; The Collected Works of C. G. Jung*, Vol. 7 (Princeton: Princeton University Press, 1966).

———. *The Structure and Dynamics of the Psyche; The Collected Works of C. G. Jung*, Vol. 8 (Princeton: Princeton University Press, 1969).

———. *The Archetypes of the Collective Unconscious; The Collected Works of C. G. Jung*, Vol. 9i (Princeton: Princeton University Press, 1968).

———. *Aion; The Collected Works of C. G. Jung*, Vol. 9ii (Princeton: Princeton University Press, 1968).

———. *Civilization in Transition; The Collected Works of C. G. Jung*, Vol. 10 (Princeton: Princeton University Press, 1970).

———. *Psychology and Religion: West and East; The Collected Works of C. G. Jung*, Vol. 11 (Princeton: Princeton University Press, 1969).

———. *Psychology and Alchemy; The Collected Works of C. G. Jung*, Vol. 12 (Princeton: Princeton University Press, 1968).

———. *Alchemical Studies; The Collected Works of C. G. Jung*, Vol. 13 (Princeton: Princeton University Press, 1968).

———. *Mysterium Coniunctionis; The Collected Works of C. G. Jung*, Vol. 14 (Princeton: Princeton University Press, 1970).

———. *The Spirit in Man, Art, and Literature; The Collected Works of C. G. Jung*, Vol. 15 (Princeton: Princeton University Press, 1966).

———. *The Practice of Psychotherapy; The Collected Works of C. G. Jung*, Vol. 16 (Princeton: Princeton University Press, 1966).

———. *The Development of Personality; The Collected Works of C. G. Jung*, Vol. 17 (Princeton: Princeton University Press, 1954).

———. *The Symbolic Life; The Collected Works of C. G. Jung*, Vol. 18 (Princeton: Princeton University Press, 1954).

Other Readings

Bolen, Jean Shinoda. *The Tao of Psychology: Synchronicity and the Self.* (HarperSanFrancisco; 25th Anniversary edition, 2005).

Borg, Marcus. *Jesus and Buddha: The Parallel Sayings* (Berkeley: Ulysses Press, 2004).

Cambray, Joseph, and Carter, Linda, eds. *Analytical Psychology: Contemporary Perspectives in Jungian Analysis* (London: Brunner-Routledge, 2004).

Clark, Ronald W. *Einstein: The Life and Times* (New York: Random House Value Publishing, 1995).

Cooper, John, ed. *Plato: Complete Works* (Cambridge, MA: Hackett, 1997).

Durant, Will, and Durant, Ariel. *The Story of Civilization*, 11 volumes, Volumes 7, 10 (New York: MJF Books).

Evans, Richard. *Jung on Elementary Psychology* (Hialeah, FL: Dutton, 1976).

Gandhi, Mohandas. *The Story of My Experiments with Truth* (Boston: Beacon Press, 1993).

Giannini, John L. *The Compass of the Soul: Archetypal Guides to a Fuller Life* (Gainesville, FL: Center for the Application of Psychological Type, 2004).

Jones, Rufus. *Spirit in Man* (Garland, TX: Peacock Press, 1963).

Jung, C. G. *Analytical Psychology: Its Theory and Practice: The Tavistock Lectures* (New York: Vintage Books, 1970).

———. *Introduction to Jungian Psychology: Notes on the Seminar Given in 1925*, ed. Sonu Shamdasani and William McGuire (Princeton: Princeton University Press, 2012).

———. "Introduction." *The Secret of the Golden Flower: A Chinese Book of Life*, trans. Richard Wilhelm (New York: Harcourt Brace, 1962).

———. *C. G. Jung Letters*, Vol. 1, 1906–51, trans. G. Adler and R. F. C. Hull (Princeton: Princeton University Press, 1973).

———. *Memories, Dreams, Reflections*, ed. Aniela Jaffé (New York: Vintage Books, 1989).

———. *Nietzsche's Zarathustra: Notes of the Seminar Given in 1934–1939*, ed. James Jarrett (Princeton: Princeton University Press, 1988).

———. *Psychological Types, or The Psychology of Individuation* (London: Routledge & Kegan Paul [archives], 1923).

———. *Visions: Notes on the Seminar Given in 1930–1934*, ed. Claire Douglas ((New York: Bollingen Foundation, 1997).

Jung, Carl G., ed. *Man and His Symbols* (Garden City, NJ: Doubleday/Windfall 1964).

Kant, Immanuel. *Critique of Pure Reason*, ed. Paul Guyer and Allen W. Wood (Cambridge: Cambridge University Press, 1998).

Keirsey, David, and Bates, Marilyn. *Please Understand Me: Character and Temperament*

Types (San Diego: Prometheus Nemesis, 1984).

Lisle, Laurie. *Portrait of an Artist: A Biography of Georgia O'Keeffe* (Seaview Books, 1980).

Loomis, Mary E. *Dancing the Wheel—of Psychological Types* (Willmette, IL: Chiron 1991).

MacCaffrey, Wallace. *Elizabeth I* (London: Edward Arnold, 1993).

Marshall, I. N. "The Four Functions: A Conceptual Analysis." *Journal of Analytical Psychology* 13, no. 1 (1968).

Maslow, Abraham. "Toward a Psychology of Being." *Psychological Review* 50 (1998) (Hoboken, NJ: Wiley, 1998).

McGuire, William, and Hull, R. F. C., eds. *C. G. Jung Speaking: Interviews and Encounters* (Princeton: Princeton University Press, 1977).

Miller, Jeffrey C. *The Transcendent Function: Jung's Model of Psychological Growth through Dialogue With the Unconscious* (New York: State University of New York Press, 2004).

Moore, Robert, and Gillette, Douglas. *King, Warrior, Magician, Lover* (New York: HarperOne, 1991).

Nasaw, David. *Andrew Carnegie* (London: Penguin Press, 2006).

Politzer, Anita. *A Woman on Paper: Georgia O'Keeffe* (New York: Simon & Schuster, 1988).

Portman, Adolph. "Metamorphosis in Animals: The Transformations of the Individual and the Type," in *Man and Transformation,* ed. Joseph Campbell (New York: Bollingen Foundation, 1964).

Samuels, Andrew; Shorter, Bani; and Plaut, Fred. *A Critical Dictionary of Jungian Analysis* (New York: Routledge, 1986).

Sanford, John. *The Kingdom Within: The Inner Meaning of Jesus' Sayings* (New York: HarperOne, 1987).

Schopenhauer, Arthur. *The World as Will and Representation,* Vols. 1 and 2 (Mineola, NY: Dover, 1966).

Serrano, Miguel. *C. G. Jung and Hermann Hesse: A Record of Two Friendships* (New York: Schocken, 1968).

Shirer, William L. *Gandhi: A Memoir* (Simon & Schuster, 1979).

Spoto, Angelo. *Jung's Typology in Perspective* (Wilmette, IL: Chiron, 1995).

Stein, Murray. *Jung's Map of the Soul: An Introduction* (Chicago: Open Court, 1998).

———. *The Principle of Individuation* (Willmette, IL: Chiron, 2006).

———. *Transformation: Emergence of the Self* (Carolyn and Earnest Fay Series in Analytical Psychology) (Texas A&M University Press; rev. ed., 2004).

Stevens, Anthony. *Jung: A Very Short Introduction* (Oxford: Oxford University Press, 2001).

Tsu, Lao. *The Way and Its Power,* trans. Arthur Waley (New York: Grove Press, 1994).

von Franz, Marie-Louise. *Conversations on Aion.* Interview by Claude Drey (Wilmette, IL: Chiron, 2004).

———. *The Feminine in Fairy Tales* (Boulder, CO: Shambhala, 2001).

———. *The Interpretation of Fairy Tales* (Boulder, CO: Shambhala, 1996).

———. *Shadow and Evil in Fairy Tales* (New York: C. G. Jung Foundation, 1995).

von Franz, Marie-Louise, and Hillman, James. *Jung's Typology: Lectures on Jung's Typology* (Spring 1971, Seminar Series, Book 4).

Wolpert, Stanley. *Gandhi's Passion: The Life and Legacy of Mahatma Gandhi* (Oxford: Oxford University Press, 2001).

Index

About the Author

James Graham Johnston has formal educational training in the liberal arts, fine art, architecture, and business. He has also pursued a lifelong interest in philosophy, psychology, and religion. He has lectured and delivered workshops on psychological types to various groups, including the International School of Analytical Psychology, Zurich (ISAP-Zurich); the Ohio Valley Association of Jungian Analysts (OVAJA); the International Association for Jungian Studies (IAJS); and the Netherlands Association for Analytical Psychology (NAAP).

Other Books by the Author:

The Call Within
Joshua, the Light of the World
Thriving on Collaborative Genius

He is founder of **Gifts Compass Inc. (www.giftscompass.com)** and the architect of the **Gifts Compass Inventory (GCI),** an online self-assessment that helps people orient to their preferred psychological types.

The Gifts Compass Inventory

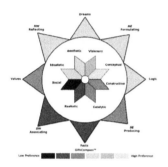

The Gifts Compass Inventory (GCI) is an online self-awareness instrument that helps navigate personal transformation toward one's full and unique potential. The GCI reports a person's graduated preferences for each of C. G. Jung's original eight psychological types.

The GCI does not purport to create a new or improved model of "typology." Rather it is intended to reaffirm Jung's original type model and to help clarify the type dynamics that were at the center of Jung's psychology. It illustrates both conscious and shadow dispositions.

The GCI affirms the value of unique individuality while it helps to explain one's orientation to life experience. With the guidance of a trained advisor, it opens new possibilities and pathways for personal growth. It helps people orient to optimal career paths, understand preferred learning styles, and gain confidence about personal strengths.

Content and construct validities have been scrupulously analyzed and successfully confirmed. The GCI has been objectively determined to be highly congruent with Jung's model of eight types.

A fifteen-page *GCI Personal Profile* provides direct, easily understood language for clients. The profile includes a compass diagram and narratives organized by key themes: Introversion/Extraversion, Orientation, Compass Headings, and Gifts (types).

A thirty-five-page *GCI Advisor Report* provides in-depth information for trained GCI advisors. It includes advisor alerts, a thorough review of dominant and auxiliary types, and a discussion of the *shadow type*—the least developed type, yet the one that plays a leading role as a catalyst for personal growth.

TRAINING IN JUNG'S PSYCHOLOGICAL TYPES

Gifts Compass Inc. offers certification training in the use of the GCI and the application of Jung's model of psychological types. The faculty includes an international group of Jungian analysts, psychologists, and experts in Jung's type model. Because the training is online, with full video-conferencing, people from different parts of the world can meet in the online training "room" together. No travel is required. In addition to illuminating some of the practical uses of the types, the training focuses on engaging the types for individuation. Individuation was a centerpiece for Jung's original work and is a centerpiece of the training.

People learn to "read the melody" of type dispositions, recognizing that there are often three or four types playing a role in consciousness, and one or two playing a "contrapuntal melody" in the shadow. Each profile, like each individual, is unique and is considered for its own special array of type dispositions.

Various advanced training seminars and conferences are available to the growing international network of GCI Advisors.

For more information, visit **www.GiftsCompass.com**.

Lightning Source UK Ltd.
Milton Keynes UK
UKOW06f2316120617
303208UK00007B/828/P